Conference Price $12

Retail Price $28

Sino-Malay
Trade & Diplomacy

Heng

Sino-Mala[y]

Tenth th[...]

Final Day Sale
$10

Heng

D1527307

This series of publications on Africa, Latin America, Southeast Asia, and Global and Comparative Studies is designed to present significant research, translation, and opinion to area specialists and to a wide community of persons interested in world affairs. The editor seeks manuscripts of quality on any subject and can usually make a decision regarding publication within three months of receipt of the original work. Production methods generally permit a work to appear within one year of acceptance. The editor works closely with authors to produce a high-quality book. The series appears in a paperback format and is distributed worldwide. For more information, contact the executive editor at Ohio University Press, 19 Circle Drive, The Ridges, Athens, Ohio 45701.

Executive editor: Gillian Berchowitz
AREA CONSULTANTS
Africa: Diane M. Ciekawy
Latin America: Brad Jokisch, Patrick Barr-Melej, and Rafael Obregon
Southeast Asia: William H. Frederick

The Ohio University Research in International Studies series is published for the Center for International Studies by Ohio University Press. The views expressed in individual volumes are those of the authors and should not be considered to represent the policies or beliefs of the Center for International Studies, Ohio University Press, or Ohio University.

Sino-Malay Trade and Diplomacy from the Tenth through the Fourteenth Century

Derek Heng

Ohio University Research in International Studies
Southeast Asia Series No. 121
Ohio University Press
Athens

© 2009 by the
Center for International Studies
Ohio University
www.ohioswallow.com

To obtain permission to quote, reprint, or otherwise reproduce or distribute
material from Ohio University Press publications, please contact our rights and
permissions department at (740) 593-1154 or (740) 593-4536 (fax).

Printed in the United States of America
All rights reserved

18 17 16 15 14 13 12 11 10 09   5 4 3 2 1

The books in the Ohio University Research in International Studies Series
are printed on acid-free paper ⊗ ™

Library of Congress Cataloging-in-Publication Data

Heng, Derek Thiam Soon.
Sino-Malay trade and diplomacy from the tenth through the fourteenth century
/ Derek Heng.
    p. cm. — (Ohio University research in international studies. Southeast Asia
studies series ; no. 121)
Includes bibliographical references and index.
ISBN 978-0-89680-271-1 (paper : alk. paper)
1. China—Commerce—Malacca, Strait of, Region. 2. Malacca, Strait of,
Region—Commerce—China. 3. China—Economic conditions—To 1644. 4.
Malacca, Strait of, Region—Economic conditions. 5. Malay Peninsula Region—
Economic conditions. 6. China—Relations—Malacca, Strait of, Region. 7.
Malacca, Strait of, Region—Relations—China. 8. China—Relations—Malay
Peninsula Region. 9. Malay Peninsula Region—Relations—China. I. Title.
HF3838.M35H46 2009
382.0951'0595—dc22

2009027735

Contents

Illustrations

Maps

Tables

Preface

One of the most important events in the late twentieth and early twenty-first centuries is the rise of China in the international economic and political arena. China has emerged as one of the most important economies in the world. This development began in the 1970s along the southern Chinese coastal provinces as part of an experiment in controlled capitalism under the initiation of former premier Deng Xiaoping. By the end of the twentieth century it had come to include the entire Chinese market, progressively opening the whole of China to the rest of the world. At the same time, the Chinese economy has increasingly been privatized, although the Chinese state has maintained firm guidance through governmental regulations and control over the value and circulation of the Chinese currency.

While access into and out of the Chinese market has been progressively established across the northwestern Central Asian and northern Southeast Asian hill-lands, the main access to this vast market remains the eastern Chinese coastline. Maritime linkages have provided China with large-scale access to the international economy, connecting its production capabilities and material consumption with economic regions both near and far.

China's maritime orientation and the state's firm management of the economy have had a fundamental impact on the economy and foreign-relations perspectives of countries that engage China economically and diplomatically. This is especially true of countries near China, such as those of Southeast Asia, that have been fundamentally affected by China's development in the last three decades. To the countries in Southeast Asia, China represents a market capable of consuming large volumes of the primary and secondary products they produce, while at the same time serving as a source of relatively cheap manufactured products that they could in turn import. Consequently, these countries, and in particular the countries of maritime Southeast Asia—Singapore, Malaysia, Brunei, Indonesia—which historically have not had significant population bases on which to develop their respective economies, have begun in recent times to gravitate toward China both economically and diplomatically.

There has been much anticipation and anxiety over the possible trajectory of China's ascendance in the twenty-first century. Much of the latter sentiment has been due, in large part, to current discussions casting its phenomenal development within the context of globalization as an unprecedented occurrence in China's history. While this may be true of China's and Southeast Asia's experiences in recent centuries, throughout much of the first and second millennia AD, China was an important player in the international economy. Its economic output, its high level of urbanization, and the sophistication of its monetary system and economy made it an important market for Southeast Asia. China has historically exerted an enormous amount of influence over the development and nature of the political and economic affairs in the regions beyond its borders. Changes to the way China regarded and conducted its external relations and economy had immediate and profound effects on how trade and diplomacy were conducted between China and the states and polities of Southeast Asia. The closer these states and polities were to China in geographical terms, the more important these economic and diplomatic ties with China were, and the more profound the effects of the structural changes in China were to them. The experiences of the last two millennia are therefore relevant to our understanding of the developments in the present-day context of East Asia and to our understanding of the relationship between China and Southeast Asia.

This book seeks to understand the changing dynamics of the diplomatic and economic interaction between China and a subregion of Southeast Asia—the Malay region, centered on the Strait of Malacca—from the tenth to the fourteenth century. During these four centuries, China, under Song (960–1279) and Yuan (1279–1368) rule, was one of the most important economies of Asia. As China's foreign and maritime trade policies changed over time, the coastal polities of the Malay region reacted and adapted to them, as well as to the resulting changes in the economic interaction and market demand in both China and South-east Asia, so as to ensure their relevance and sustainability over time.

Acknowledgments

Nothing can be done alone. This book is a testament to that truth. A great number of people have contributed tremendously to the present study. It represents a culmination of my relationship with these wonderful scholars, many of whom had a fundamental impact on my scholarship over the last ten years. I thank Jan W. Christie, who between 1999 and 2004 was my PhD supervisor. Her resourcefulness, insight, and intelligence, as well as the maturity of her scholarship, compelled me to strive to attain the highest levels of scholarship in my own research.

Between 2000 and 2004, in an effort to map the economic linkages between the Malay region and southern China in the premodern era, I spent much research time studying and classifying the ceramic artifacts excavated from archaeological sites in Singapore and southern Kedah. I am indebted to a number of individuals who helped me gain access to the materials I needed for this study. John N. Miksic of the Southeast Asian Studies Program, National University of Singapore (NUS), generously granted me access to the archaeological material that his team had recovered from various fourteenth-century sites in Singapore; Ng Ching Hwei of the National Heritage Board, Singapore, tirelessly helped, between 2000 and 2003, in making the recovered material at the archaeological laboratory at Fort Canning Hill readily accessible; the director-general of the Jabatan Muzium dan Antikuiti, Malaysia, Dato Adi Haji Taha, kindly granted me access to the archaeological material at the Muzium Negara and the Archaeological Museum Lembah Bujang, Kedah; and curator Shamsul Rijal of the Lembah Bujang Archaeological Museum (2003–4) gave me his kind assistance at the museum in late 2003 and took me to site 31 at Sungai

Mas, Kota Kuala Muda, Kedah. I also thank Masni bt. Adeni (curator, DG Office) of the Jabatan Muzium dan Antikuiti, Malaysia, for allowing me access to the archaeological reports at the resource library of the Muzium Negara, Kuala Lumpur, in early 2004.

Throughout the writing process, many scholars read my initial drafts. Their comments, criticism, and questions enabled me to improve my manuscript immensely. These individuals include Jane Leonard, Professor Emeritus of History, University of Akron, who was the Isaac Manasseh Visiting Fellow at the Department of History, NUS, in 2003; Kwa Chong Guan, Adjunct Fellow at the Department of History, NUS, and Senior Fellow at the Institute of Defence and Strategic Studies, Nanyang University (Singapore), whom I regard as a mentor as well as a fellow scholar of Singapore history; and Cynthia Brokaw, Professor of History at Ohio State University, who has generously supported the success of her younger colleagues.

This book would not have been possible without the support of the various institutions where I have worked since 2000. I thank the staff at the Department of History, NUS, for their encouragement and constructive comments throughout the research and writing process. In particular, I thank Tan Tai Yong and Ian Gordon, both of whom were heads of the Department of History during my tenure as teaching assistant and visiting fellow (2002–6), for allowing me time off from teaching to complete my PhD thesis in 2004, upon which this book is based. I also thank Ohio State University, and the Marion campus in particular, for funding my travels to Singapore and Malaysia during the final stages of my research and writing.

Finally, I dedicate this book to my wife, Wendy, and my four children, Bethan, Lauren, Keane, and Megan. Even though I wrote the text, this book is the fruit of a family effort. The sacrifices that they made for my academic success are too numerous to chronicle here. I can only say that I will not forget these sacrifices and that my family is more important to me than all that this book may represent.

Sino-Malay Trade and Diplomacy from the

Tenth through the Fourteenth Century

INTRODUCTION

The Malay region, comprising the Malay Peninsula, the eastern coast of Sumatra, and the northern coast of Borneo, has, throughout history, played an important and strategic role in the international maritime economy of Asia. Located at the southern periphery of the Asian continental landmass, the Strait of Malacca has been an important maritime passage, linking the Indian Ocean to the South China and Java seas, while the annual pattern of the northeast and southwest monsoon winds has made the Malay region and the East Java Sea area the interface between the Indian Ocean littoral, maritime and mainland Southeast Asia, and Northeast Asia. This region was a natural meeting place where vessels sailing between eastern and western Asia would await the change in direction of the monsoon wind and merchants from east and west could exchange goods. Numerous ports emerged along the coastlines to capitalize on the shipping and trade that congregated in or passed through the region. It has also been, throughout history, an important geographical region, famed for its indigenous products, which have long been in high demand in the major Asian markets and, in the modern era, in Europe.

Given their dependence on international trade for survival and prosperity, changes in the political fortunes of key Asian states, which determined the economic outlook and policies of these states and, in turn, the overall state of the international economy of Asia, had a direct impact on the nature of the interaction of the polities of the Malay region with the international maritime trade, on the key Asian states,

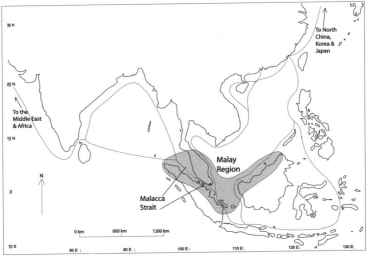

Map I.1. Trade routes linking the Indian subcontinent, Southeast Asia, and China, tenth through fourteenth century

and ultimately, on the fortunes of these individual port-polities. China was one such state in Asia.

The economic relationship between China and the Malay region can be traced back two millennia, and this dynamic interaction between the two regions may be periodized into several watershed cycles— the second century BC to the third century AD, corresponding to the Han period;[1] the sixth to the eighth century AD, corresponding to the Sui and early Tang periods;[2] the tenth through the fourteenth century, corresponding to the Song and Yuan periods; the fifteenth century, corresponding to the early Ming period; and the eighteenth century, corresponding to the mid-Qing period.[3]

These key cycles, however, were not entirely similar. More significantly, fundamental changes appear to have occurred from the tenth to the fourteenth century. Before the late tenth century, the trade between China and the states and polities of the Malay region was characterized by small-volume exchanges carried by traders and shipping from the latter, and high-value Middle Eastern and Indian Ocean littoral products were the chief items brought to China's ports. By the fifteenth century, however, the trade had changed dramatically; it consisted mainly of high-volume exchanges carried by Chinese traders and shipping and predominantly involved low-value maritime Southeast Asian products sourced directly from the Malay region. Diplomatic relations between China and the Malay region began with representatives of the Malay region interacting with the Song court at the advent of its rule. This state of affairs, however, devolved, by the end of Song rule, in 1279 AD, to the point that there were no concerted or coherent diplomatic overtures between China and the Malay region—a situation characterized by the near absence of any state-level interaction between the two.

These dramatic changes in the interaction between China and the Malay region during this period took place against the backdrop of major internal developments in the two. Politically, China experienced the rule of two dynasties—the Song (960–1279) and Yuan (1279–1368)—of which the latter was non-Chinese. During this period the dynastic capital shifted between three different cities. Economically, China underwent a revolution characterized by the monetization of the Chinese economy, regional specialization in agricultural and manufactured products, the rise of the merchant class and the increasing sophistication of mercantile trade, and the expansion of international maritime trade. Socially, China's population became increasingly urbanized.

The Malay region was also characterized by significant political and economic developments during this time. Between the tenth and the early thirteenth century, the region was dominated by Srivijaya, a port-polity that had managed to raise itself to a position of preeminence by the eighth century AD. The political center of Srivijaya was located initially at Palembang, along the Musi River in Sumatra, but in the latter half of the eleventh century it shifted to Jambi, along the Batang Hari River in Sumatra. The capitals functioned, through the eighth through the thirteenth century, as the region's chief maritime hub for shipping and trade between the Indian Ocean and the South China Sea, and transshipped foreign products to the Chinese, Indian, and island Southeast Asian markets, where they were in high demand.[4]

By the early thirteenth century, however, a number of port-polities that appear to have engaged independently in international trade had begun to emerge in the northern part of the Strait of Malacca, the northeastern tracts of the Malay Peninsula, and the northern coast of Borneo. Srivijaya's position as the key entrepôt port of the region was gradually being eroded.[5] In 1275 the capital of Srivijaya was sacked by invading Javanese forces, and from that point the region was characterized by the mushrooming of a plethora of minor ports, a number of which fell under the influence of such regional powers in Southeast Asia as Sukhothai, in Thailand, and Majapahit, in Java. Such dramatic developments in the region's political history can no doubt be directly linked to changes in the international and regional economic context upon which the Malay region's polities were highly dependent for their political sustainability.

The tenth to the fourteenth century must have been a pivotal phase in the history of Sino-Malay interactions. Significant changes must have occurred in both regions that led to such fundamental shifts evident by the fifteenth century, changes that have continued to characterize the relationship between the two regions up until the present time. What was the nature of this relationship, within the context of evolving diplomatic and economic links between China and its foreign trading partners, particularly those in Southeast Asia? What changes occurred in both China and the Malay region that consequently affected maritime trade between the two? What were the channels of trade at the various levels of economic interaction, and how did they evolve in response to the changes in the maritime trade? What commodities were exchanged between the two regions, and how did the nature of that trade evolve from the tenth to the fourteenth century? What social developments and commercial practices resulted from these changes?

Themes and Approaches

Although there is a large body of literature on the economic and diplomatic interaction between China and the Malay region in the tenth through the fourteenth century, most studies deal with the histories of the two regions' relations separately. Only a select few explore the interaction in its own right. The gaps in the literature help shape the issues I shall address here.

There is also a large number of studies on the economy of China's Song and Yuan periods.[6] These works deal in considerable detail with the development of China's economy, including such aspects as China's monetary system, the sources and administration of state finance, and the commercialization of the Chinese economy. However, the links between developments in China's overall economy and its maritime economy have not been adequately addressed, even though the maritime economy became a crucial aspect of the overall economy during the tenth through the fourteenth century and an important source of state revenue by the twelfth century.

Several studies have explored China's maritime economy during this time.[7] These works—in particular those of J. Kuwabara, Yu Chang Sen, and So Kee Long—deal primarily with the institutions governing maritime trade, the nature of Chinese participation in that trade, and the types of products traded at both the state and provincial levels. Nonetheless, there is insufficient discussion pertaining to the changes and development in China's maritime economy over these four centuries. This is due, in large part, to the types of sources used by these scholars—predominantly Chinese historical texts and some Chinese archaeological reports. Often no foreign sources of historical data are used. Consequently, these studies have not taken into account, in any significant way, the role that China's foreign trading partners played in the development of Chinese maritime trade. The studies that do extend beyond China include only brief, cursory discussions of the role that the states and polities in Southeast Asia and the Indian Ocean littoral played in China's maritime economy.

Furthermore, current studies of the Chinese maritime economy are centered predominantly on the Song period. The amount of scholarship pertaining to the Yuan period is relatively insignificant. This is a critical gap; even though China's maritime trade was quite different during the two periods, the changes that occurred in the Yuan grew out of developments in the Song. The Song and Yuan periods need to be viewed together for the progression in the diplomatic and economic aspects of China's maritime relations in the tenth through the fourteenth century to be fully understood.

A number of studies presently available do attempt to explore the interaction between the Malay region and China.[8] These works place a certain emphasis on the mutual importance of both regions in this economic relationship, and they approach this issue from two key angles. The first approach deals with historical geography, namely the identification of regional ports and the development of trade routes between southern China and maritime Southeast Asia during the period in question. However, subtle changes in the nature of the interaction between China and the Malay region over the course of the tenth through the fourteenth century have not been captured. This is due in large part to the heavy reliance on historical texts, in particular those from China, and epigraphic and philological data from the region and the Middle East. Archaeological data—particularly data collected from research at Malay-region settlement sites over the last thirty years—have been distinctly absent from the body of information used by these studies, most of which appeared before the 1980s.[9]

The second key approach is that of commodities studies, which inquires into the products that were exchanged between China and the Malay region. Here two main methods have been employed—looking at the sources and uses of these products in both China and Southeast Asia, and the evolution of the trade of individual products; and providing information on a large number of products that were traded between China and the region. In this regard, the works of Paul Wheatley and Roderich Ptak stand out.[10] These unique works continue to be important to present-day scholars working on the history of China–Southeast Asia trade, as they provide both a broad overview and detailed discussions of the products involved in the Sino-Malay trade. However, apart from the individual products examined by Roderich Ptak, the evolution of the commodities trade as a whole through the tenth to the fourteenth centuries has not been examined In addition, we do not at present fully understand the respective roles that China and the Malay region played in shaping the commodities trade.

The exposure and dependence of the Malay region on the international economic context has received significant discussion—especially the region's involvement in and response to international trade and foreign relations from the tenth through the fourteenth century.[11] Bennet

Bronson, in particular, has formulated a model for the economic and social interaction between the coastal port-settlements of the Malay region and their immediate hinterlands in the era before European colonialism. The model, known as the dendritic model, has also been used to contextualize the dynamics of the links between these hinterland economies and their societies, the coastal port-settlements, and the external world. This model continues to be adopted by historians and archaeologists studying parts of Southeast Asia that have inland groups as well as coastal settlements and are located along the major routes of the international maritime economy. Nonetheless, this model is not without its flaws. The dendritic model assumes that the nature of the international maritime economy, particularly that which flowed between the South China Sea and the Indian Ocean, remained relatively unchanged until the arrival of the Europeans in Asia in the late fifteenth and the early sixteenth centuries. The key states of the South China Sea and Indian Ocean regions definitely did not remain static until the early modern era, and this poses a critical problem with the consistency of the dendritic theory.

A number of important works, particularly those of Jan Wisseman Christie, have attempted to address the impact that changes experienced by key Asian states had on the Malay region. [12] Christie focuses on the economic and political relationship between the Malay region and the Indian subcontinent, and they provide us with a crucial understanding of the impact that social, political, and economic developments in India had on the ports and coastal polities of the Malay region.

Unfortunately, similar works on the impact that the political and administrative changes in China and the changes to the structures of the Chinese maritime economy had on the region and its port-polities are largely absent. The only works that do study the interrelated nature of the diplomatic and economic interaction between China and the Malay region in the period in question are centered largely on Srivijaya, the preeminent Malaccan port-polity between the seventh and thirteenth century. O. W. Wolters has explored the causes of the rise and fall of this polity as the Malay region's key emporium along the international maritime trade circuit and the role it played as the representative in the region's economic and political interaction with China during its seven-century existence.[13]

One of the most important aspects of the Sino-Malay interaction that Wolters has examined pertains to state-level exchanges. Wolters assumes that state-level exchanges were the main channel through which the Malay region, under the auspices of Srivijaya, conducted its trade with China. Consequently, he examines Sino-Malay relations during the Song and Yuan periods through this interpretative lens and explains the economic, social, and political implications that this channel of trade had for Srivijaya and the Malay region.

However, Wolters has placed too much emphasis on the importance of state-level exchanges as the main channel through which trade was conducted with China during the Song period.[14] Most of his arguments have been based on the assumption that the Song court's conduct of maritime trade remained largely unchanged from the tenth through the thirteenth century, and indeed into the Yuan period. The impact of the changes in the conduct of maritime trade by the Chinese, and of China's maritime trade institutions and structures, on Srivijaya and the Malay region's conduct of its economic and diplomatic relations with China, have therefore not been taken into account.

Nor has Wolters satisfactorily explained the continued flourishing of trade between the Malay region and China, despite the complete decline of state-level missions from Srivijaya to China by the latter half of the twelfth century. In fact, the works presently available do not sufficiently address the role of Chinese private traders in China's maritime trade or the impact that increasing private Chinese participation in this trade had on the Malay region and on Sino-Malay relations. These inadequacies in the scholarship remain unresolved.

Finally, almost none of the currently available literature on Sino-Malay relations explores the interaction between smaller port-polities of the Malay region and China—even though textual and archaeological information indicates that a large number of coastal settlements in the Malay region interacted economically with China during the tenth through the fourteenth century. The gap in the scholarship on smaller port-polities is partially filled by a number of studies that have been carried out on individual ports in the region. These include research on Kota Cina, southern Kedah, and Singapore Island, as well as Barus, on the northwestern coast of Sumatra. The focus, however, is primarily archaeological, since textual information concerning such smaller ports tends to be very sparse or even nonexistent. While they are important in revealing certain characteristics of the region's international trade at the port level—such as the material culture of the polities' population and the port's trade in such nonperishable products as ceramics and metal items—no longer-term overview of the region's economy at the port level, based on archaeological data, has yet been assembled. This is further hampered by the fact that no single site spans the entire period of the tenth through the fourteenth century; normally any single site was active for only one to two hundred years.

The present study thus aims to explore the changes in the nature of the economic and diplomatic relationship between China and the Malay region and to impart a sense of continuity in the developments over the course of the four hundred years. I also aim to move away from the confines of state-sponsored exchanges to explore such other aspects as port activities, the impact of the subregional demand markets in the Malay region on the export of Chinese products, and the meeting of changing market demands in China for foreign products.

These topics will be explored through three key themes. First, changes in China's political and economic contexts and the administration of maritime trade had a direct and profound impact on the Malay region. This included the manner in which the region's polities conducted their diplomatic relations with China, the manner in which those polities related economically with China and with each other, and ultimately the formation, viability, and hierarchy of the polities in the region. Second, these developments ultimately determined the types of products that were exchanged between the two regions. Third, these structural changes and developments in China and the Malay region had an impact on how maritime trade was conducted between the two regions. From the tenth through the fourteenth century, that trade evolved from a state-controlled and state-sponsored exchange to one largely driven by Chinese private concerns, and one that went from being initiated by regional polities and confined to the regional level to one that was highly diffuse. This was accompanied, and often spurred on, by developments in how the traders conducted their commercial and social activities in the respective foreign regions.

Three key approaches have been adopted in this study. First, the relationship between the two regions will be explored from the perspective of the economic interaction itself, not centered on one region or the other. Second, the economic relationship will be examined at three levels—the region, state, and individual. Third, the nature of the economic interaction will be reconstructed as one that changed over time. In this regard, the Song and Yuan periods will be studied together, since the Yuan period, with regard to China's maritime trade, represents a period of continuity, rather than change, from the Song.

A Note on Sources

This study draws its information from two key sources—historical texts and epigraphy, and archaeological data. Although a number of Indian and Middle Eastern texts and epigraphic data have been used, Chinese historical texts and epigraphic information dominate the first source. Chinese texts constitute a significant source of data for the study of the nature of, and changes in, the economic relations between China and the Malay region during the Song and Yuan periods. These texts provide both contemporary information and later syntheses of, and commentaries on, information concerning such topics as the products that were traded, the administrative structure of China's maritime trade, and the practices of those involved in the trade between China and the region.

Although sixty-three known texts published or written during the Song period contain information on Southeast Asia, only a few contain information pertaining to the Malay region and to China's economic and political relations with the polities in the region.[15] Among these latter texts, I focus on five here: *Pingzhou ketan* (Zhu Yu, 1116),[16] *Lingwai daida* (Zhou Qufei, 1178),[17] *Yunlu manchao* (Zhao Yanwei, 1206),[18] *Zhufanzhi* (Zhao Ruguo, 1225),[19] and *Songhuiyao jigao*.[20] They provide information on this relationship between China and the Malay region from the late eleventh to the thirteenth century.

These texts mainly reflect the Chinese administrative perspective on Sino-Malay relations and China's maritime trade. Even though the authors of these texts, with the exception of the authors of the *Songhui-yao jigao,* wrote and published their literary works on a private basis, they were employed in various capacities during their lifetime by the Song bureaucracy. Anyone using these texts in the study of Malay history has to bear in mind this unbalanced perspective.

Yuan-period texts containing information pertaining to China's relations with the Malay region fall into two general groups. The first comprises texts that provide an account of this relationship in the Song and Yuan periods. These texts consist mainly of historical studies that contain sporadic references to the Sino-Malay relationship, in particular the trade and diplomatic exchanges that took place between the two regions. Although these texts are considered to be primary documents, they are in themselves historical works. They were assembled entirely from earlier textual sources. The texts thus present a late-thirteenth- or fourteenth-century interpretation of the earlier historical data. The *Wenxian tongkao* (Ma Duanlin, 1307),[21] *Songshi* (ed. Tuo Tuo et al., 1345),[22] and *Yuanshi* (1370)[23] are texts that belong in this category. The first two are Yuan-period historical works containing information on the Song period, the third being an early-Ming-period work containing information on the Yuan period.

The second group of Yuan-period texts comprises contemporaneous accounts of Sino-Malay relations during the Yuan period. Three texts of this group have been used in this study—the *Dade nanhaizhi* (Chen Dazhen, 1304),[24] the *Yuandianzhang* (anon., ca. 1321–24),[25] and *Daoyi zhilue* (Wang Dayuan, ca. 1349).[26] The first, written by a Chinese official, reflects the personal perspective of a Chinese official on the trade centered at Guangzhou. The second, an administrative guide written and published under the auspices of the Yuan court, provides the perspective from the political center of Yuan China. The third, an eyewitness account of the ports and other areas in Southeast Asia written by a Chinese trader, provides a unique view of the Sino-Malay trade from the perspective of a Chinese participant in the trade who was operating outside China.

All these Song and Yuan texts are already known to scholars. However, this body of information has been underused in the study of the Malay region's economic interaction with China during the period in question. In addition, although a number of these texts have been drawn upon by sinologists in their discussions of China's history, not all have been translated into Western languages. As a result, important as they are as a source of information on Southeast Asia's early history, many are not accessible to historians of Southeast Asia. Nor have previous studies used the textual data in furthering our understanding of the nature of the trade between the two regions at levels below that of the state. The present study brings together information through a critical rereading of these texts and in the process extends the boundaries of our understanding of the topic at hand.

Archaeological data, the second major body of information used here, are derived from the two geographical regions of maritime Southeast Asia and southern China. The sites from which this study draws its information fall into three categories: kiln sites in southern China; shipwrecks found both in Chinese and Southeast Asian waters; and settlement sites in the Malay region.

The ports of Guangzhou and Quanzhou provide information concerning relations with Southeast Asia, the Indian Ocean littoral, and the Middle East through epigraphic records on tombstones and the remains of places of worship of foreign religions, such as mosques and temples. However, the archaeological data most useful for the study of Sino-Malay patterns of trade are derived from kiln site excavations. The ceramic remains from such sites can be directly compared with the ceramic finds in shipwrecks and settlement sites in Southeast Asia. This also provides insight into the economic links between the Chinese ports and their economic hinterlands within which the kiln sites were located.

Archaeological reports on tenth- to fourteenth-century kiln sites in southern China are primarily concerned with the fine stoneware produced by these kiln districts. A good deal is currently known about the types of fine stoneware—as well as the glazes, forms, and decorative techniques—associated with various kiln districts. While there was a general exchange of knowledge between potters concerning ceramic production—as witnessed by similarities in decorative techniques, forms, glazes, and kiln construction—differences in the physical characteristics of the wares from different kiln districts are discernible, and that has enabled the provenance of many excavated shards and whole examples to be fairly confidently assigned. The sources of fine ceramics found at Southeast Asian archaeological sites can therefore be fairly accurately identified at the Chinese provincial, and in some cases even the district, level.[27]

Studies on coarse Chinese stoneware have focused on vessel forms and types of decoration, such as molded and incised motifs, character, and motif stamping and decorative lugs. However, most of the forms and the types of decoration used by Fujian and Guangdong kilns were not exclusive to any particular district or even province, and many of the kilns produced a wide range of forms and decorations that were similar to those produced by other kilns. The clay body thus stands as the best means of distinguishing the different sources of coarse stoneware. Unfortunately, no scientific analysis of the clay used by the different kiln districts has yet been conducted, and the precise nature of variations in the clay used by the potters is still unclear. The classification of coarse stoneware from Guangdong and southern Fujian is thus based on visual identification of clay types currently known, and on vessel forms attributable to a particular kiln area or larger kiln district.

The only southern Chinese area in which a study has been made both of the development of the ceramics industry and of the role that local ceramics played in domestic and international economy is southern Fujian.[28] No major study has yet been made of the Guangdong ceramics industry, or for that matter of those of provinces north of Guangdong and Fujian, such as Zhejiang, Jiangxi, and Jiangsu. The implications of the archaeological data for the Chinese export trade have been discussed only briefly in the current body of works. Most of the studies of the role of the southern Chinese kilns in the Southeast Asia–China trade of the tenth through the fourteenth century have been carried out by Southeast Asian archaeologists and historians, with heavy reliance on secondary sources, since most of the reports resulting from the archaeological surveys on the southern Chinese kiln districts conducted by Chinese archaeologists remain unpublished. Our present understanding of the economic links between southern China and maritime Southeast Asia, and in particular the Malay region, remains limited.[29]

Shipwreck excavations, the second body of archaeological data, provide a different form of information. Data from shipwrecks reflect the shipping patterns and other characteristics of the shipping trade that was taking place between the two economic regions at the time the ship foundered, as well as types of products traded at that time. Despite the snapshot nature of shipwreck data, with data from a sufficient number of wrecks spread over a substantial period, we get a picture of the development of this maritime trade.

In dating wrecks, both the ship's contents and its hull are relied upon. An approximate date can often be assigned on the basis of coins—in particular Chinese copper cash bearing reign marks—along with trade wares such as ceramics or metal wares, the decoration and forms of which often reveal their period of manufacture, and any other items that may have inscriptions or stylistic characteristics to which a date or period may be attributed. When parts of a vessel are recovered, organic samples may be sent for radiocarbon dating. The resulting composite date can often be precise to within a few decades, and occasionally to within a few years or even months.

Five wrecks have been drawn upon in this study for information concerning the maritime trade patterns between the Malay region and China. The Intan, Pulau Buaya, Java Sea, Quanzhou, and *Turiang* wrecks have been assigned to the early tenth, early twelfth, thirteenth, late thirteenth, and late fourteenth centuries respectively.[30] The data from these wrecks thus provide snapshots of the development in the shipping and products trade between the two regions at fairly even intervals over four centuries.

Not all the ships originated from the same port or region. The Intan and Java Sea wrecks appear to have been Southeast Asian vessels, while the

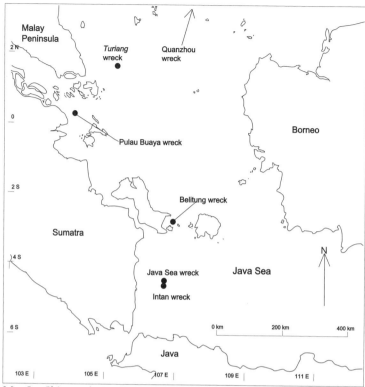

Map I.2. Shipwrecks in maritime Southeast Asia, tenth through fourteenth century

Quanzhou and *Turiang* wrecks were probably Chinese vessels. Whence the Pulau Buaya ship originated is not known because of the absence of any hull structure at the wreck site. Also, these ships sank off parts of southern China and maritime Southeast Asia. The Intan, Pulau Buaya, and Java Sea wrecks were discovered in the Java Sea off the southeastern coast of Sumatra. The Quanzhou wreck was discovered in Houtu harbor, in Quanzhou Bay, southern Fujian. The *Turiang* wreck was discovered off the southeastern coast of the Malay Peninsula. Nor were all the ships on the same route. While the contents of the tenth-century Intan wreck reflect the types of goods exported or transshipped from the Malay region to Java, the Pulau Buaya, Java Sea, and *Turiang* wrecks reflect the types of goods imported by the

Malay region, largely from China and mainland Southeast Asia. The picture that these wrecks provide is not focused on one segment of the maritime trade between China and maritime Southeast Asia, and it does not reflect the flow of goods in one direction alone. The Quanzhou wreck provides an important counterpoint to the otherwise one-dimensional view of the region's participation in international maritime trade evidenced by data from land-based archaeological sites.

Land-based excavations and survey reports from the Malay region form the third important source of the archaeological data used in the present study. Land-based archaeological data provide information concerning trade only in imperishable commodities, such as ceramics, glass, and metals. Other commodities, including such organic products as textiles and foodstuffs, are absent from the data. Even the identity of the commodities that were transported in ceramic containers can only be inferred, and conclusions are not definite. The picture of the trade between China and the Malay ports, as reflected by the data from land-based excavations, is therefore not complete. Nonetheless, it is important.

Settlement sites on the coasts of Sumatra corresponding to the tenth through the fourteenth century include Palembang, Muara Jambi, Kompei, Lobu Tua (Barus), and Kota Cina.[31] Of these, a detailed report is available only for Kota Cina. A number of tenth- to fourteenth-century sites along the coast of the Malay Peninsula have also been studied archaeologically over the last sixty years. These include southern Kedah (Pengkalan Bujang and Sungai Mas), Tioman Island, and Temasik (present-day Singapore). The finds include ceramics from China, Southeast Asia, and the Middle East as well as other trade goods such as glass beads and fragments of glassware. In the case of the southern Kedah sites, these include monumental remains and inscriptions as well as sculpture and images in stone, bronze, gold foil, and terra-cotta. Two key settlement sites along the northern Borneo coast have also been discovered and systematically surveyed. These are at Santubong (Sarawak) and Sungai Limau Manis (Brunei).[32] Ceramic shards are the primary finds recovered from these sites, although a large quantity of Chinese copper cash and fragments of the hulls of several wooden vessels have also been recovered from Sungai Limau Manis.

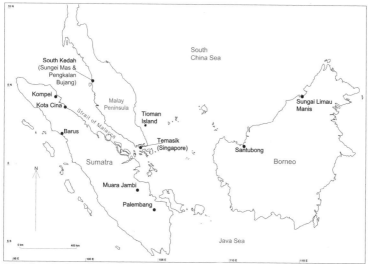

Map I.3. Archaeological settlement sites in the Malay region, tenth through fourteenth century

Each of the two groups of historical data—texts and archaeological finds—has its strengths and weaknesses. Textual data provide a good understanding of the structures of the economic relationship from the Chinese perspective, in particular the administration of trade. Textual data also remain the only source of information on certain types of products carried by the trade, in particular those that were perishable. However, as Chinese texts provide the bulk of this group of data, the information reflects a Chinese perspective on this economic relationship. Archaeological data, on the other hand, provide, where available, information on the development of trade in such imperishable goods as ceramics, currency, and metals. In addition, quantitative data on these groups of goods are often made available, supplying information that the texts do not provide. This information may be used to link the Malay ports to key economic areas and ports in southern China, where these products were produced and from which they were exported, as well as changes in the patterns of demand for them over time. By integrating both the archaeological and textual sources of information, the resulting synergy provides for levels of analysis and perspectives not immediately apparent in the textual data. The result is a more complex and complete picture of the developments of China's economic and diplomatic relations with the Malay world, and the changes that occurred between the tenth and the fourteenth century.

Chapter 1

SINO-MALAY INTERACTION IN THE FIRST MILLENNIUM AD

Since the late first millennium BC, the Malay region has played a pivotal role in the international maritime economy that encompasses maritime Southeast Asia, the South China Sea region, and the Indian Ocean littoral. This role has been as much the result of the region's strategic location in maritime Asia as the geographical and demographic characteristics of the region's islands. Unlike land-based polities, which have internal economies based on agrarian hinterlands that enabled them to be self-sufficient, the islands of the Malay region have throughout history maintained two distinct types of societies—coastal societies and upland social groups. The polities of the Malay coastal region did not extend very far inland. The islands' mountainous interiors have been occupied by groups who were ethnically and even linguistically distinct from the coastal societies.[1] Although the coastal and inland groups interacted with each other economically, the prosperity and political stability of the coastal groups were determined mainly by their ability to capitalize on the international maritime trade that flowed through the region.

The ports of the Malay region participated in the international trade in three ways. The first was by acting as an entrepôt in the trade between the Indian Ocean, the South China Sea, and island Southeast Asia. From the middle of the first millennium AD onward, the port-settlements along the Strait of Malacca and the northeastern parts of the Java Sea were able to capitalize on the region's geographical advantages, under the leadership of a succession of port-polities that were able to project themselves as the key entrepôt in different eras.

They also traded by carrying transshipped products to states bordering the Indian Ocean, South China Sea, and island Southeast Asia. The key port-polities of the Malacca Strait and northeastern Java Sea were able to obtain and transship foreign products in high demand in the Chinese, Indian, and island Southeast Asian markets, supplying international products directly to the various Asian markets. Indigenous products that were in demand in these Asian markets were also collected by these ports, either from the hinterland through commercial exchanges with inland groups or from the region's feeder ports that fell within the sphere of influence of the key port-polities, and shipped by the region's ports to these foreign markets.[2]

Finally, ports in the region could make available key products to foreign traders who were passing through and could in that manner conduct some maritime trade by attracting some of the passing mercantile shipping to call at their ports directly. Ports located along less strategic stretches of the Malay region's coastline, such as those along the eastern coast of the Malay Peninsula and the northern coast of Borneo, participated in international trade in this manner. This, however, depended on a high level of diffused trade taking place in the region and usually occurred during the transitional periods between the passing of a key port-polity and the ascendance of a succeeding one, a political and economic situation that often led to intense competition between the region's ports for external trade.

Given the middleman role that the Malay region's port-polities played in the international economic context, the commencement of relations with specific external regions or states, the importance of these port-polities in the diplomatic and economic arena, as well as the nature of the interaction they established with external regions or states, depended on the market demands as well as the diplomatic positions adopted by the key states of Southeast Asia, the South China Sea region, and the Indian Ocean littoral.

Exchanges between the Malay region and India appear to have commenced as early as the late first millennium BC. One of the earliest references to these contacts can be found in the Ramayana, a Hindu epic poem composed some time in the second half of the first millennium BC, which mentions Suvarnabhumi (Land of Gold), an early Sankritic reference to the Malay Region. The coastal areas of India had historically maintained a maritime outlook and were by the first millennium BC traversing the Bay of Bengal and trading at ports located on the northern tip of Sumatra as well as landing along the western coast of the Isthmus of Kra, near the Andaman Sea, and engaging in trade with such Southeast Asian polities located along the Gulf of Siam as Funan.

The Malay region's interaction with China, on the other hand, began only in the first millennium AD. The lateness of China's engagement with maritime Southeast Asia and the Malay region, as opposed to India, was due primarily to China's development of its maritime orientation only from the third century AD. Even though, as early as the third century BC, China as a political entity had begun to encompass the southern Chinese coastal areas, it was not viewed by the Chinese court as imperative that China develop an external orientation beyond the mainland Southeast Asian states with which it shared a common border.

It was only after the collapse of the Han dynasty in AD 220, and the subsequent political fragmentation that ensued, that the need for this maritime avenue began to manifest. In particular, the kingdom of Wu, which was centered in the Yangtze delta and controlled the entire southern Chinese coastline until AD 280, began to establish links with maritime Southeast Asia, not only because it shared a common border with such mainland Southeast Asian polities as Vietnam, but also because the international maritime economy began to be regarded as a potentially important source of revenue for the Wu court. Indeed, the earliest record of economic or diplomatic interaction between China and maritime Southeast Asia appears only during the early third century AD, in the form of an account by the Chinese officials Kang Tai and Zhu Ying. Both were dispatched by the ruler of the kingdom of Wu on a diplomatic mission to Funan during the 230s to ascertain the state of affairs in maritime Southeast Asia and presumably to establish economic links with that state, which until the fourth century AD maintained an important international port at modern-day Oc Eo, southern Vietnam, along the Gulf of Siam. This was the start of a pattern of external relations maintained by the southern coastal provinces of China, and by subsequent Chinese kingdoms or dynasties that regarded maritime linkages with maritime Southeast Asia, the Indian Ocean littoral, and the Middle East as significant to their well-being, in particular when key parts of inland China were not accessible to them economically or when they could not access the states in India and the Middle East, and their respective markets, via the central Asian route. Products from these regions were shipped to China, and in return, such Chinese products as silk and ceramics were distributed to the markets of these regions.[3]

Despite some semblance of China's interest in maritime Southeast Asia and the Indian Ocean littoral, the political upheavals that China was experiencing during the early centuries of the first millennium AD appears to have caused this interest to appear to maritime Southeast Asian polities as being sporadic. Consequently, the linkages that these polities established with China were indirect, and no textual reference to direct contact between the two can be found. Whatever interaction that did exist was conducted via the ports and polities of mainland Southeast Asia.

By the fifth century AD, however, there was a further increase in interest, on the part of China, in the potential benefits that could be derived from its southward maritime linkages. In particular, the consolidation of southern China under a single rulership (the Liu Song dynasty, AD 420–79) appears to have provided a political and economic climate along the southern Chinese coast in which the southward maritime linkages grew to be regarded as a viable source of economic gain. The increased significance of the exchanges with maritime Southeast Asia even led, in AD 446, to the Liu Song court dispatching several punitive maritime patrols in the South China Sea and the Gulf of Tonkin to keep Cham piracy around the maritime approaches from Southeast

Asia to southern China in check, perhaps reflecting the viability and importance of the government in southern China investing in the security of this southward maritime route.[4]

The polities of maritime Southeast Asia quickly reciprocated this renewed interest, and they began to engage China directly. By the fifth century the names of maritime Southeast Asian polities had begun to appear in Chinese official records. These textual references were made in connection with state-level missions that were dispatched by these polities to China and most likely reflected attempts on their part to establish and maintain diplomatic and economic relations with China. The political consolidation of southern China under Liu Song rule appears to have provided the impetus for maritime Southeast Asian polities to begin investing in and wooing China into a direct economic and diplomatic relationship. Polities that began to engage China at the state level during the fifth century AD included Holotan, which dispatched six missions; Pota, which sent three; and Pohuang, which dispatched eight. Kantoli sent seven missions in the fifth and sixth centuries, while Poli sent five between the fifth and the seventh century.[5] In addition, Topoteng dispatched a mission in 647,[6] while Polo dispatched one in 642 and one 669.[7]

The diplomatic and economic links appear to have been established in tandem with direct shipping links. Although maritime Southeast Asian polities no doubt continued to gain access to the Chinese market via the mainland states that had economic ties with China, direct maritime links with southern China had already begun to appear. Traders, diplomatic representatives, and passengers were able to travel between the Indian Ocean littoral and China via maritime Southeast Asia. In particular, maritime passage to India and thence to the Middle East could be obtained via the Malacca Strait. This connection facilitated cultural interaction between China, maritime Southeast Asia, and the Indian Ocean littoral during the second half of the first millennium AD. Maritime Southeast Asia, and in particular the Strait of Malacca, became one of the main routes along which the exchange and transmission of Buddhism from India to China took place during this time. Thus, Fa Xian, a Chinese Buddhist monk who visited India some time in the early fifth century and returned from India to China via the Malacca Strait, was able to obtain direct passage from Sumatra to Guangzhou.[8]

While southern China became increasingly engaged in diplomatic and economic relations with maritime Southeast Asia, there did not appear to have been any concerted state-level response or coherent foreign policy in this area of Chinese foreign relations. Chinese administration of maritime trade was also ad hoc, despite the consistent economic exchanges between China and maritime Southeast Asia occurring by this time. Few specific regulations concerning the administration of maritime trade were promulgated, and trade was subject to significant abuse by the local officials who handled the foreign traders arriving at the Chinese ports at which they were stationed. This led, in at least one instance during the seventh century AD, to maritime Southeast Asian traders complaining to the Chinese court concerning the corruption of Chinese officials at Guangzhou as a major factor inhibiting the smooth and profitable conduct of trade with China, culminating in the foreign traders taking such matters as the corrupt and extortionist conduct of Chinese officials at the ports into their own hands.[9]

By the late seventh century, however, China, under the Tang dynasty (618–906), did attempt to govern its maritime trade in a more accountable manner, a move that suggests that the Tang court was becoming increasingly aware of the growing importance of maritime trade both as an aspect of China's economy as well as a source of revenue for the state. Some time before 714, the post of superintendent of mercantile shipping was established at Guangzhou, the purpose of which was to appoint an official specifically tasked with insuring that maritime trade could be conducted unimpeded.[10] The administration of maritime trade was consequently established as a separate area of jurisdiction from the other administrative functions of the Guangzhou prefectural officials. Presumably this move was an attempt to redress the long-standing problem of Guangzhou officials being involved in the trade in a clandestine manner, which was characterized by the abuse of their official authority.[11] It also provided for a state-level approach toward the handling of diplomatic and economic relations between China and maritime Southeast Asia, which had clearly developed into a significant aspect of China's external economy, with Guangzhou becoming the most important Chinese international port during the Tang period.

To create a conducive environment for the conduct of international trade at its ports, the Tang court also undertook, at around the same time, a number of measures to ensure that the welfare of foreign traders who were arriving annually at these ports was taken care of. These included, in 695, an edict that provisions were to be made available for all foreign traders in China.[12] These measures were aimed at ensuring that trade with China was sufficiently profitable for foreign traders, in particular those who were arriving from or via maritime Southeast Asia, and thus to encourage them to continue to trade with China.

The more concerted policies that were instituted during the Tang period, as opposed to the lack of any coherent state policy toward maritime relations and trade during the preceding periods before the seventh century AD, appear to have had a fundamental impact on the manner in which maritime Southeast Asian polities regarded their relationship with China. A more coherent pattern of state-level missions dispatched from maritime Southeast Asia to China began to emerge. During this period, the overtures by several maritime Southeast Asian polities began to give way to a state of affairs whereby only two key subregions in maritime Southeast Asia were eventually engaged in state-level discourse with China—Java, representing the Malay Archipelago, and the Malacca Strait, representing the Malay region. Of the former, two polities vied for China's attention. Holing, a central Javanese kingdom, dispatched a total of ten missions to China between the seventh and the ninth century.[13] By the early tenth century, however, a new Javanese polity appears to have taken over the mantle of initiating diplomatic relations with China. Shepo, which emerged by the tenth century as the chief polity in Java, dispatched four missions in the ninth century.[14]

In the Malay region, two polities began dispatching missions to China, competing for the Chinese court's attention. Melayu, a port-polity at Muara Jambi, in Sumatra, was recorded in Chinese texts to have dispatched only one mission. This occurred in 644.[15] Melayu's attempt to assert itself as the regional port-polity of the Malay world, however, appears to have been short-lived. According to the Chinese Buddhist pilgrim Yi Xing—who sojourned at Srivijaya, a port-polity centered at Palembang in southeastern Sumatra, in 671 and again sometime between 685 and 695—Melayu was absorbed by Srivijaya by the late seventh century.[16] In the second-half of the seventh century, Srivijaya began to initiate a series of diplomatic overtures toward the Tang court. Chinese texts note that this newly ascendant Malay port-kingdom dispatched six missions to China between the seventh and the ninth century—one sometime between 670 and 673, and then one each in 702, 716, 728, 742, and 904.[17]

Such missions from maritime Southeast Asian polities were often recorded to have presented many and varied foreign products to the Chinese court, and consequently have often been viewed by historians as one of the chief means by which these polities conducted trade with China. However, the occurrence of the missions suggests that they were more likely occasions spurred by diplomatic and economic motives and not necessarily dispatched primarily as commercial exchanges to be conducted at the state level. The points of time at which they occurred, which often coincided with important political changes or changes to the administration of maritime trade in southern China, suggest that such diplomatic overtures were more likely to have been attempts by the key polities in the Malay region and the Malay Archipelago at establishing, in the eyes of the Chinese courts, their political hegemony over the respective subregions or a means of reaffirming their economic position in the eyes of the new Chinese dynasties establishing their rule over southern China. Such missions were also occasions for these polities to advertise the products that they could obtain and transship to China. In the case of the Malay region, it would appear that by the eighth century, Srivijaya had quickly established itself, in China's eyes, as the preeminent polity of that subregion of maritime Southeast Asia. It became the only Malay polity to continue to maintain diplomatic ties with China by that time.

In spite of these diplomatic and economic developments between China and maritime Southeast Asia during the second half of the first millennium AD, China was by and large a passive partner in this relationship. From the fifth through the tenth century, while tribute missions were being dispatched by maritime Southeast Asian polities to China, the Chinese court sent only one mission to the region. That was dispatched by the Tang court in AD 683 to Srivijaya.[18] The absence of any other Chinese mission dispatched to maritime Southeast Asia suggests that China's perception of, and response to, the region would have almost entirely been dependent on the diplomatic and commercial efforts of the region's polities, and on the accounts of the state of affairs in their respective subregions, which their envoys presented to the Chinese court whenever their missions arrived and were received in China. The dispatch of the sole mission to Srivijaya also suggests that the Malay port-polity had managed to achieve a major political coup in China by the late seventh century, having convinced China that it was the most important regional polity in maritime Southeast Asia, and therefore of vital importance to China's foreign and economic policies toward that region and even such regions further afield as the Indian Ocean littoral. This perception was also evident in the policies that the Tang court promulgated concerning the ensuring of the welfare of foreign traders present at China's ports. As an example, Srivijayan traders were highlighted, in a 695 edict concerning the supply of provisions to foreign traders, as one of the groups of beneficiaries of this concession.[19]

China's reliance on the Malay region as a proxy between itself and the rest of maritime Asia was manifest in the cultural realm as well. Such Chinese travelers as the Buddhist pilgrim Yi Xing note that by the seventh century AD, Chinese pilgrims on their way to obtain sacred scriptures from the Buddhist university at Nalanda, in India, would sojourn at Palembang, the capital of Srivijaya, for a time to develop their language skills. Srivijaya had developed a level of exchange with the Indian subcontinent that was sufficiently intense to enable it to develop as a Buddhist center of learning that was renowned both in China and India. This cultural achievement would no doubt have been established by the economic and cultural interaction that Srivijaya, and the Malay region in general, maintained with India, and which came subsequently to be capitalized in Srivijaya's efforts to promote itself in the eyes of China's political and cultural elite.[20]

The interaction between China and the Malay region, and the role of the Malay region as a proxy between China and the Indian Ocean littoral, appears to have been facilitated by ships from the Malay region as well as further afield. Two networks of shipping developed along the China–maritime Southeast Asia leg of the maritime circuit during this period. The first was maritime Southeast Asian shipping. The ability of maritime Southeast Asians to sail between China and the Malay region appears to have been based primarily on their time-honored seafaring tradition. Indian textual sources suggest that as early as the late first millennium BC, the expertise of these sailors had already enabled them to establish contact with the Indian subcontinent. Establishing contact and more permanent linkages with China would not have been a challenge for them. By the fifth century AD, Chinese texts were beginning to record maritime Southeast Asian vessels in southern Chinese waters. Chang Qingchen and Wei Shun, in the fifth and sixth centuries AD respectively, note that products were shipped by foreign traders to Tongkin and Guangzhou in vessels of *kunlun* origin,[21] apparently referring to maritime Southeast Asian vessels. No distinction as to subregion may be inferred from the Chinese texts. By the seventh century, however, the term *kunlun* appears to have been used exclusively to denote the coastal people of western Indonesia, or the Malay region.[22] By the ninth century, Malay shipping to China had apparently become vibrant. In the *Yiqiejing yingyi* (815), Hui-Lin notes that *kunlun bo,* or Malay seagoing vessels, were arriving regularly at the Gulf of Tonkin and along the southeastern Chinese coast.[23]

Maritime Southeast Asian shipbuilding capabilities and maritime traditions are not well documented in historical sources. Some information, however, is available from archaeological research. The earliest known wreck of Southeast Asian construct comes from the Sambirejo site in southern Sumatra, dated to between AD 610 and 715. Constructed with the dowel-peg and lash-lug techniques, the ship has been estimated to have been almost twenty-three meters long and six meters wide, most likely a seagoing vessel of substantial displacement.[24] Such large seagoing vessels appear to have been used to ply the Sino-Malay route by this time. Xuan Zhang's account of the fifth century, for example, notes that the vessel on which he was traveling from Palembang to southern China was carrying around two hundred traders.[25] Although most likely an exaggeration, the displacement of that particular vessel would nonetheless have been fairly significant, capable of carrying a fairly large number of passengers and their cargo.

The size and displacement of maritime Southeast Asian vessels appear to have grown larger through the course of the first millennium AD. Another wreck—the Intan—a tenth-century maritime Southeast Asian vessel that was probably on its way from Palembang to a Javanese port when it foundered in the northeastern Java Sea, was approximately thirty meters long and may have had a displacement of around three hundred tons.[26] The volume of shipping between China and the Malay region would have been fairly significant by the end of the first millennium.

The second network that facilitated the Sino-Malay trade was Indian Ocean shipping. In particular, Arab merchants and sailors stood out as an important group of traders who helped carry the trade between the Malay region and China in the first millennium. Chinese and Middle Eastern records of this period note that by the Tang period Middle Easterners had established a significant presence in southern Chinese ports, in particular Guangzhou, where a large sojourning Middle Eastern community thrived until 873, when a rebellion led by Huang Chao attacked the port and massacred many Middle Easterners and other foreigners.[27] The Middle Eastern presence at Guangzhou must have also contributed significantly to the facilitation of trade between China and the Malay region during the second half of the first millennium.

There is no known textual reference to Middle Eastern or Indian Ocean vessels throughout much of the first millennium. However, by the ninth century, Arab texts containing navigational information of the passage from the Indian subcontinent to China via the Malay region begin to emerge, with fairly detailed descriptions of the key ports in maritime Southeast Asia. In particular, accounts of a port in the Malacca Strait, known as Zabag to the Arabs, are provided in Arab texts from the eighth century onward, suggesting that Arab traders and ships were by this time beginning to use the key port in the Malay region, most likely the regional port of Palembang, as a transit point between the Indian Ocean littoral and southern China.[28]

Archaeological information pertaining to Arab shipping between the Malay region and China is presently available only in the form of the Belitung wreck, recovered just north of the Java Sea in the vicinity of the Belitung Islands in 1998 and 1999. Dated to the ninth century and identified as an Arab vessel, the ship was carrying a cargo of Chinese products, including ceramics, metal ingots, and metalware, and apparently en route to Srivijaya-Palembang when it foundered.[29] Arab vessels were thus sailing from the Indian Ocean to China by the late first millennium AD, with Arab traders aboard conducting some form of long-distance trade between the two bastions of the trans-Asiatic economy. The bulk of the cargo arriving in the Malay region from China, however, would most likely have been dispersed at a port in the region first, to cater to the region's demand for such Chinese products as ceramics, metals and metalware, and textiles. The absence of any discovery of any other Middle Eastern or Indian Ocean vessel in Southeast Asian or Chinese waters suggests that, although these vessels were used in trade between China and Southeast Asia during the first millennium AD, the proportion of the trade that they carried was most likely much smaller than that carried by Southeast Asian and Malay ships and that Middle Eastern traders operating between maritime Southeast Asia and China were likely to have relied heavily on ships from those two regions.

Malay and Indian Ocean shipping were the main channels through which the economic and diplomatic exchanges between China and the Malay region were conducted. It does not appear that Chinese shipping carried any of the trade between Southeast Asia and China throughout the first millennium AD. In addition, we know nothing about Chinese shipbuilding technology for this period.[30] Information on Chinese participation in maritime shipping to the Malay region is not forthcoming until the eleventh century, when Chinese provincial accounts, particularly in Fujian and Guangdong, begin to mention the Chinese sailing abroad for the purpose of trade.[31] Archaeologically, no seagoing vessel of Chinese construct, dating to before the thirteenth century, has as yet been discovered in Chinese or Southeast Asian waters. The passive stance of the Chinese courts in their diplomatic and economic interaction with maritime Southeast Asia appears to have greatly discouraged active Chinese participation in shipping between the two regions during this period.

Instead, the Chinese appear to have been eager recipients of whatever products were shipped to their shores, relying completely on the arrival of foreign ships for the inflow of foreign goods. Demand for specific types of foreign products would have been relayed to foreign traders through their representatives residing in the Chinese ports. This state of affairs was perpetuated by the administrative stance of successive Chinese courts concerning the conduct of maritime trade at the ports that they controlled. By and large, the Chinese courts appear to have maintained a state monopoly over the external and domestic sectors of China's trade in foreign products throughout the first millennium AD. The only people with whom foreign traders carried out commercial transactions at the Chinese ports were the Chinese officials.[32] As a result, Chinese demand for foreign products appears to have been based largely on the demands of the bureaucracy and the imperial courts, even though the general Chinese market did exhibit some interest in foreign products. The Malay region, as a proxy between China and maritime Asia, became an important channel through which the Chinese political and social elites' demands for foreign products were fulfilled. The result was that the Malay region became one of southern China's most important foreign maritime trading partners.

By the seventh century, Malay traders had established a significant presence at the port of Guangzhou. The presence of Malay agents at the coastal port cities of southern China suggests that the volume and value of the trade between the Malay region and China was sufficiently high to warrant a more permanent presence at these ports. By the late ninth century Malay commercial operations in southern China were no longer confined to Guangzhou. A memorial issued by the Tang court in 896 notes that "island barbarians" (a reference to maritime Southeast Asians, including Malays) were by this time residing in the provinces of Fujian and Zhejiang as well.[33] Malay ships, and the trade that they carried with them, were thus arriving at the Chinese ports along the length of the southern Chinese coastline. Diplomatic missions, however, appear to have been confined largely to Guangzhou, the chief Chinese port in the south.

Initially, the products shipped to China via the Malay region were mainly from the Indian Ocean littoral and the Middle East. These included such resinous aromatics as frankincense, storax (liquidambar), myrrh, and dragon's blood, glassware from the Middle East, ivory, gems, and such foodstuffs as rosewater and dates,[34] reflecting the sophisticated tastes of the consumers to which maritime trade was catering. These products were already familiar to the Chinese market, having been available via the central Asian route. The trade between China and maritime Southeast Asia was primarily a duplication of the transcontinental overland trade that had been established by the early first millennium AD. In the case of the maritime trade circuit, most of these products were probably transshipped by Malay traders to China, having first been obtained from Middle Eastern and Indian traders calling at the Malay region's key entrepôt port of Palembang. However, as ties between China and maritime Southeast Asia became increasingly firm over the second half of the first millennium AD, a number of products from the region began to be introduced to the China market. These included cloves and nutmeg, which originated only from the eastern Indonesian islands,[35] both of which were quickly regarded by the Chinese as high-value medicinals.

For China, the Malay region did not feature as an important source of foreign products during this period. Only a very select number of indigenous Malay products managed to be accepted in the Chinese market. These included such aromatics as gharuwood, and other products of lower value, including betel nuts and sappanwood (most likely used as a dyestuff). Three other products, however, appear to have made significant headway in the Chinese market. Camphor, a product from Borneo and northwest Sumatra, particularly Barus, began to be exported to China only in the sixth century. Benzoin began to be shipped to China and marketed as a substitute for Middle Eastern storax some time in the second half of the first millennium, while at around the same time Malay pine resin appears to have been marketed in China as a substitute for frankincense.[36] These three products were traded under the category of aromatics and medicines and were regarded by the Chinese market as high-value items.

In return for the items brought to its ports, China exported such products as ceramics, metals, textiles and foodstuffs to its foreign trading partners. Chinese ceramics were a very important class of products demanded by maritime Southeast Asia and were imported in large quantities. *Yue*-type wares produced by southern Chinese kilns and such provincial ceramics as Changsha ware have been recovered from Malay sites, notably Palembang and southern Kedah, as well as in Java.[37] Other high-value ceramics, such as the *sancai*-type ("three-color") wares, white wares, and unglazed blue-and-white wares produced by kilns in northern China, have also been recovered from the Belitung wreck.[38] The bulk of the ceramics exported to maritime Southeast Asia were produced in kilns near southern Chinese ports, although a small proportion of the ceramics exports appear to have been sourced from renowned inland kilns, which would have made them more costly to procure.

Metals were another important class of Chinese products demanded by maritime Southeast Asia.[39] While there is a dearth of textual information on the trade of metals, archaeological information, particularly the data accrued from the Belitung and Intan wrecks, indicates that by the ninth century, China's export of metals—including lead, iron, copper, silver, and gold—to maritime Southeast Asia was already a well-established aspect of the trade between the two regions.

These metals were exported in workable as well as manufactured forms. Lead was exported to maritime Southeast Asia predominantly in the form of ingots, which often doubled as ballast on the ships that were used to carry them,[40] while copper, given its scarcity and the consequent high value placed on it by the Chinese, appears to have been exported exclusively as high-value manufactured items, such as bronze mirrors.[41] Iron, on the other hand, was exported in the form of utilitarian items, such as cauldrons and cooking pots mounted on tripods, as well as such partially worked forms as bars and rods.[42]

Chinese iron, which was cast-iron, was much poorer than the iron that was produced in India and Southeast Asia at the time. However, the economies of scale attained by the Chinese iron industry by late in the first millennium allowed Chinese iron to be produced and sold cheaply. This enabled China to serve as an important source of iron to places in maritime Southeast Asia, especially Java and Bali, that lacked natural deposits of iron ore. In particular, Java and Bali became reliant on China as a source of iron.

By the early tenth century direct economic links between China and maritime Southeast Asia were already well established, with Guangzhou as the chief port of call for ships arriving from the south.[43] Only two of maritime Southeast Asia's polities had, by this time, managed to maintain diplomatic and economic links with China—Srivijaya, in the Malay region, and Shepo, or Java, in the East Indonesian Archipelago. These two polities represented the general nature of the China–maritime Southeast Asia interaction by the tenth century—essentially that of two subregions maintaining their distinct links with China under the auspices of their respective preeminent polities.

The Malay region, in particular, under the auspices of Srivijaya, had established itself as strong in China's eyes. Chinese perception of Srivijaya as a vital proxy in China's economic and diplomatic policies toward maritime Asia remained unchanged in the face of the political upheaval unleashed by the Huang Chao rebellion at the end of the ninth century, which rocked China and eventually led to the collapse of the Tang dynasty in 906. In the ensuing interregnum, which lasted until 960 in northern China and the 970s in the south, the southeastern coastal provinces effectively became autonomous kingdoms. The fiscal needs of these kingdoms led their respective courts to continue to maintain as well as develop the maritime economic and political links that had already been established between China and the polities of maritime Asia.[44] In the early tenth century the kingdom of Min, in southern Fujian, began to develop Quanzhou and Fuzhou as major ports for foreign ships,[45] while the southern Han kingdom, with its administrative capital at Guangzhou, continued to maintain that port as the center of China's maritime economic relations with maritime

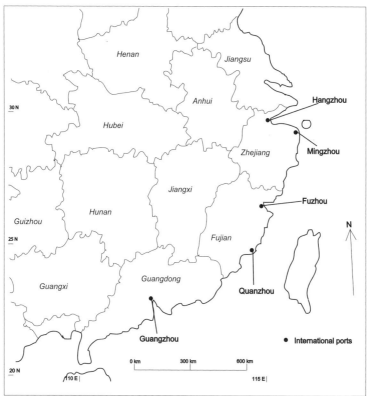

Map 1.1. International ports along the southern Chinese coast, late first millennium AD

Asia throughout the tenth century.[46] The foreign products arriving at these ports were redistributed to the rest of the Chinese market through domestic mercantile networks.[47]

In this regard, the Malay region appears to have benefited from the vacuum left by the Huang Chao massacre of foreign traders at Guangzhou in 873, and apparently seized the opportunity amid the political upheaval in southern China to establish itself as a major player in the Asian maritime economy and an important trading partner of China. Malay representation at the southern Chinese ports, in particular Guangzhou, was regarded by the Chinese as having been important enough by the early tenth century to warrant the southern Han court to appoint as the foreign official of that port, in 905, the Srivijayan envoy who had arrived in China on a diplomatic mission the year before.[48] The presence of sojourning communities from the Malay region at the southern Chinese ports, and Srivijayan official representation at Guangzhou, enabled the region, during the tenth century, to react and adapt to any changes in maritime trade policies, as well as to be attuned to shifts in the political situation in China, which often had a fundamental impact on the flow of maritime trade and the commercial and political position of foreign polities in the eyes of the Chinese court. This included its apparent awareness of the political changes that swept through China during the mid-tenth century, which culminated in the establishment of the Song dynasty in China in 960, a decade before the eventual extension of Song rule over the southern coastal provinces of Fujian and Guangdong in 970, when Song rule eventually began to have an impact on the administration of China's economic and diplomatic relations with the polities of maritime Asia.

Thus, upon the establishment of its rule over the coastal provinces of Guangdong and Fujian in 970, the Song court inherited a legacy of direct economic and diplomatic relations with the Malay region that had developed over the course of the first millennium AD. The Malay region began its relations with the Song court as one of China's important foreign trading partners, and as a state with which China had significant foreign relations. China had by this time also become an important factor in the political and economic life of the Malay region. The overall absence of a coherent state-level approach by China toward its relations with maritime Asia prevented it from having a more significant or active role in shaping the course of the Malay region's political and economic developments in the first millennium. It was only in the Song period that China's impact, particularly that of its maritime trade policies, on these aspects of the region's coastal societies and polities became more pronounced.

Chapter 2

CHINA'S ECONOMIC RELATIONS WITH MARITIME ASIA IN THE SONG AND YUAN PERIODS

In AD 960 a Chinese general named Zhao Guangyin usurped the imperial throne of northern China, thus uniting most of northern and southern China under the Song dynastic house for the next three centuries. From 960 until the capitulation of northern China to invading Jurchen forces in 1126, the capital of the Song court was at Kaifeng. Song rule initially began as a northern Chinese political entity, with its political and economic orientation directed to a significant extent toward central Asia and the regions beyond the northern Chinese borders. It was only in 970, when Song forces eventually prevailed in the southern Chinese coastal provinces of Guangdong and Fujian, that the Song court managed to begin to implement direct administrative control over China's economic and diplomatic interaction with the polities of maritime Asia. As such, China's relations with the maritime regions of Asia, in particular Southeast Asia and the Indian Ocean littoral, was essentially a continuation of the Tang period, and were not seen by the Song court as a vital aspect of the political and economic imperatives it had to address during the first decades of its rule.

However, as China began to face military and political pressures from the north, successively from Liao, Jurchen, and subsequently Mongol forces, the Song court was forced to reconsider the nature of its foreign relations with the polities in maritime Asia. The importance of these polities that lay south of China became increasingly important to the political and economic well-being of Song China, as the Liao through the eleventh century, and the Jurchens and the Mongols through the twelfth and the thirteenth centuries respectively, systematically pressed southward and encroached into Chinese territory. Finally, in 1279, the whole of China fell under the rule of the Mongols. Consequently, a shift in the perspective of the Chinese court toward maritime Southeast Asia and the Indian Ocean littoral may be discerned from the eleventh to the fourteenth century, and the Song court was compelled to increasingly adopt a southward approach in its economic and diplomatic policies.

At the same time as these international developments were taking place, several important developments were occurring within China itself. Chief among them were the burgeoning government bureaucracy and the increase in the generation of wealth by the Chinese economy as a result of monetization and of increasing urbanization. These developments led to increases in the number of affluent consumers, who could appreciate the high-value exotic products made available via maritime trade, as well as the popularization of the consumption of low-value foreign products by the Chinese market in general. These trends in consumption had a fundamental impact on the evolving nature of Chinese maritime trade through the course of the Song and Yuan periods.

The Northern Song: From State Monopoly to State Stewardship

Following the advent of Song rule, the Chinese court's stance concerning the administration of diplomatic and economic relations with the polities of Southeast Asia and the Indian Ocean littoral was, at first, essentially a continuation of the policies that had developed by the late first millennium AD. Initially, the Song rulers saw themselves as at the head of a tribute system, and indeed tribute missions began to arrive at the Song court as early as 960, bringing foreign products to exchange for Chinese ones. However, China's maritime trade effectively took off only after 971, when the Song court finally defeated the southern Han kingdom in Guangdong, reunified the southernmost coastal province of China under Song rule, and established bureaucratic departments to administer this trade at the ports of southern China. A mercantile shipping superintendency was established at Guangzhou in 971, and, later, similar offices at Hangzhou and Mingzhou. The creation of these superintendencies at the major Chinese ports facilitated and stimulated trade with the Dashi (Middle Eastern Arabs associated with the 'Abbasid caliphate),[1] Kollam (India), Java, Champa (a kingdom along the eastern coast of modern-day Vietnam that had maintained economic links with southern China throughout the first millennium), Boni (the northern coast of Borneo, most likely centered in modern-day Santubong), Mait (in the Philippines), and Srivijaya in the Malay region. All these states were able to establish regular trade relations with Song China.[2]

However, trade was limited to that which could be conducted through the mercantile shipping superintendencies, which conducted trade solely at the state level. The chief means of conducting trade was through ritualized state-level exchanges. Foreign missions from China's trading partners arrived in China and presented tributes of products that were either obtained from their respective spheres of influence or were transshipped through one of their trading ports. In return, Chinese products, as well as status gifts such as ceremonial attire and headdresses that denoted official rank, were given to the mission envoys. The reliance on tribute missions as the chief source of foreign products is reflected in the high frequency of tribute missions from China's trading partners from the advent of Song rule until the second decade of the eleventh century. This period witnessed the largest number of state-level exchanges between China and its foreign partners in the entire Song period. A total of seventy-one missions were received by the Song court between 960 and 999, while thirty-five missions were received during the first two decades of the eleventh century. The Song court actively encouraged maritime commercial exchanges via this channel.

The Song court did not initially look favorably on the participation of private Chinese traders in overseas voyages. The role of Chinese private enterprise in this import trade appears to have been severely curtailed, with the Song court monopolizing the domestic trade in imports. The mercantile shipping superintendencies, the key Chinese maritime trade administrative organs, were established purely to facilitate the maritime trade carried by China's foreign trading partners to its shores, and not with the view to facilitating trade between Chinese merchants and foreign traders. Indeed, in 976 overseas trading voyages were actually prohibited, and severe penalties were meted out to those who contravened the ban.[3] The ban was reiterated in 994 and the penalties for the offense made harsher.[4]

The Song court also instituted a total monopoly over the domestic trade in foreign products. The fiscal regime governing maritime trade reflected this monopoly. Commercial transactions between private Chinese citizens and foreign traders within China were prohibited in 976.[5] Although some foreign products were permitted to be traded among Chinese citizens in 982, the Song court's grip on the domestic trade was nonetheless very tight. Between 984 and 987, the customs duty was levied at 10 percent of a ship's cargo, and then the whole of the net cargo was purchased by the mercantile shipping superintendency.[6] The foreign products were then sold to the Chinese domestic market through official markets.

However, toward the end of the tenth century, the Song court's attitude toward maritime trade began to change. As early as 982 the Song court modified its total monopoly over this domestic trade by permitting thirty-seven types of aromatics to be freely traded among Chinese citizens.[7] This change appears to have been triggered by the complaints of Chinese citizens concerning the lack of access to foreign products. The official markets, which were the sole sources of foreign products available to Chinese citizens, were apparently not able to meet this demand.

The impact of the change was limited, since the official markets remained in control of all foreign products as they entered China. The Song court continued to acquire all incoming foreign products through the levying of customs duties and official purchases. Only after purchasing goods at official markets could Chinese traders sell them on to other customers. In addition, eight high-value products, all of which had significant status value, were declared to be state monopoly items.[8] Nonetheless, this shift in the stance of the government represented a break from the court's previous insistence on total state control over the domestic trade of foreign products. From this point on, the Song court began a protracted process of scaling back its participation in maritime trade.

The scaling back of state involvement began with the reduction in the proportion of the domestic trade in foreign products in the Song court's hands. This was achieved through changes in the rate of customs duties and the proportion of the imported products that the court purchased. In 991 the customs duty rate was doubled from 10 percent to 20, while the mercantile shipping superintendencies had the right to purchase no more than half of the better-quality products of a ship's net cargo (after import duties had been levied).[9] These two measures immediately reduced the Song court's market share of foreign products, obtained through tax and compulsory purchase, to no more than 60 percent. This proportion was further reduced during the reign of the emperor Renzong (1023–63). Compulsory purchases of all products, regardless of their quality or value, were imposed at 30 percent of the net cargo.[10] Since the customs duty rate remained at 20 percent, the Song court's market share was consequently reduced to 44 percent. The reduction of state-level participation was accompanied by the growing involvement of Chinese private traders in this trade. Thus, within less than a century after 982, the domestic trade in foreign products shifted from being a total monopoly of the Song court to the point where a marginal majority of the trade was in the hands of Chinese private trading concerns.

These changes were part of a larger movement in the Song court's move away from ritualized state-level exchanges carried out at the imperial court, to a more mundane trade conducted at the ports. Toward the end of the tenth century, China's foreign trading partners appear to have been encouraged to establish commercial presences and operations at China's international ports. It is likely that the establishment of local agents at these ports, who could relay orders for specific foreign products, would have led to a shift in trade from that which was channeled through tribute missions to that received at the port by the foreign states' own representatives. Tribute missions continued to be regarded as important by the Song court as diplomatic exchanges, conducted for the purpose of reaffirming the economic links with its foreign trading partners. Tribute missions as state-level trade exchanges, however, were in decline. Between 1020 and 1050 the Song court received only fourteen missions from the states of Jiaozhi (Tonkin), Champa (modern-day coastal Vietnam), Srivijaya, India, Chola, and the Arabs, its key foreign trading partners in Southeast Asia and the Indian Ocean littoral.

The Song court was apparently encouraging the growth of maritime trade outside the official framework it had instituted following the advent of its rule. These efforts were given a further boost by developments taking place in the early eleventh century in central Asia, traversed by the transcontinental trading route that linked the Middle East and the Mediterranean to China. By the 1020s this overland route, traditionally important for the Middle East–China trade, had become so unsafe that the Song court had to advise the Dashi Arab envoys in 1023 to no longer use it for tribute missions to China but to use the maritime route through Southeast Asia instead.[11] This advisory no doubt gave maritime shipping and trade flowing between the Indian Ocean, Southeast Asia, and China, which had to funnel through the Strait of Malacca, a significant boost, both in terms of the volume of shipping as well as the value of trade.

Chinese traders were, from the outset, eager to participate in the external sector of this trade, and the initial ban that the Song court had imposed on private Chinese shipping operating abroad had not been entirely successful. In 989 the Song court began to permit Chinese private shipping to sail abroad for the purpose of trade. Regulations were imposed, requiring all Chinese traders going on overseas voyages to first register themselves at the Liangzhe mercantile shipping superintendency at Hangzhou and Mingzhou.[12] The Song court also stipulated that upon their return, Chinese ships had to return to the ports at which they had registered before departure, so that they could be subjected to customs inspection.

Very quickly many Chinese entrepreneurs became engaged in maritime shipping. A 995 memorial notes that many Guangzhou traders had become involved in the shipping trade by that time,[13] presumably traveling to Southeast Asian and Indian Ocean littoral ports. Guangzhou-based traders were not the only ones involved in overseas trading ventures. A poem written by the Chinese official Xian Li, stationed at Quanzhou in the mid-eleventh century, refers to the annual departure of ships from Quanzhou to foreign lands for trade.[14]

However, even as maritime trade was devolving out of official hands through the course of the late tenth and the eleventh century, China continued to rely largely on its foreign trading partners to act as the main carriers of its maritime trade. Chinese shipping did not develop at an exponential rate before the late eleventh century. The need to report to one of the two officially designated international ports of Hangzhou and Mingzhou both before a ship's departure and upon its return meant a year's extra travel time for traders and vessels not based at either port. This inconvenience had obvious financial implications for Chinese traders, and the restrictive regulations appear to have curtailed the growth of Chinese shipping. Thus, shipping from Southeast Asia and the Indian Ocean littoral continued to be the chief means through which China's import of foreign products from these regions was sustained, even though Chinese shipping gradually increased through the course of the eleventh century. This policy was subsequently broadened during Renzong's reign to include Guangzhou as a designated port of departure for southbound Chinese shipping, a move that was of tremendous benefit to the Chinese traders based at that port.[15]

These changes to the domestic and shipping sectors of China's maritime economy led to a boom in China's maritime trade during the eleventh century. Between 1049 and 1054 the annual value of foreign products imported by China was 530,000 strings of cash.[16] By 1064 this annual figure had risen by another 100,000 strings.[17] These figures refer only to the import of products through Guangzhou, Hangzhou, and Mingzhou, the only Chinese ports officially permitted to handle foreign trade before 1087. The figures do not include the trade in foreign products conducted at unauthorized ports such as Quanzhou.[18] Primarily, by lowering the proportion of the domestic trade it controlled and breaking away from the reliance on tribute missions as the key means of importing foreign products, the Song court stimulated sustained growth in China's trade in foreign products. It is not clear whether the Song court intended for this protracted process of scaling back the state's direct involvement in maritime trade to spur growth in the maritime sector, but that was its effect.

Toward the end of the eleventh century the liberalization of China's maritime economy reached its peak. The fiscal regime governing maritime trade was eased significantly during the reign of the emperor Shenzong (1067–85), under the Wang Anshi reforms. Begun in 1069, the reforms were instituted in order to encourage the expansion of the tax base of the Song court, and to enhance the overall fiscal health of the Song empire. This need to increase the revenue collected by the Song court was caused by an exponential increase in the court's state expenditures, which, as a result of the massive buildup of the Song army through the course of the eleventh century as well as the increase in the size of bureaucracy following the change in China's political power base from military to civilian government at the inception of Song rule in the late tenth century, had by this time ballooned out of control. Interestingly, while the reforms pertaining to the sources of state revenue garnered from the Chinese domestic economy, such as the Song court's monopoly on the production, distribution, and sale of salt, was streamlined into the hands of the central administration, the reforms relating to international maritime trade were intended to have completely different results.[19] Instituted in 1072 as part of the restructuring of the Trade and Barter Regulations,[20] the maritime trade reforms were aimed at raising the level of economic exchange between China and its foreign trading partners, as well as to expand maritime-related economic activities within China itself. Whereas the Chinese domestic economy was to increasingly be under the tight rein of the central administration with private participation being heavily regulated, China's maritime economy was to be further liberalized into private hands.

The reforms affected China's maritime trade in three ways. First, all commercial exchanges with foreign traders were henceforth to be handled at the port level. Before the reign of Shenzong, although the Song court had decreased its reliance on tribute missions for the import of foreign products, there had been ambivalence toward such missions. However, during the first half of Shenzong's reign, all trade exchanges were dealt with at the port of arrival. None was received at the imperial court, regardless of the status of the trading partner involved, nor were ceremonial reciprocal gifts conferred on the representatives of these trading missions. Only diplomatic missions were received at the imperial court in Kaifeng.

The second effect of the reforms related to the monetization of China's maritime economy. In 1074 the embargo on the export of copper cash from China, which had been instituted at the advent of Song rule in 960, was lifted so as to encourage an increase in foreign trade, as copper cash was a Chinese item in high demand among China's trading partners.[21] China's maritime trade at all levels was, after that, conducted within a monetized system.

The move toward a monetized system of foreign trade had already been taking place progressively throughout the eleventh century. In the Taizong Chunhua era (990–95), although China's maritime trade had been on the increase and compulsory purchases of up to 50 percent of a ship's net cargo had been imposed, cash disbursements from the imperial coffers to facilitate the conduct of official maritime trade had apparently remained insignificant. However, by the mid-eleventh century trade at the Chinese ports had already made an important move away from a barter system toward one that would eventually be based on currency. During the Renzong Huangyou era (1049–54), a valuation in copper cash terms was conducted for the first time of the maritime trade at China's ports.[22] Similar valuations were conducted again during the Yingzong Zhiping era (1064–68)[23] and in 1086.[24] China's shift to evaluating its maritime trade in currency terms during the reign of Renzong (1023–63),[25] at a time when compulsory purchases of 30 percent of net cargoes were levied by the mercantile shipping superintendency, suggests that maritime trade products were valued in cash terms as part of the normal fiscal administration of maritime trade.[26]

This new method of accounting introduced a new factor into China's maritime trade. Hitherto, the only fiscal measure imposed on maritime trade had been import duties levied in kind, based on a stipulated quantitative proportion of the incoming cargo. Purchases of the remaining cargo by the mercantile shipping superintendency had presumably been conducted through barter, since the Song court held a monopoly over trade with foreigners. Trade exchanges between China and its foreign trading partners, which had until the second decade of the eleventh century taken place mainly in the form of tribute exchanges, had consisted of reciprocal exchanges of goods rather than currency. The introduction of compulsory purchases under Renzong, although based on a stipulated percentage of the quantity of the cargo, was valued and most likely carried out in monetary terms, as the correct value had to be ascertained and cash paid out to the foreign traders, who would in turn use the money to purchase goods to bring home with them. These developments coincided with an increase in the production of copper cash during the Renzong Baoyuan era (1038–40).[27]

Nonetheless, the impact of this process before the Wang Anshi reforms must have been felt only in the domestic sector of China's international maritime economy. Before the 1074 lifting of the export embargo on copper, although silver and gold were already exported by China, the Song court vigilantly guarded against the outflow of Chinese copper cash due to its vital role in the Chinese economy. Copper cash had previously been disbursed by the Song court to foreign traders with the intention that it be used to purchase Chinese commodities at the ports before the foreign traders returned home.

The 1074 lifting of the copper embargo, however, effectively extended the monetized system to include the international sector of China's maritime economy. Chinese copper cash of this period is the most commonly found Chinese coinage at sites in maritime Southeast Asia, particularly in Java and the Malay region.[28] Increases in the production of copper cash were officially sanctioned to facilitate the smooth implementation of fiscal reforms. The annual production of copper cash thus increased from 1.3 million strings annually in the early eleventh century to almost 6 million by 1078.[29] This outward extension of the Song monetized economy is apparent from the shift in reciprocal gifts presented to tribute missions that arrived between 1072 and 1086. During the fifteen-year Wang Anshi reform period, no prestige article, with the exception of imperial letters, is recorded as having been presented to the foreign missions that made presentations of tribute to the Song court. The Song court reciprocated solely with copper cash and silver bullion to the value of the tribute presented. The recipients of such cash disbursements included the Cham missions of 1072 and 1086, the Dashi Arab mission of 1073, and the Chola mission of 1077.[30] The Malay region was also a recipient of such currency payments. The 1078 Srivijayan mission received sixty-four thousand strings of copper cash and 10,500 taels of silver in return for its tribute of white gold, camphor, frankincense, and other foreign products.[31]

The third effect of the Wang Anshi reforms was the further scaling back of state participation in the domestic trade in foreign products. A change in customs duties during the first half of the reign of Shenzong saw the import tax lowered from 20 to $6\,^{2}/_{3}$ percent. The compulsory purchase rate remained unchanged.[32] The proportion of the domestic trade in foreign products that the Song court controlled was thus not more than $34\,^{2}/_{3}$ percent, with the proportion in private hands consequently increasing from 54 to $65\,^{1}/_{3}$ percent. This proportion of the domestic trade in private hands was the highest at any point during the Song period. Market share in the domestic trade, an issue consistently lobbied for by Chinese private trading concerns, was apparently the most satisfactory when it was at around 65 percent. Subsequent memorials submitted by mercantile shipping superintendency officials to the Song court always referred to the customs duties and compulsory purchase rates of the first half of the reign of Shenzong as the most equitable for the trade in both high- and low-value foreign products by Chinese private traders.[33] Apparently, this proportion encouraged the development of maritime trade by Chinese private traders, while the Song court's level of participation played a stabilizing role in China's maritime economy.

The structural changes instituted through the Wang Anshi reforms were fundamental to the growth of Song China's maritime economy, and their impact on the value and volume of the trade was immediate. The value of China's maritime import trade in the nine years following the end of the first half of the reign of Shenzong, in 1085, amounted to approximately 1 million strings of cash annually,[34] almost double the average annual value noted between 1049 and 1064. The Wang Anshi reforms were therefore successful in achieving the ultimate objective of increasing the amount of revenue that could be garnered from China's maritime trade through encouraging the growth of the maritime economy. The reformers correctly understood that, unlike domestic economic activities, where revenue could be increased only by streamlining the existing economy into state hands and under direct state execution, the maritime economy, which was dependent on the external world, had to be liberalized for it to grow. The resulting structural changes signaled the success of the Wang Anshi reforms in achieving their ultimate goal. More important, however, these changes provided the necessary framework within which China's maritime economy made the next quantum leap when the right impetus appeared. This occurred in 1090.

In 1090 the Song court decreed that instead of having to register at one of the designated ports of departure, Chinese ships would henceforth be permitted to depart on overseas voyages from any prefecture, so long as their departure was officially registered and a permit for the trip had been issued. The authority to issue departure permits was no longer limited to the mercantile shipping superintendencies. Any prefectural administration willing to take on the administrative responsibilities of allowing ships to depart from their respective prefectures were permitted to maintain documentary records for the issue of departure permits.[35] This liberalization of Chinese shipping had been preceded, in 1087, by the establishment of a mercantile shipping superintendency at Quanzhou, and another at Banqiao in 1088, enabling Chinese shipping based at those ports to participate directly in the shipping trade, instead of having to register at Guangzhou, Hangzhou, or Mingzhou before proceeding abroad.[36]

The 1090 liberalization was a major departure from previous Song policy. The additional financial and operational burdens of having to report to one of a small number of designated ports of departure were no longer a factor, and Chinese private maritime shipping was no longer under the burden of the state administrative procedures and regulations it had experienced throughout the eleventh century. In addition, the liberalization exposed large areas of the hinterlands of the Chinese coastline, linking the Chinese domestic economy, its demands and its industries, to Chinese shipping. The domestic economy and its industries no longer had to funnel through the Chinese ports that had mercantile shipping superintendencies. Instead, they could now be integrated with maritime shipping at the local level, creating the context for the development of a highly diffused maritime economy.

There were two effects of the 1090 liberalization of maritime shipping. First, Chinese trade figures showed a twofold jump in the amount of revenue from customs duties, from approximately half a million strings of cash collected annually during the mid-eleventh century to approximately a million in the last years of the eleventh century.[37] This indicates that the volume of international shipping had increased significantly. For foreign shipping, the Chinese climate of trade remained essentially unchanged from the first half of the reign of Shenzong until the fall of the Northern Song capital, in 1126. Although the Wang Anshi reformist faction fell from favor under the new emperor in 1085, the reforms that affected maritime trade were not rescinded, even as most of the other Wang Anshi reforms were. There was no change in the conditions under which foreign traders operated in their maritime trade with China.

Instead, the increase in shipping during the last decades of the Northern Song was most likely fueled to a large extent by the expansion of Chinese maritime shipping following the 1090 liberalization. This was private Chinese shipping, since the Song court did not officially participate in or sponsor any trading voyages. The increase was accompanied by the advancement of Chinese maritime technology, which included Chinese technical knowledge in the construction of seaworthy vessels, as well the development of such navigational instruments as the magnetic compass.[38] These developments pushed Chinese international shipping toward a tipping point, the effects of which became manifest by the twelfth century.

The other effect of the 1090 liberalization was on the range and nature of Chinese imports and exports via maritime trade. Until the late eleventh century, China had largely remained a recipient of the shipping trade that was carried chiefly by foreign shipping. Although Chinese demand for specific foreign products would no doubt have been noted by foreign traders who arrived regularly at Chinese ports, as well as by the representatives of China's key trading partners who were based at the Chinese international ports, the Chinese market would not have been able to project its consumption patterns into its maritime trade to the fullest extent, given the absence of Chinese official participation in maritime shipping and the limited amount of Chinese private shipping during the late tenth and the eleventh century. The nature of the domestic trade in foreign products as it developed in China during this period was still largely determined by the products that China's foreign trading partners brought to its ports. The 1090 liberalization, however, paved the way for the Chinese market to no longer be dependent on foreign shipping to meet its demands or determine its consumption patterns. China could now shop abroad. New products were consequently added to those already traded, and the expansion in trade encouraged the large-scale presence of Chinese traders and shipping in a number of foreign ports. As Chinese commercial presence at the foreign ports increased, Chinese knowledge of the availability of indigenous and entrepôt trade goods in specific subregions and ports, and the consumption patterns and demands of the settlements in these places, deepened. This led to a significant expansion of the range of products in both China's import and export trade.[39]

In turn, the expansion of Chinese shipping and the growing presence of Chinese traders at foreign ports led to the increasing importance of the trade in low-value products from the late eleventh century onward. Low-value products gained increasing significance throughout the twelfth century. The relatively low unit value of these products necessitated a high turnover volume for reasonable profits to be generated. A significant increase in the volume of shipping was therefore a critical precondition for the development of China's import trade in low-value foreign products.

The increasing significance of the trade in low-value imports is reflected in the change in the Chinese fiscal regime governing the import of foreign products. Until the end of the eleventh century, only one customs duty and one compulsory purchase rate had been instituted. While there must have been different prevailing market and official prices for different products, the Song court apparently regarded all of them as belonging to a single value band. China's maritime import trade was, until the end of the eleventh century, essentially based on high-value products. Although there were already low-value products from Southeast Asia in China's import trade—such as sandalwood incense, sappanwood, and ebony, all of which were listed as coarse-category or low-value products later in the twelfth century—the shipment of such products to China had hitherto apparently been in such limited quantities that a specific customs duty and compulsory purchase rate had not been instituted.

However, by the beginning of the twelfth century, this situation had clearly changed. Different rates for low- and high-value foreign products were instituted for the first time in China. During the reign of Huizong (1102–25), a customs duty of 30 percent was levied on low-value imports, while 10 percent was levied on high-value imports.[40] The Chinese textual records do not note the reason behind the new rates. However, the setting of a separate rate for low-value products most likely reflected an increase in the volume and range of such imports. The low unit value of these products, and the variety imported by the beginning of the twelfth century, in the context of a high turnover in shipping volume, had clearly necessitated a change in the Chinese administrative approach.

Although liberalization was a fundamental factor in changing the trajectory of China's maritime economy, its effects were mitigated by the Song court's attempts to control the extent of Chinese private shipping abroad. The Song court had, as early as the second half of the eleventh century, restricted Chinese vessels from remaining abroad for more than nine months, or approximately one cycle of the northeast-southwest monsoons. Chinese ships were also required to declare to the mercantile shipping superintendency or prefectural administrations their

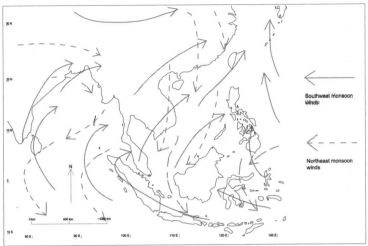

Map 2.1. Northeast and southwest monsoon winds across the Bay of Bengal, maritime Southeast Asia, and the South China Sea

intended port of call. The shipowners and captains were liable to investigation by the superintendency if any one of these two restrictions was violated, and punishment would be meted out if the violations were not due to unforeseen circumstances or difficulties while the vessel was abroad.[41] These restrictions are first noted in an official's memorial dated to 1164, although the memorial records that the restriction was imposed as early as the reign of the emperor Shenzong (1067–85).

Limiting a vessel's stay abroad to one monsoon cycle would have restricted the operation of southbound Chinese ships to areas east of the Bay of Bengal. Ships bound for Southeast Asia from China departed annually on the northeast monsoon, between November and February. Ships intending to proceed to the Bay of Bengal and the Indian Ocean had to wait, in the southern end of the Strait of Malacca or the Java Sea, for the southwest monsoon, which occurred between April and September. The time restriction not only limited the geographical extent of China's projection of its maritime shipping activities but its domestic consumption pattern. Coupled with the need to declare the intended port of call, these restrictions caused Chinese maritime traders to concentrate on Southeast Asia as one of the key markets that they could access directly on a large scale from the late eleventh century onward, as well as to build knowledge of other ports and markets they could access directly. Knowledge of Southeast Asian ports, even among Chinese who did not personally travel to that region but were engaged in China's internal maritime trade, increased dramatically from the late eleventh century on.

By the end of the Northern Song period, in 1126, China's maritime trade had evolved from a rigid system of ritualized state-level exchanges to a trade conducted wholly at the international ports by the late eleventh century. Tribute missions lost their economic function and instead came to be viewed as manifestations of the Song dynastic rule's imperial virtue, as laid out in Confucian precepts, and treated as affirmations of a foreign state's status by the Song court.

From the reign of Renzong (1023–65), the proportion of the domestic trade in both high- and low-value products had remained fairly constant, at 30 to 40 percent of all products imported into China. This stability of the domestic market with regard to trade in foreign products was apparently intended by the Song court to provide an environment conducive to maritime trade, one in which the domestic trade in foreign products could develop unimpeded. It is also clear that the court's stance toward low- and high-value products was essentially the same, the only differentiation being made between the values of these products. The possibility that the volume of trade in low-value products might overtake that of high-value products—and thus have a marked impact on the volume of shipments, rate of turnover, and profit margins—appears not to have been taken into consideration when the fiscal regime was devised.

Within China, the domestic trade in foreign products shifted from being a state monopoly to being dominated by Chinese private traders. China's maritime trade, which had hitherto been dominated by foreign shipping, began to witness an increase in Chinese participation from the end of the eleventh century. As a result, the domestic and external sectors of China's maritime trade, which had functioned and been governed separately, were integrated from the late eleventh century on.

The Song court continued to maintain a reduced but nonetheless significant level of participation in the domestic sector of the maritime trade, although it refrained from participating in the international carrying trade even after the 1090 liberalization of Chinese mercantile shipping. This state position gave the domestic market a measure of stability, while at the same time left sufficient space to private traders so that the development of China's maritime economy could be driven by the private sector. The result was sustained growth in China's maritime trade with Southeast Asia through the eleventh and the early twelfth century.

The Southern Song: Consolidation and Popularization of Maritime Trade

In 1126 the Song capital at Kaifeng was overrun by the Jurchens of the north, marking the end of the Northern Song period. The Song court moved south and in 1127 established its capital at the coastal port-city of Hangzhou, in Jiangxi.[42] The loss of the territories north of the Huai River to the Jurchens, and the ensuing peace treaty with the invaders, was a severe blow to the Song court, in terms of both the legitimacy of its rule and its finances.[43] The Song court lost not only its northern agricultural and commercial hinterland but also such important economic resources as the northern copper mines.[44]

In the face of such dire political and economic stresses, the Song court in 1127 attempted to impose some measure of financial austerity by instituting an almost total ban on the import of luxury products. That year, the newly enthroned emperor Gaozong decreed that the importation of foreign products, in particular such luxury items as jewelry and aromatics, depleted state coffers and had to be stopped. Only ivory (for producing audience tablets) and rhinoceros horns (for producing officials' belts) could be imported, under strictly enforced quotas. The mercantile shipping superintendencies of Liangzhe, Fujian, and Guangnan circuits were disbanded and their responsibilities taken over by the respective circuits' tax transport bureaus. Chinese shipping was also prohibited.[45]

This austere stance against maritime trade did not, however, last long. With the economic limitations it faced, the Song court was forced to look southward for its sources of state revenue. The external economy, in particular international maritime trade, very quickly was viewed by the court as an important source of state revenue. Its recognition of the importance of maritime trade to the Chinese economy led the court to permit maritime trade once again. By 1130 mercantile shipping superintendencies were reestablished at Hangzhou, Mingzhou, Quanzhou, and Guangzhou.[46] In 1133 the court reinstituted compulsory purchases of luxury products and of aromatics that were in high demand in the Chinese market, purchasing, at the Chinese ports, a large proportion of these products that were being shipped to China.[47] The Southern Song court thus resumed the position that the Northern Song court had adopted during the late tenth century, with the state becoming once more the chief participant in the Chinese maritime economy.

However, whereas Northern Song China was by and large a land-based entity with its economy centered inland, Southern Song China, with its capital at Hangzhou and its territories centered along the southeastern Chinese coastline, was, as a result of its geographical orientation, a maritime entity. The compelling importance of the maritime economy to the Southern Song court forced it to rethink its position. Consequently, from the 1130s to the 1160s, the Song court implemented a series of administrative changes, reflecting a major shift in Song China's economic and diplomatic orientation from that which had been maintained during the Northern Song. The changes that were effected were manifested in two ways—active state encouragement of maritime trade and the restructuring of the administration of that trade.

Official encouragement of maritime trade was two pronged. First, in 1136 a decree was issued that official ranks were to be conferred on traders who managed to import foreign products to China worth at least fifty thousand strings of cash.[48] This opportunity was open to both foreign and Chinese traders. There had been several precedents for such official recognition before 1136. In addition, Chinese officials who had collected more than one million strings of cash in revenue from the frankincense trade were to be promoted by one rank.[49] The Song court was thus trying to encourage both large-scale private trade and the initiative of officials of the mercantile shipping superintendencies in increasing the trade flowing to and from China. In 1131 a significant shipment of ivory and rhinoceros horns arrived at the port of Guangzhou,[50] indicating that the trade in high-value products to China resumed almost immediately, despite the turmoil of the early years of the Southern Song. In 1134 an official title was conferred on the foreign ship captain Cai Jingfang for having carried products to China worth nine hundred and eighty thousand strings of cash between 1127 and 1134.[51] In 1136 an Arab trader named Luoxing was granted an official title for having imported frankincense worth three hundred thousand strings.[52]

Second, the Song court sought to encourage foreign traders to carry out commercial activities in China by welcoming their presence in Chinese ports every year. In 1144, Quanzhou was allocated an annual budget with which to organize a celebratory feast in honor of the foreign traders before their departure for home. For several years before that, similar festivities had already been organized annually at Guangzhou, to show the Chinese administration's appreciation.[53]

Administratively, China's maritime economy was subjected to several stages of restructuring. In 1133 a number of foreign products, of both high and low value, were permitted by the Song court to be freely traded by Chinese merchants at the point of entry into China, after the customs duties and compulsory purchases had been levied, even as the Song court continued to retain control over the domestic trade of a number of high-value products through the official markets.[54] This development was accompanied by a decrease in the court's taxation of China's maritime trade. In 1136 the customs duties on high- and low-value products were reduced to 10 and 6 $^2/_3$ percent respectively.[55] The compulsory purchase rate for both categories of products appears to have remained unchanged at 30 percent. This brought the court's control of the domestic trade in high-value products down to 37 percent, and in low-value products to 34 $^2/_3$ percent, thereby restoring the proportions of the domestic trade held by the state and by private traders to the levels that they were at during the late eleventh and the early twelfth century. The 1136 rate changes effectively returned the major portion of both the domestic and external sectors of China's maritime trade to Chinese private traders. Finally, in 1141 the domestic trade in all foreign products was reopened to Chinese merchants.[56]

The development of China's maritime trade from then on resumed along the trajectory that had previously been set at the end of the eleventh century.

Several other administrative changes intended to develop greater private participation were also implemented. In 1141 the Song court published a classification of all foreign products into high and low value categories for the purpose of standardizing customs duties and compulsory purchases.[57] The reorganization of the administration of maritime trade culminated in a decree passed in 1159 that all the mercantile shipping superintendencies of the three circuits of Guangnan, Fujian, and Liangzhe be abolished, the administrative practices and regulations pertaining to maritime trade be written and standardized, and new superintendencies be reestablished at the end of the process. A rationalized approach was also formulated to monitor the movement of Chinese citizens in and out of China.[58] Throughout the course of this restructuring process, decrees were issued to tackle the problem of the waste of operating funds through inconsistent adherence to the mercantile shipping regulations, as well as cases of official corruption and fraud.[59] By the 1160s the administration and organization of the bureaucratic departments that administered China's maritime trade were reformed and restructured.

These changes represented a concerted effort on the Song court's part at reshaping the governance of maritime trade into a coherent, streamlined administrative system. By the 1160s the process of rationalizing the administration of maritime trade, which had lasted for about thirty years, was largely complete. The entire process of streamlining the governance of maritime trade was intended to give greater administrative control to the court, and that in turn reflected the importance the court had come to attach to the maritime economy. The Song court had come full circle to the position it had adopted at the end of the eleventh century, which was essentially the acceptance of a maritime economy driven by private trading concerns, with the state maintaining a level of participation in the domestic trade sufficient to act as a stabilizing factor and to reap the benefits of the growth in trade through taxation.

These changes in the immediate decades following the advent of Southern Song rule apparently had a significant positive impact on China's maritime economy. There was a sustained increase in maritime trade activity at the Chinese ports, reflected by the growth in revenue collected by the Song administration from the inflow of maritime products. By 1137 revenue collected annually from customs duties alone amounted to approximately one million strings of cash.[60] Between 1147 and 1159 the value of this source of revenue rose to 2 million strings of cash annually.[61] Other economic benefits would have been derived from such activities as manufacturing and other value-added industries catering to the increased demand for Chinese products by the foreign markets with which China engaged in maritime trade during this period. These included the production of ceramics, silk textiles, and processed foods.[62]

The contributions of China's Southeast Asian and Indian Ocean Littoral trade partners to this sustained growth in maritime trade were significant. The reestablishment of the mercantile shipping superintendencies between 1128 and 1130 was a move that would have encouraged and facilitated foreign shipping and trade to return to China. Consequently, China's maritime economy does not appear to have suffered any serious setbacks in the early years of the Southern Song. The trade in luxury products continued to be sizeable, while the trade in lower-value products began to constitute a significant part of China's maritime imports.

Southeast Asia became a source of foreign products that were or could be demanded and absorbed by the Chinese market. By 1141 the types of high- and low-value Southeast Asian products imported into China had increased significantly. This increase in the importance of the trade with Southeast Asia, and in particular island Southeast Asia, is reflected by the rate increase instituted in 1144, which saw the import duties on frankincense, cloves, *chen* (sinking) gharuwood incense, and cardamoms increase to 40 percent.[63] The rate increase appears to have been applied mainly to aromatic and medicinal products sourced from or transshipped by island Southeast Asia. Frankincense was a reexport item from the Middle East that was transshipped to China, Srivijaya being the main participant in this trade. Cloves, chen, and cardamoms were key island Southeast Asian products exported to China by the twelfth century. While they were known to the Chinese market since the beginning of the Song period, before the twelfth century, these products were transshipped to China mainly by mainland Southeast Asian states such as Champa. The twelfth century witnessed these products being increasingly shipped directly from island Southeast Asia to China. This development can also be seen in the shift in the products presented by tribute missions from island Southeast Asian states such as Srivijaya to the Song court during the second half of the twelfth century, from being predominantly Middle Eastern and Indian Ocean to Southeast Asian products.

The impact of Chinese shipping activities in Southeast Asia, which had begun on a large scale by the late eleventh century, continued through the twelfth and thirteenth centuries. Chinese mercantile knowledge of and economic interaction with maritime Southeast Asia, and in particular the Malay region and its minor ports, became increasingly intense. However, Chinese maritime shipping continued to be confined to Southeast Asia throughout the Southern Song period. The restriction on overseas voyages by Chinese ships to a single monsoon cycle continued into the twelfth century.[64] In addition, the absence of any textual record during the rest of the Song suggests that it remained in force until the end of Southern Song rule, in 1279.

In 1164 expansion of Chinese private participation in the trade of Southeast Asian products was inadvertently precipitated by changes to the customs duties and compulsory purchase rates levied on certain luxury products that had previously been declared state-monopoly products in the tenth and eleventh centuries. The customs duties on rhinoceros horns and pearls were set at 20 percent and 10 percent respectively.[65] At the same time, the compulsory purchase rates were increased significantly: 40 percent for rhinoceros horns and 60 percent for pearls.[66] As a result, the Song court controlled 52 percent and 64 percent respectively of the domestic trade in rhinoceros horns and pearls. It is likely that the domestic trade in other former state-monopoly products, such as tortoise shells, elephant tusks, turtle carapaces, coral, agate, lac, and frankincense,[67] was similarly affected.

For foreign traders, the 1164 increases in customs duties were regarded as unreasonably high and affected the profitability of the foreign shipment trade in these products to China. The overall profitability of the trade in these luxury products was determined by the proportion of the cargo that could be sold to the official markets after customs duties had been levied. As a result, foreign traders appealed for the customs duties rate to be reduced to 10 percent.[68] The increase in the compulsory purchase rates, which would have translated to a proportional reduction in access to the domestic market, was of minor concern to them, since, with the exception of locally born foreigners resident in China, most foreign traders were not permitted to have access to the Chinese domestic market outside the port or prefecture at which they had arrived.

The reaction of Chinese traders, on the other hand, was more marked. In addition to the negative impact of higher customs duties, which would have been similar to that experienced by foreign traders, they were also severely affected by any increase in the compulsory purchase rates. These traders had commercial networks extending into the Chinese domestic market beyond the port area. Private domestic trade in foreign products thus constituted an important aspect of their commercial activities. Any loss of access to the domestic market would have adversely affected this group of traders. Consequently, Chinese traders complained of losses in the trade of these products as a result of the rate changes.[69]

The immediate impact on the trade in these luxury products was severe. Chinese shippers ceased importing these products almost immediately.[70] Shipment to China by foreign traders appears to have ceased for a time as well. Luxury goods were not included in the long list of foreign products brought into China in the late twelfth century.[71] By the beginning of the thirteenth century the shipment of these products to China appears to have somewhat recovered, but it was exclusively carried only by Arabs and Srivijayans.[72]

Chinese participation in the shipment trade in luxury products is no longer mentioned in any Chinese texts after 1164, and was most likely minimal. The compulsory purchase rates levied on these products were not reduced for the rest of the Song, until 1279. The chief complaint of the Chinese traders—that they lacked profits because they had no access to the domestic market—thus remained unresolved. On the other hand, the customs duties and compulsory purchase rates for nonluxury high-value products, set in 1147, remained unchanged, and trade in those products expanded. Consequently, Chinese trade in high-value products became increasingly confined to nonluxury products, particularly those from Southeast Asia.

The 1164 rate changes also led to a marked expansion of Chinese private participation in the trade in low-value foreign imports. The fiscal regime applied to low-value products imported into China had remained unchanged after 1136. The low customs duty rate, and the lower level of participation in the domestic trade in these products by the Song court, allowed for adequate profitability for Chinese maritime traders. As a result, after 1164 Chinese traders shifted from participation in the luxury products trade to trade in low-value products.[73] The maintenance of a favorable tax regime for both high- and low-value products (though not for luxury goods) in the late twelfth and the thirteenth century contributed to a sustained expansion of China's import trade in these products. By the early thirteenth century the trade in low-value products was beginning to surpass that of high-value products. Southeast Asia, and in particular the Malay region, became the most important source of low-value products shipped to China and remained so until the end of the Song period.

The connection of private trading networks in the domestic Chinese economy to Chinese international maritime shipping appears to have been crucial to the commercial viability of Chinese private participation in maritime trade during the Song. The permission accorded by the Song court to Chinese private traders to exploit their domestic trade networks, and to distribute at least 60 percent of their foreign imports directly into the Chinese market—rather than having to depend on the bureaucracy to absorb their imports—provided the impetus for the growth of China's maritime trade until the end of the Song. However, the Song court, through the use of administrative regulations, maintained a near monopoly on the domestic trade in foreign luxury goods after the 1160s. The result was a development of two distinctive sectors within China's trade in foreign products—the luxury products trade, which was largely in the hands of the Song court, and the trade in high- and low-value products, which remained in the hands of Chinese private traders. Of the latter, low-value foreign products came, by the end of the Song, to dominate Chinese maritime trade with Southeast Asia.

In assessing China's maritime economy during the Southern Song period, it can be noted that the Song court's active administration of China's external trade, coupled with the building of its substantial stake in the domestic trade in foreign products (while permitting private trade to flourish), reflected the administrative attitude toward maritime trade that the court had adopted during the Southern Song. Apart from the maritime trade bans from 1127 to 1133, the Song court placed no restrictions on foreign shipping during the Southern Song. The Song court sought to rely on Chinese private and foreign maritime shipping to bring foreign products to China. Official participation in the trade in foreign products was confined to trade within China. At no time during the Song period did the Song court intend to control maritime trade beyond its borders.

The court thus strove to provide an environment conducive to the private development of external trade, while maintaining strong control over the domestic market. Rather than control foreign trade the court seemed content in the role of steward. This stewardship was achieved both by gradually liberalizing the Chinese sector of the maritime trade in Southeast Asia, and by maintaining fairly tight control over the domestic trade in foreign products, without stifling this increasingly vibrant and important sector of the Song economy, the growth of which was generated by Chinese private traders in the establishing and extending of their commercial networks, integrating the maritime and domestic economies.

The control exerted by the court over the domestic trade in foreign products, which would have been substantial even though it represented a minor portion of that trade, enabled the Song court to maintain a significant measure of stability in the Chinese maritime-based economy.

The court's stance recognized that maritime trade had become a vital source of state revenue, in particular during the Southern Song. The court's stewardship of the maritime economy reflected China's coming to terms with the economic realities of the Song political entity.

At first glance, this appears to have been in direct contrast to the Song court's position with regard to it control and administration of the domestic Chinese economy, such as the production and trade in salt, tea, and grain. The Song court consistently sought to increase its control of the production, distribution, and sale of these staples, which were important sources of revenue, and control over all stages of the economic activities related to these staples translated to control over the revenue they could generate.

In the trade of foreign commodities, over which the Song court had no control, the court sought instead to enlarge its revenue source by encouraging their consumption. The court then benefited by taxing the transactions involved in their import, distribution and sale. It was apparent to the Song court that liberalizing the trade in these products, which translated into the liberalization of China's maritime economy, was the best way of enlarging this part of China's economy. The end goal of the Song court, to increase the revenue from all economic activities, would have been achieved, even if the means were starkly different.

The Yuan: Oscillating between Economic Stewardship and Monopolistic State Participation

In 1279, the southern Chinese coastal administrative circuits of Fujian and Guangnan capitulated to pressure from Mongol forces, ushering in Yuan rule throughout China. The advent of Yuan rule brought China into the orbit of the larger Mongolian empire. The structures of Chinese maritime trade were then modeled after practices throughout the Mongolian empire, while the motivation behind Yuan diplomatic policies were no longer based on the integrity of the Chinese state but instead on the furthering of the prestige of the trans-Asian Mongolian empire. These changes had a fundamental impact on Yuan China's maritime economic and foreign policies in the late thirteenth and the fourteenth century.

Whereas the period between 969 and 1279 witnessed the Song court systematically attempting to maintain the integrity of China's southward foreign and economic policies, the late thirteenth and the fourteenth century saw the Yuan court drastically modifying the structures and basis of China's southward economic and diplomatic interactions with the states and polities of maritime Asia from that which had been developed over the first three centuries of the second millennium AD.

The first few years of Yuan rule over southern China saw the government's administration of China's maritime trade remain largely the same as during late Song. The permitting of private maritime trade as well as customs duties rates remained unchanged. However, unlike the Song period, references to restrictions on the length of a ship's voyage outside China are distinctly absent from Yuan period texts. The geographical extent of Chinese maritime shipping thus appears to have been substantially enlarged. Chinese shipping reached as far as the Indian Ocean during the Yuan period. This development is substantiated by the accounts of such travelers as Marco Polo (1272–95) and Ibn Battuta (1325–54), who noted that travel between India, Southeast Asia, and China was by this time predominantly accomplished on Chinese ships. Chinese shipping thus expanded beyond Southeast Asia to include the Indian Ocean littoral ports as well, in particular the Bay of Bengal. This major structural change to Chinese maritime shipping may have been a reflection of the transregional nature of the Mongol empire that had been established across central and eastern Asia by the late thirteenth century, and may have been a means of integrating and enhancing the maritime communication networks between the different centers of the Mongolian khanates.

As a result of the expansion of its geographical range into the Indian Ocean, Chinese shipping appears to have begun to take over the Malay region's role of transshipping products from the Indian Ocean littoral and Middle East to China, and vice versa. The *Yunlu manchao* (1206) and the *Zhufanzhi* (1225) which reflect the maritime trade in the early thirteenth century, note that Srivijaya continued as a key port through which China's supply of frankincense was obtained, the way that it had been since the advent of the Song period.[74] The *Daoyi zhilue* (ca. 1340s), suggests, however, that by the first half of the fourteenth century, frankincense was no longer available for export from Jambi or Palembang, the two chief ports of the Malay region and Srivijaya in the tenth to the thirteenth century.[75] This although frankincense continued to be imported into Guangzhou during the late thirteenth and the early fourteenth century.[76]

In 1284, however, the Yuan court made a major departure in China's participation in maritime trade from the position taken by the Song court for most of its reign. In that year, the Yuan court began official participation in China's maritime trade by monopolizing Chinese shipping. After almost three centuries of the flourishing of private maritime trade, the Yuan court instituted a ban on this commercial activity, with harsh sanctions for any violations.[77] This policy, however, was not consistent throughout the Yuan period. The ban was revoked 1294,[78] reinstated in 1314,[79] and lifted again in 1320, following the official admission of clandestine trade.[80] After being reinstated in 1322,[81] the ban was lifted for the last time in 1323,[82] after which private Chinese trade was permitted until the end of the Yuan.

The Yuan court's attempts at monopolizing the shipping trade were administratively supported by the establishing of the mercantile shipping superintendencies at designated Chinese international ports, through which official participation in maritime trade was conducted. In 1284 the chief Mercantile Shipping and Transportation Bureau was established at Quanzhou, whereupon it became responsible for providing capital and ships and for appointing traders to venture overseas to trade on behalf of the Yuan government.[83] Subsequent periods of official monopoly over China's maritime shipping were similarly marked by the establishment of superintendencies for the conduct of maritime trade.

The mercantile shipping superintendencies of the Yuan period were different from those of the Song. Whereas during the Song they were administrative departments dealing with the governance of maritime trade, during the Yuan they were responsible for organizing and dispatching overseas trading voyages. Whenever the superintendencies were abolished (i.e., in periods when private shipping was permitted), customs inspections were taken over by the various provincial administrations.[84]

Official participation in Chinese shipping trade appears to have been devolved by the Yuan court to provincial-level initiatives, which came under the purview of the Ortaq clique. This clique, the economic equivalent to the Darahachi (the political overseers of the Mongol government), was a group of central Asian traders favored by the Mongol rulers and granted access to large amounts of capital supplied by the latter to conduct trade in and across in various regions under Mongol rule. Initially monopolizing the trade between and within Mongol-ruled China and central Asia from 1206 on, their maritime trade interests were firmly established when the Bureau of Ortaq Affairs was established in 1281. In 1285 it assumed responsibility over the mercantile shipping superintendencies,[85] thereby placing in its hands the administrative arm with which official participation in maritime trade was conducted. In 1287 its position in southern China was further strengthened when the provincial Bureau of Ortaq Affairs was established at Quanzhou,[86] the officially designated center of Chinese maritime trade and trade administration during the Yuan period. Ortaq maritime commercial interests and their control over China's shipping trade were thereby secured at the provincial level, under the patronage of the Yuan court.

The Ortaq clique's ability to use the superintendencies in its efforts to monopolize Chinese shipping was further enhanced by the appointment to important administrative positions in the superintendencies of local residents of the Chinese ports who were from Middle Eastern and Persian Muslim maritime merchant families, such as Pu Shougeng in Fujian.[87] Many locally born members of these families had some access to the Chinese domestic economy from the early twelfth century onwards. The Ortaq clique needed these China-based foreign traders as collaborators, since, as new entrants to China's maritime trade with Southeast Asia and the Indian Ocean littoral, they lacked the necessary experience and networks for operating in this sector of the Chinese economy.[88]

Although the Ortaq clique's participation in maritime trade was clearly done with the court's approval as well as its financial and administrative support, it is not apparent that the commercial gains made by the Ortaq clique ultimately filtered back up to the Yuan court. Texts from the Yuan period contain no record of revenue generated from the shipping trade and domestic trade of foreign products. The Yuan court appears to have benefited only from the tax regime it instituted at the Chinese ports. Even then, the low customs duties and additional tax rates instituted during the Yuan period benefited more those who were importing foreign products into China. At the beginning of Yuan rule, the rates for both coarse and fine products remained the same as those of the late Song,[89] at 6 2/3 and 10 percent respectively, as the Yuan court essentially adopted the position of the Song court in its administration of Chinese maritime trade. These rates remained in place for the whole of the Yuan period, despite the dramatic shifts in the Yuan court's position toward maritime trade between 1284 and 1323. This fiscal stability was reiterated in 1293, when the review of the maritime regulations, which resulted in the issue of twenty-four maritime trade stipulations, saw the customs duties rates remain unchanged.[90]

An additional tax levied on maritime trade products entering China, which began to be imposed in 1280,[91] was also kept very low and would have benefited those participating in the maritime trade. In 1292 the rates were set at 4 percent and 3 1/3 percent for fine and coarse products respectively. In turn, foreign products were exempted from local trade taxes.[92] In 1293, following the review of the maritime regulations, the additional tax was set at 3 1/3 percent for all products regardless of their value or quality.[93] No compulsory purchases were instituted during the Yuan period.

Altogether, the fiscal regime of the Yuan period was more favorable for those engaged in China's import trade of foreign products than the regime imposed during the Song. This would have benefited both China-based and foreign traders that were involved in China's trade in foreign products. It is therefore apparent that the fiscal environment created by the Yuan court was very conducive to international trade whenever the ban on private trade was not imposed. On the other hand, at times when the ban was in place, the tax regime would have benefited those who were officially sanctioned to conduct China's trade, since they would technically have had a monopoly over the Chinese sector of the import trade of foreign products into China. The profits gained from such an administrative context would have been significant. However, they were not necessarily available to all throughout the Yuan period.

The economic outlook of the Yuan court was set to a large extent by its favoring of the Ortaq clique in commercial affairs through the farming out of licenses for trade and tax collection to this commercial group.[94] The official Yuan position and the way in which official participation in this trade evolved by 1323 was determined by the nature of operations that had been established by the commercial interests of the Ortaq clique and their foreign collaborators resident in the Chinese ports during the first two decades of the Yuan period. However, the economic influence and control that the Ortaq clique and its foreign collaborators had over Chinese maritime trade appears to have been confined mainly to the ports and the seas beyond. The domestic trading networks of foreign traders based in China would not have been as pervasive as those of Chinese traders.

Official participation in maritime trade, which had, during the Song, been limited to a substantial court participation in the domestic trade in foreign products, shifted during the Yuan period to that of monopolizing the Chinese sector of the import-export trade by means of officially sponsored trading voyages and intermittent bans on private Chinese maritime shipping. The position of the state thus shifted from economic stewardship during the Song period, to active participation in the shipping trade during parts of the Yuan. The state intermittently acted in direct competition to the private sector of Chinese maritime shipping, relying heavily on its administrative muscle to establish and maintain a distinct advantage for itself.

The collaboration between the Ortaq clique and the Middle Eastern and Persian traders resident at the southern Chinese ports lasted for only thirteen years and ended when the Provincial Bureau of Ortaq Affairs was abolished in 1297. That year the mercantile shipping superintendencies were brought under the direct authority of the Imperial

Secretariat.[95] This reorganization appears to have been initiated by a faction in the Yuan court that was keen on eliminating the Ortaq clique's role in maritime trade. Instead, after 1297 the superintendencies became the administrative tool by which the Yuan court attempted to engage and possibly to monopolize the Chinese sector of the shipping trade. The subsequent contest between the Yuan court and the Ortaq clique for control over the shipping trade is reflected in the oscillation between the abolition and reestablishment of the Provincial Bureau of Ortaq Affairs and the superintendencies between 1297 and 1323. The Yuan court eventually emerged triumphant in this prolonged contest, and the superintendencies were reestablished for good in 1323.[96] In addition, the following year the provincial governments were granted the sole right to levy customs duties and the additional maritime import tax.[97] The Ortaq clique was thus left with no more influence or power over the administration of China's maritime trade and no preferential treatment by the Yuan court at the provincial level.

While the periodic bans on private maritime voyages were aimed solely at private Chinese traders and shipowners, foreign traders and foreign mercantile shipping were apparently not subjected to the restrictions imposed by the Yuan administration, reflecting the administration's awareness of the continued importance of foreign traders in China's maritime trade. While the activities of foreign traders could not be easily controlled, marginalization of Chinese private traders in the import trade could be carried out easily by way of a ban on Chinese private maritime trade. The ban on private trade was thus aimed at both traders who had substantial capital backing and petty traders who initially were not in alliance with the Ortaq clique, and later not operating under the court's purview.

However, the Yuan court made no effort to control the domestic trade in foreign products. Official attempts to break into the domestic trade were confined to the exemption of traders from the market tax if foreign products were purchased from the official markets. Such official participation in the domestic trade in foreign products appears to have been confined to the ports. Unlike the Song period, no structural institutions appear to have been developed during the early Yuan for official participation in domestic trade. In addition, the foreign collaborators of the Ortaq clique had few networks that extended beyond the port areas. Foreign traders resident at the ports had been under severe restrictions during the Song with regard to traveling and trading within China. They had been permitted to trade only in the prefecture or port where they were based. Limited access to the domestic economy had been accorded in 1104 only to locally born foreigners.

In addition, the Ortaq clique was a newcomer in the trade in foreign products in southern China, having begun participating in maritime trade only with the advent of Yuan rule in 1279. Thus, the proponents of official participation in maritime trade during the early Yuan did not possess the domestic trading networks within China to fully exploit the domestic trade in foreign products. In light of this reality, official participation in maritime trade, which was first carried out by the Ortaq clique and their foreign collaborators, could only exploit the shipping trade. Once private trade was permitted again in 1323, Chinese traders quickly resumed their maritime trade activities, reintegrating the Chinese domestic market with the Chinese maritime carrying trade. This continued until the early Ming period, when private trade was once again prohibited, and tributary trade, coupled with the proactive foreign policy of projecting China's maritime capabilities and might into Southeast Asian waters and the Indian Ocean littoral, became the maritime policy of China.

The way in which China regarded and governed its maritime economy during the Song and Yuan periods underwent significant changes over time. While these governmental changes affected the way in which Chinese maritime economy developed, their impact was also felt abroad. China was a key player in the international maritime economy. Structural changes to the way China conducted its maritime trade had immediate and profound effects on how maritime trade was conducted between itself and such external regions as those in Southeast Asia. Whereas for the Chinese, the impact was felt in both the domestic and international sectors of China's maritime trade, mainly characterized by the evolving nature of both state and private participation, for China's trading partners in Southeast Asia, the impact was felt on the manner in which trade and diplomatic relations were conducted. One of the regions fundamentally affected by the changes in China was the Malay region.

Chapter 3

THE MALAY REGION'S DIPLOMATIC AND ECONOMIC INTERACTIONS WITH CHINA

Sources for the study of contact between the Malay region and China in the early second millennium AD are fairly limited. Almost all the information available comes from Chinese textual sources, particularly the official histories of the various dynasties that ruled over China. Other sources, such as archaeological and epigraphic data, are sparser. Thus, the study of the Malay region's economic relations with China is necessarily unbalanced, slanted toward a more Sinocentric state-level perspective.

Due to the official nature of the textual data, state-sponsored exchanges are those about which most information has survived. Since such exchanges were often imbued with diplomatic overtones, China's court policies toward foreign relations and maritime trade clearly had an impact on them. As the Chinese court's perspectives on foreign relations changed, so did the rationale for the conduct of state-level exchanges.

State-level exchanges between China and the countries of Southeast Asia and the Indian Ocean littoral initially took place through tributary missions. Envoys from these countries were dispatched to China, carrying gifts for the Chinese court. The court reciprocated with gifts of metal bullion and such manufactured items as metal goods, ceramics, and silks, and by granting them official titles and items of official stature, such as headdresses, robes, and letters.

However, tribute missions were not only the major channel through which these states promoted and maintained their diplomatic status in the eyes of the Chinese court but also the chief means by which they advanced their economic relationships with China. The Chinese court by and large remained the passive recipient of the overtures of its foreign counterparts. Its perception of the wealth and political authority of these states was therefore shaped to a great extent by their missions and the tribute that they brought. Ordinary economic exchanges appear to have been highly dependent on the success of the state-level relations. It is in this framework that we should view the Malay region's interaction with Song China, initiated by Srivijaya, the preeminent port-polity of the region from the tenth through the thirteenth century.

In 987, soon after reestablishing internal order in China, the Northern Song court dispatched its sole diplomatic mission to various foreign states. The exploratory nature of this mission is indicated by the fact that its members carried, along with gold and silks, imperial documents with blanks for the names of the states they visited, to be filled in upon arrival. The purpose of the mission was to express the court's desire for foreign states to dispatch presentations of tribute to China, as well as to purchase important trade products such as aromatics and medicines, rhinoceros horns, elephant tusks, pearls, and camphor from these states.[1] The court's interest in tribute missions from distant foreign states in the tenth century was economic rather than political. Moreover, the move strongly suggests that the court, at least during the late tenth century, regarded tribute missions as a key means by which foreign trade, and therefore foreign products, was to arrive in China.

It was in this context that a number of states dispatched missions to present tribute to the Northern Song court. Most of these states were substantial political and economic entities within their respective regional spheres of influence. More important, they were also key participants in the international maritime trade and therefore important trading partners of China. Aside from the mission of 987, the Northern Song court was not active in its conduct of, or attitude toward, its relations with these states. Unlike the preceding and succeeding dynastic periods, when diplomatic missions were sent from China to inquire about specific countries,[2] the Northern Song period was characterized by an apparent complacency concerning relations with states beyond China's borders, with two exceptions—Tonkin, which had been a Chinese province until the end of the Tang period, and the Dashi (Arabs), at that time the powerful 'Abbasid caliphate. Apart from these two states, the Northern Song court appears to have conducted its diplomatic relations with the states of Southeast Asia and the Indian Ocean littoral solely on commercial considerations.

However, as the Song court began to liberalize China's maritime trade from the late tenth century onward, tribute missions began to be differentiated into two classes—diplomatic and trade. Diplomatic missions were received by the mercantile shipping superintendency at the port of arrival and escorted to the imperial court, where they presented tribute to the emperor in person. Trade missions, on the other hand, presented their tribute to the superintendency at the port of call, where the tribute items were registered and processed under prevailing trade regulations. The Song court already practiced such differentiation as early as 971, when an edict was issued instructing the superintendency of Guangzhou to forward only the diplomatic missions to the imperial capital of Kaifeng.[3]

This apparent distinction also led to differentiations in the gifts that the Song court made in exchange for the tribute presented. Missions that appeared before the imperial court and received in return gifts of a ceremonial nature, comprising items of great value and ceremonial trappings, were most likely diplomatic ones. On the other hand, those that had the tribute items assessed according to the prevailing market values, and that received in return gifts of bullion or products of equivalent value, were most likely trade missions. While the reciprocal gifts given to trade missions also included ceremonial trappings, they were generally not as significant as those presented to diplomatic missions.

Inevitably, the distinction the Chinese made between diplomatic missions and trade missions, along with the generally passive stance adopted by the Northern Song court toward tributary relations with foreign states, led to the development of different strategies by which these foreign states exploited China's perception and reception of tribute missions in order to advance their own objectives. States that were primarily interested in developing their trade with China may have tended to focus their efforts on the preferred Chinese port of call, and their efforts appear to have been reciprocated by the respective prefectural administrations.[4] Diplomatic efforts that focused on the Northern Song court were undertaken by these states in order to initiate or preserve this primary relationship. Other states, for which direct trade with China was not the primary preoccupation, tended to regard tribute missions as a diplomatic channel.

These developments came to a head during the Southern Song period (1127–1279). The political defeat of the Song court at the hands of the Jurchens shortly before 1127 led the Southern Song court to take a more proactive role in its interaction with foreign states after 1127, in a bid to demonstrate that the dynasty continued to receive the mandate of heaven. Changes in the administration of maritime trade and the reorganization of the departments responsible for foreign affairs contributed significantly to the reshaping of China's foreign policy. The role that tribute missions had previously played in shaping the court's impression of, and attitude toward, each of these states became less important. Although tribute missions continued to arrive in China, the Southern Song court chose to regard them as the manifestation of its own imperial virtue rather than as demonstrations of the importance of the states presenting tribute. At the same time, the development of Chinese maritime trade from the late eleventh century onward, particularly the increased Chinese participation in the import trade of low-value products into China, the general participation in the trade in high-value products from Southeast Asia, and the development and increase in the volume of Chinese maritime shipping that these developments brought about, led to a significant enlargement of China's maritime economy by the early twelfth century.

This had a marked impact on the relationships that China had established with the various foreign states through the course of the

Northern Song. Foreign states whose primary preoccupation in diplomatic relations with China was trade, and whose contributions to China's maritime economy continued to be significant, continued to be diplomatically important to the Song court. Foreign states whose contributions remained largely the same through the course of the Song period suffered significant setbacks in their diplomatic relationship with the Southern Song court from the twelfth century on.

It is within this changing framework that the approaches adopted by the Malay region's port-polities in their economic interaction with China from the tenth through the fourteenth century must be understood. Malay social and political organization, and the regional structure of Malay port-polities, was highly fluid. Similarly, the approaches that these polities adopted in their economic relations and interactions with China were not monolithic but multifaceted and were highly adaptable to the context of the economic relationship between the two regions. The Malay port-polities were not inherently confined to a regional hierarchical structure, although, when such structures allowed the exploitation of the key Asian markets to be optimized, the polities would order themselves into one. Once the economic context changed, the polities would reorganize themselves with the aim of maximizing their economic gains through the maximization of trade.

The Late Tenth Century

From the tenth through the thirteenth century, the Malay region's diplomatic relations with China was initiated and maintained by Srivijaya, the region's preeminent port-polity, which existed between the seventh and the thirteenth century. Until the early thirteenth century, Srivijaya was the only polity in the region to be recorded in Chinese texts as having maintained continuous contact with China, Borneo being the only other polity to have dispatched a single mission to China during the early decades of Song rule in China. The unique nature of the thalassocracy of Srivijaya dictated that its prosperity, and even its survival, depended on maintaining its role as the region's major entrepôt for international maritime trade, providing the Chinese market with the products of Southeast Asian, Indian, and Middle Eastern origins, and Indian Ocean states with Chinese and Southeast Asian goods in return. Srivijaya's conduct of its tribute relations with Song China was shaped by this need to ensure its economic, and hence its political, survival. Diplomatic initiatives were intended to sustain and enlarge this all-important trade relationship.

The importance that Srivijaya placed on being recognized by the Song court as China's major trading partner in maritime Southeast Asia caused it to be highly sensitive to any administrative or political changes within China. Srivijaya carefully followed the events taking place in China, and its rulers appear to have kept themselves updated on the political changes there. The first presentation of tribute took place in the ninth month of 960, the year the Song dynasty was founded. This was the first tribute to be offered by a foreign state to the Song court.[5] The 960 mission was followed by a rapid burst of three missions over the next two years. Over the next thirty years, Srivijaya dispatched a total of fourteen tribute missions to China. These missions occurred in three series. The first series, consisting of four missions, was dispatched by the Srivijayan ruler Silihu Daxialitan and his successor, Shili Wuya[6] in 960,[7] 961 (twice),[8] and 962.[9] The next four missions were sent in 971,[10] 972,[11] 974,[12] and 975 by an unnamed king.[13] The third series, consisting of six missions, was dispatched by King Xiachi in 980,[14] 983,[15] 985,[16] 987,[17] 988,[18] and 990.[19] This flurry of tribute missions stands in marked contrast to the absence of any immediate missions from the other maritime Southeast Asian states. Borneo dispatched only one tribute mission, in 977,[20] while Java dispatched two missions, in 971 and 992.[21] Apart from Tonkin (northern Vietnam) and Champa, Srivijaya was the only foreign country to send tribute missions to China at such a frequency during these three decades.

The frequency with which Srivijaya dispatched its tribute missions to China at the beginning of the Song period reflected its aim of promoting itself as the premiere maritime player in the Southeast Asia–China leg of international trade. Its reliability in shipping products from Southeast Asia and from the Indian Ocean to southern China would have been demonstrated. Srivijaya's display of its shipping capabilities was complemented by the types of products it was clearly advertising itself as being able to deliver. Of the items recorded as dispatched as tribute between 960 and 990, many were from the Middle East and India. The earlier missions of this period presented high-value products that were in great demand in China, especially frankincense, ivory, rhinoceros horns, rosewater, coral, foreign textiles, and various aromatics, all of which, apart from foreign textiles and ivory, were declared to be subject to Chinese state monopoly in 982.[22] By 988 the range of items Srivijaya presented in the tribute missions had expanded to include intricate handicrafts, furniture, grooming instruments such as combs, and Buddhist scriptures from India.

Srivijaya was also highly attuned to the requests of the Song court in matters pertaining to trade. Hence, when the Chinese envoys were sent abroad in 987 to encourage the dispatch of tribute by the states of Southeast Asia and the Indian Ocean to Song China, Srivijaya responded with a tribute mission in the following year. The mission, which presented an impressive range of items from Southeast Asia, the Middle East, and India, appears to have been a calculated effort to highlight to the Song court Srivijaya's familiarity and access to these two major Asian economic zones, and the reliability and flexibility of its trade relations with them. It also demonstrated Srivijaya's keen awareness of, and responsiveness to, the needs of the Chinese market.

Srivijaya's ability to remain attuned to the Chinese market's demands was due, to a large extent, to the presence of Srivijayan representatives at the key Chinese ports, in particular Guangzhou. By the beginning of the tenth century, the Malay region, under the auspices of Srivijaya, had already established a sojourning population at Guangzhou that was regarded by the Han kingdom at Guangdong to have been sufficiently significant for the Han court to appoint the Srivijayan envoy that had arrived in 904 as the foreign official of the foreign community of Guangzhou.[23] Malay representatives were apparently encouraged by the Srivijayan court to act on their own initiative. Srivijaya's presentation of tribute immediately after the Song dynasty was founded in 960, and its occurrence during the ninth month—instead of during the fifth and sixth months when ships from maritime Southeast Asia would normally arrive in China, carried by the southwest monsoon winds—suggests that this initial mission may not have been dispatched from Sumatra. It is more likely that the representatives of the Srivijayan court, who were residing at Guangzhou, had dispatched tribute on the Srivijayan court's behalf to the Song court in Kaifeng, which at that time still did not exercise control over Fujian and Guangdong.[24]

Srivijaya's connections in Guangzhou were to be an important factor in its relations with China through the course of the Song period. During the first three decades of Song rule in China, Srivijaya appears to have engaged in economic relations with China primarily through state-level exchanges. The 960 mission was the only mission dispatched by Srivijaya during the tenth century that was clearly stated to have been presented to the Song court, although a memorial submitted by the administration of Guangzhou in 992 to the imperial court referred to the Srivijayan mission leader of the 990 mission to China as an envoy to the court, providing indirect evidence that this tribute was also presented directly to the Song court.[25] In contrast, four of the eight missions dispatched by the Arabs before 990 were clearly stated to have been received by the Song court. Between 990 and 1000, the Song court received another two (out of the six) missions dispatched by the Arabs. Where the tribute of all the other missions dispatched until 990 has not been recorded. The absence of such references may be an indication that most of the Srivijayan missions were received at Guangzhou. This suggests that Srivijaya's missions were, by and large, regarded by the Song court as trade missions rather than as diplomatic ones.

Apart from the first tribute mission, in 960, and the one in 990, all the Srivijayan tribute missions in the late tenth century were probably dispatched as a means of carrying out trade exchanges with China. This is apparent from the items that were given by the Chinese to the missions in return for the tribute submitted. Harnesses, white yak tails, white stoneware, lacquerware and silks were given to the envoys of the 962 mission. Headdresses, gold and silver wares, and copper cash were given to the 975 mission. With the exception of the headdresses and gold and silver wares, the items given to these missions were normal trade products, given in accordance to the stipulations recorded in the *Songhuiyao*.[26] This is in contrast to the list of reciprocal gifts awarded to the Arab diplomatic mission of 993, consisting of a printed gown, a purple brocaded turban, stamped gold and silver, a pair of phoenix jars (ceremonial jars with tops in the form of a phoenix heads), and twenty bolts of silks,[27] which was drawn up in accordance with the regulations dealing with diplomatic missions.[28] The list of reciprocal gifts awarded to the Srivijayan missions of 962 and 975 suggests that for missions that were not strictly regarded as diplomatic, the list of reciprocal gifts was to comprise two sections—Chinese trade products and a minimal number of accompanying ceremonial gifts. The harnesses and headdress awarded to the envoys of the 962 and 975 Srivijayan missions were not normal trade products. It is most likely that they were included in recognition of the official status of these missions, while still regarding them as trade missions.

The differentiation between diplomatic and state-level trade missions is never explicitly noted in the Chinese texts. Nonetheless, from the records of the different reciprocal gifts, as well as the treatment of the envoys that accompanied the missions from China's various foreign trading partners, it would appear that the Song court and the mercantile shipping superintendency were able to differentiate between the two types of missions and sought to handle them differently. This differentiation was to become apparent during the early eleventh century, when Srivijaya's missions to the Song court were accorded treatment that befitted diplomatic missions from states that the Chinese court regarded as first-tier trading partners.

Srivijaya's efforts to promote its entrepôt shipping capabilities to China, as well as its conduct of trade through tribute missions, appear to have been handled almost exclusively by its political elite, who were based in the Srivijayan capital, Palembang, in the Malay region.[29] All the tribute missions it dispatched between 961 and 990, except for that of 985, in which tribute was submitted by a Srivijayan shipowner, were headed by royal emissaries, even though they were probably trade missions. The presentation of tribute by all these missions took place either in the third or fourth month, or in the eleventh or twelfth month of the Chinese lunar calendar, coinciding with the sailing seasons.[30] The presentations of tribute during the third and fourth months were most likely made immediately upon the arrival in China of the emissaries from Srivijaya, while tribute presented during the eleventh and twelfth months would indicate that the emissaries executed their official responsibilities before leaving China for Srivijaya with the northeast monsoon. This indicates that these missions originated from Sumatra, rather than from Srivijaya's local representatives at Guangzhou. Since they accompanied shipments of trade goods, this is not unexpected.

After 990, no official tribute missions from Srivijaya were received by China for another thirteen years. In 992, according to a memorial submitted by the administration of Guangzhou to the imperial court, the Srivijayan envoy of the 990 mission had returned to the Chinese port. Having initially stayed for a year in Nanhai district in Guangzhou because of reports of Java's attack on Srivijaya, he had then tried to return home the following year. However, after sailing down to Champa and there receiving negative news concerning the conflict, he had decided to return to Guangzhou.[31] The Srivijayan envoy's inability to return home suggests that the maritime route to Srivijaya may have been severely disrupted by the conflict with Java.

The Srivijayan-Javanese conflict had continued intermittently since at least the eighth century, when Srivijaya had exercised political influence over central Java through the Sailendra dynasty.[32] By the ninth century, however, Srivijayan influence had receded from Java, and by the 930s Java had become the aggressor in the ongoing rivalry.[33] The conflict had come to the fore along the Sunda Strait during this time, culminating in the conflict in the late tenth century in the western Java Sea and the southern end of the Malacca Strait noted in the Chinese records.

The conflict may have temporarily damaged Srivijaya's position as an entrepôt, undermining its trade with China. During the period between 991 and 1002, six Arab missions and three Indian missions arrived in China to present tribute.[34] The absence of any mention of the arrival of these missions via the overland route through mainland Southeast Asia suggests that ships were still able to sail from the Indian

Ocean to China despite the ongoing conflict in the Malacca Strait. The absence of any record of Srivijayan tribute missions having been received by China during this period suggests that this conflict, or the consequences it inflicted on Srivijaya's internal politics and external trade, may have lasted for around twelve years.

The conflict between Srivijaya and Java may have been exacerbated by the Song mission of 987 to Southeast Asia. During the late tenth century, Srivijaya's tribute to China comprised only Middle Eastern and Indian products. It did not include important products from Java and the eastern Indonesian Archipelago, such as sandalwood incense, cloves, and black pepper, the supplies of which were apparently under Javanese control. Java may have refused to supply Srivijaya with products from its sphere of influence. Srivijaya, having attempted to make up for its inability to supply key Southeast Asian spices to China by including artisan crafts of high value from India, may have tried to gain access to Java's trade sphere by force, thus precipitating a power struggle between the two powers in maritime Southeast Asia.

In 992, Java dispatched an impressive tribute mission to China.[35] Received by the Song court, the diplomatic mission was an obvious portrayal by Java of its wealth in trade products and resources, many of which could only be sourced from its sphere of influence and were in high demand in the Chinese market. Absent from the list of tribute items were some of the standard Middle Eastern and Indian products. While there were Southeast Asian sources for products such as rhinoceros horns and elephant tusks, other products such as dates, rosewater, and frankincense, customarily offered by Srivijaya, had to be obtained from Middle Eastern and Indian sources. It therefore does not appear to have been Java's intention to promote itself as an alternative entrepôt to Srivijaya for the transshipment of products from these regions to China. Java was instead advertising to China its position as an important trade partner—with a regional authority that surpassed that of Srivijaya—able to supply the Chinese market with products from its sphere of influence.

Java's naval ascendancy in 991, and the diplomatic overture toward China in 992, did not go unchallenged by Srivijaya. A memorial from the Guangzhou administration concerning the plight of the Srivijayan envoy was submitted to the Song court in 992, conveying the envoy's request for the court to intervene on Srivijaya's behalf by ordering Java to cease the conflict. The timing of the memorial, which was sent sometime during the winter of that year, suggests that the Srivijayan envoy's appeal was a response to the Javanese diplomatic mission, which had been received just a few months earlier. Although the appeal succeeded in getting the Song court to advise Java to cease its military campaign against Srivijaya, China did not receive another tribute mission from Srivijaya for over a decade, suggesting either that the conflict or its consequences were not immediately resolved or that Srivijaya's trade with China may have been at a low ebb for other reasons at the end of the tenth century. However, the effectiveness of Srivijaya's representatives at Guangzhou in maintaining its economic interests and presence in China were eventually to bear fruit in the eleventh century.

The Eleventh and the Early Twelfth Centuries

In 1003, after a lull of twelve years, Srivijaya resumed tribute relations with China. The Srivijayan mission that arrived in China that year presented itself in a manner that differed from the missions dispatched during the late tenth century. During the imperial audience, the Song court was informed that a Buddhist monastery, dedicated to the Song emperor, was being built in Srivijaya, presumably at the capital, which at that time was probably located at Palembang. The envoy requested that the Song emperor give a name for the temple, and for a bronze bell to be cast and given to the Srivijayan envoys to be brought back to Palembang and to be housed at the temple.[36] The building of a monastery would have sent a strong signal to the Song court of Srivijaya's intention to deepen this patron-client relationship beyond mere commodity exchanges. Although Srivijaya had, until 990, made tremendous efforts to foster a commercial patron-client relationship with China, the missions that had been sent did not appear to have gone beyond state-level commercial exchanges. The 1003 mission marked the beginning of a diplomatic courtship of China that was to last for the next twenty-five years—over three reigns—and was to witness the establishment of a more intimate diplomatic relationship between the two states that lasted until the end of the eleventh century.

The conflict between Srivijaya and Java in the late tenth century may have been a major determinant in this diplomatic courtship on the part of Srivijaya. Srivijaya appears to have arrived at the conclusion that a reciprocal relationship with China beyond mere commercial exchanges was necessary to protect and advance its political and commercial interests. The 1003 Srivijayan mission thus marked a shift from mere commercial exchange to diplomatic outreach with the intention of eliciting a favorable response from the Song court. This was carried out by the Srivijayan envoys through requests for Chinese imperial patronage and approval during the presentation of tribute, which included the requests for gifts and favor that would highlight Srivijaya's reverential attitude, namely permission to visit places of political importance by Srivijayan emissaries while they were in China, presentation of plaques with gold characters to the Srivijayan ruler, visits by eminent Srivijayan dignitaries, and the scattering of tribute offerings before the Song imperial throne. The missions dispatched by Srivijaya in 1003, 1008, and 1017 were clearly diplomatic missions, initiated with the intent of reinforcing the patron-client relationship between Srivijaya and China that had been established by 990.

The 1003 mission met with immediate success. The request for a name for the Buddhist temple and a specially cast bell were approved. The Song court also regarded the mission as a diplomatic one, as attested by the conferring of the honorary titles "general who admires virtue" and "general who cherishes culture" upon the mission envoys.[37] This was the first time Srivijayan envoys had been accorded such ceremonial honors, indicating that Srivijaya's status had risen in the eyes of the Song court.

This diplomatic coup was followed by another in 1008. Once again, the strategy of eliciting a response from the Song court to a flattering request for patronage had succeeded. The Srivijayan envoys were permitted, under escort, to visit Mount Taishan, in Guangdong, and to make obeisance to the Song dynastic altar there.[38] Apart from the Arab envoy, who presented tribute three months after the tribute presentation by the Srivijayan envoys in 1008, no other envoy was accorded the same privilege anytime during the Song period. By 1016, Srivijaya, along with Java, the Dashi (Arabs), and Chola (southern India), was accorded the status of first-class trading state.[39] This placed Srivijaya, at least from an economic point of view, on an equal footing with China's other three major trading partners. This favorable relationship was reinforced in 1017, when Srivijaya's envoys were given a tour of the imperial palace, again probably at the request of the envoys. The mission was subsequently rewarded with presents and an imperial document.

The efforts at eliciting a noncommercial response from the Song court appear to have been part of Srivijaya's overall strategy for gaining the favor of the rulers of the first-tier states with which it had important commercial links. In the context of its transshipment trade of high-value Middle Eastern, Indian, and from the eleventh century on, Southeast Asian products to China, and vice versa, Srivijaya was simultaneously making diplomatic overtures to the Cholas, who by the early eleventh century controlled the coastline of southern India as well as the island of Sri Lanka and the important southern Indian port of Nagapattinam. Srivijaya's diplomatic overtures to China were matched by its overtures to the Chola court in the early years of the eleventh century, reflected in a temple inscription dated 1005, indicating that Srivijaya had built a *vihara* (Buddhist monastery) at Nagapattinam. The move was viewed favorably by the Chola ruler, Rajaraja I, who set aside a village to provide for the maintenance of the temple.[40] This was followed by three donations made during the reign of the Chola king Rajendra I. According to an inscription from the wall of the Karonasvamin temple at Nagapattinam, dated to the reign of Rajendra I, a gift of several lamps was made by Nimalan-Agattisvaran, the agent of the Srivijayan king. In another inscription of 1014–15, Rajendra I records the gift of a jewel set with precious stones to the deity of Nagaiyalagar, which was commissioned by a Srivijayan agent. A third inscription, dated to 1018–19, records the gifts of Chinese gold to the deity Tirukkaronam-udaiyar and the feeding of the Brahman priests by Sri Kuruttan Kesuvan, the agent of the Srivijayan king.[41] Srivijaya was clearly wooing its two major trading partners—China and southern India—with the objective of securing its own position as the fulcrum of the trade that flowed between the two.

Srivijaya's political and economic interests had apparently been advanced by its representatives who were resident in China between 990 and 1003, during the lull in tribute missions from Srivijaya. The immediate and marked success of Srivijaya's diplomatic overtures when tribute relations resumed in 1003 and 1008, and the mutually affectionate relationship that existed during the first three decades of the eleventh century, suggest that such championing of Srivijaya's interests by these representatives met with great success. The effects of Srivijaya's successful new diplomatic strategy were felt particularly in matters of commerce.

Thus, by the beginning of the eleventh century, Srivijaya was no longer as heavily reliant on tribute missions as a means of conducting its transshipment trade with China as it had been the previous century. This was probably due to changes that occurred in China's maritime trade structure toward the end of the tenth century. The liberalization of the domestic trade since 982,[42] and, to a lesser extent, the reduction of the domestic trade in foreign products by the Song court, left the domestic sector of China's import-export trade largely in the hands of private Chinese merchants.[43] These changes would have enabled Srivijaya to establish agencies to receive and sell the products shipped by Srivijaya to China and even allowed traders on the ships to dispose of the products themselves without having to rely on the Song administrative apparatus.

By the early decades of the eleventh century, the Song court was already closely monitoring the Southeast Asian and Indian Ocean trade centered at Guangzhou and reacting to changing circumstances. In 1023 the maritime trade route had become important as a means of bypassing the overland trade routes through increasingly unstable central Asia, and countries beyond central Asia were requested by the Song court to dispatch their tribute missions via the maritime route.[44] A decree passed in 1028, noting that few ships had arrived at Guangzhou in the preceding years, indicates Chinese interest in strengthening maritime trade ties. Srivijaya was by this time regarded by the Song court as a key player in the shipping trade, and therefore of substantial importance to the prosperity of China's international maritime trade. The court's proactive stance on trade thus played to Srivijaya's advantage. That same year, a Srivijayan trade mission was dispatched to China, presumably in response to Chinese efforts to increase trade at its ports. It was distinguished by the Song court from other state-level trade exchanges, regarded as an act of affection on Srivijaya's part, and was given a special reward. This marked change indicates that Srivijaya had, with the resumption of its tribute relations with China, come to regard tribute missions as a vital channel for diplomatic interaction with China and as the key means of championing its status in the Song court's eyes.

After 1028 it was fifty years before Srivijaya dispatched its next state-level mission to the Song court. These five decades saw a general decline in the number of tribute missions from China's major trading partners arriving in China. Only fourteen missions from states in the Indian Ocean and Southeast Asia were recorded as having been received by the Song court between 1030 and 1050. This is in contrast to seventy-one between 960 and 999 and thirty-five during the first two decades of the eleventh century. The number of diplomatic missions to China hit its nadir by the fourth decade of the eleventh century. While the dispatch of tribute missions by the mainland Southeast Asian states of Champa and Tonkin picked up again by 1042, tribute missions from the Dashi resumed only in 1055, and those from the states of the Indian Ocean littoral and maritime Southeast Asia did not pick up until 1072.

This lull in tribute missions from China's key trading partners in maritime Asia between 1028 and 1077 has been attributed by some scholars to a series of raids in the Malay region conducted by the Cholas around 1025. These raids, which were part of a larger campaign of raids against the ports of the Malacca Strait and the Gulf of Siam, are believed by these scholars to have had a fundamental impact on the Malay region in particular, causing the disruption of the Malay hold on maritime trade that was flowing between the South China Sea and the Indian Ocean. They have also argued that the raids had a significant political impact on the Malay region, serving as the catalyst that sparked the beginning of the demise of Srivijaya and its control over the Malacca Strait and that resulted in the shift in the capital of Srivijaya from Palembang to Jambi sometime during the mid-eleventh century.[45]

However, there is no direct evidence to indicate that the Cholas were displacing the Srivijayans in the Southeast Asian leg of the international maritime trade during this time. The lull in state-level exchanges between Srivijaya and the Song court began several years after the Chola raids had apparently occurred, and only after Srivijaya had dispatched a tribute mission to the Song court in 1028. Moreover, the lull was characteristic of the Song court's foreign relations with all the states and polities of maritime Asia in the mid-eleventh century. The Chola raids thus do not appear to have made a fundamental impact on the Malay region or its maritime interaction with China in the eleventh century.

In fact, despite the general lull in tribute missions, maritime trade at Chinese ports does not appear to have declined. The value of China's import trade increased progressively between 1049 and 1064. The lull in tribute missions was probably due to the Song court's shift in its conduct of maritime trade away from ritualized state-level exchanges at the imperial court to the administration of general maritime trade at the Chinese ports through the mercantile shipping superintendencies and the liberalization of the domestic trade in foreign products in China to allow private participation. There was therefore no compelling reason for China's trade partners to maintain frequent state-level contact with the Song court.

Srivijayan shipping appears to have been active throughout the lull in state-level exchanges. An inscription at Guangzhou, dated to 1079, sheds light on the frequency with which Srivijayan ships were arriving at the port between 1064 and 1077, before the resumption of the next series of missions from Srivijaya. The inscription states that between 1064 and 1066, ships of the Srivijayan king Dihua Jialuo had arrived in Guangzhou, led by one of his relatives, Zhi Luoluo. Zhi Luoluo returned to Srivijaya the next year and reported to the Srivijayan king about a Taoist temple at Guangzhou that had been lying in ruins. In 1067 a representative named Sili Shawen was dispatched to Guangzhou to commence the restoration of the temple's main gate. Sili Shawen sailed back to Srivijaya in 1068 but returned in 1069 to complete the work. He returned to Srivijaya the same year, and in 1070 another representative was sent to China with various gifts to arrange for the appointment of an administrator of the restored temple and to purchase fields for its upkeep.[46]

Hence, between 1064 and 1070 four return trips were made from Srivijaya to China to handle the restoration work of the Taoist temple. While a statement from the "Older History of Guangzhou," quoted in the *Document Concerning the Treatment of Illnesses of the Districts and Countries under Heaven* by Yan Jianwu, states that the Srivijayan king dispatched Zhi Luoluo as an envoy to present tribute to the Song court sometime before 1064,[47] it is clear from the absence of mention of this mission in the Chinese official record that the Song court considered this a trade mission rather than a diplomatic one. Similar shipments of foreign products, carried by Srivijayan vessels, probably arrived at Guangzhou annually from 1028 to 1077, when tribute relations eventually resumed.

The restoration of the Taoist temple in the 1060s and 1070s had a clear impact on Srivijaya's diplomatic and commercial relations with China, culminating in the resumption of its diplomatic relations with the Song court in 1077, when an envoy of the Srivijayan king was dispatched to present tribute to the Song court to seek the court's permission to present a substantial cash donation for the construction of two buildings within the temple compound and to request that a bell be cast and a bell tower be erected.[48] Possibly occurring just after the shift of the Srivijayan capital from Palembang to Jambi, the temple restoration and the subsequent mission may have been calculated moves on the Srivijayan ruler's part to obtain recognition of the new port-capital of Srivijaya.[49] The Srivijayan ruler was also attempting to obtain recognition at the state level for his patronage and donations in Guangzhou, for which the requests for permission to carry out the restoration works and purchases of arable land had hitherto been made at the prefectural level. Furthermore, in making these requests to the Song court, Srivijaya was once again, as in the first two decades of the eleventh century, trying to elicit a favorable response from the Song court. The conferring of a title on the Srivijayan ruler following the above request, a privilege that no other maritime Southeast Asian ruler enjoyed, indicates that this protracted overture was highly successful.

Srivijaya's elevation in status also resulted in substantial benefits for Srivijaya's trade with China. Even though the trade missions dispatched by Srivijaya in 1078 and 1083 were not, in the end, received by the imperial court, they were nonetheless accorded due ceremony, and the envoys of both missions were granted honorary titles. The Guangzhou mercantile shipping superintendency was apparently aware of Srivijaya's elevated status in the eyes of the Song court, and preferential treatment was not confined to the trade missions dispatched by the Srivijayan king. All other presentations of foreign products, including those dispatched by other members of Srivijaya's political elite, were handled with great care. Hence, when a shipment of camphor and textiles was dispatched by a Srivijayan princess to Guangzhou in 1082, the cautiousness with which the Guangzhou superintendent of mercantile shipping initially handled it, by delaying its reception until instructions from the capital were received to handle it as an ordinary shipment of products, is a clear indication of the high status that Srivijaya had by this time enjoyed, both at the port and state levels.[50]

At the port level, Srivijaya benefited greatly from its donations to Guangzhou. Srivijaya's temple restoration represented a sustained effort to court the Guangzhou administration, whose commercial favors it was seeking to gain or retain. This sustained pursuit of patronage mirrors Srivijaya's earlier efforts in the building of the religious centers at Nagapattinam, in Chola, South India, in the first two decades of the eleventh century, an effort that lasted for several years and spanned the reigns of several Srivijayan kings.[51] While Srivijaya secured preferential treatment for its commercial interests at the Chinese ports as a result of the success of its overtures to the imperial court, its overtures at Guangzhou, which included such long-term commitments that lasted well beyond the completion of the restoration projects as the financial support of the religious institutions, would have enabled it to establish a significant presence at the port city. Social links both with the port administrators and the Chinese merchants established at Guangzhou, would have been secured and reinforced, and through this Srivijaya's commercial interests—its ultimate concern—would have been furthered.

Srivijaya's presence in Guangzhou was given a further boost in 1079, when the assistant envoys of the 1078 Srivijayan trade mission were appointed commandants, a title conferred on the chiefs of minority ethnic groups resident within China's borders. In the context of China's ports, this title was normally accompanied by the appointment of the its recipient as foreign headman.[52] The conferring of the title of commandant on the Srivijayan envoys was apparently a move made by the Song court in recognition of the increasing importance of maritime trade as a source of state revenue. More important, the court recognized the increasing volume of trade that was taking place between China, Southeast Asia, and the Indian Ocean littoral from the 1070s on. This can be seen from the resumption of tribute missions to the Song court by states such as Srivijaya, Chola, and Tianzhu (northern India) from 1072 on. Before 1079 there appears to have been only one foreign headman at the port. The post was held by an Arab, and the title of commandant was not conferred on this person until sometime between 1054 and 1063.[53] The 1079 appointment appears to have been the first time that more than one foreign headman was maintained by the superintendency of Guangzhou, suggesting that the size and ethnic diversity of the foreign population, at least at Guangzhou, had grown substantially by the late eleventh century, of which Srivijayan and other Malay-speaking merchants were most likely one of the most important groups.

Hence, by 1079, Srivijaya had gained a foothold in the administration of Guangzhou. This foothold was reaffirmed in 1082 and again in 1083 by the granting of the title of commandant to four more Srivijayan envoys.[54] The impact that the acquisition of the post of foreign headman and the title of commandant had on Srivijaya's commercial interests in Guangzhou must have been significant, and the Srivijayan king appears to have supplemented his links to the Chinese port administration with his own appointment of a ship captain as his chargé d'affaires at Guangzhou, a post that had already been in existence for some time before 1082.[55] Together with the post of foreign headman, the two positions provided Srivijaya with lines of communication between the Srivijayan ruler, his representatives stationed in Guangzhou, and the Chinese administration, which would have been used to facilitate Srivijaya's commercial activities in China.

In the last decade of the eleventh century there was a perceptible change in the overall pattern of tribute missions dispatched by Srivijaya. By this time, there was a move away from the pattern established in the early decades of that century, of predominantly diplomatic missions dispatched at intervals of several years, and a return to the pattern established in the tenth century, in which trade missions, forming a larger portion of the total missions, were dispatched in rapid succession. This, and the lack of details concerning the tribute and the absence of any ceremonial treatment accorded to the mission envoys, suggests that changes in the political or economic context in the Malay region may have been occurring during this time. This may have followed the succession of a new Srivijayan king or was possibly a response to increased competition from other states such as Chola, South India. It is also possible that Srivijaya was advertising itself as the preferred port of call to Chinese traders, who were by this time beginning to arrive in Southeast Asia in increasing numbers following the 1090 liberalization of Chinese shipping.

After 1095 no Srivijayan tribute mission was received by China until 1137. The forty-two-year lull in Srivijayan tribute missions took place within the context of two slow periods for all the foreign trading partners that had hitherto regularly dispatched tribute missions to China. The first of these, between 1096 and 1104, involved all of China's trading partners who had regularly sent missions to China from the 1070s, namely Tonkin, Champa, the Dashi, and Srivijaya. The absence of any indication of political turmoil or economic oppression at the Chinese ports suggests that these states were probably enjoying favorable trading conditions at those cities. Rather, there appears to have been a consensus among China's trading partners that there was no need to continue frequent dispatches of tribute missions to the Song court as long as favorable conditions prevailed both within and outside China. The 1090 liberalization of Chinese shipping, which led to the engagement of the Chinese coastline and its immediate hinterland in China's maritime trade, must have had an immediate impact on China's trade with Southeast Asia. In 1105 a further decree was issued, which enhanced the mercantile shipping superintendencies' management of foreign ships that were calling at China's ports,[56] suggesting that the number of foreign ships arriving at the Chinese ports annually had increased sufficiently to warrant the administrative changes. The foreign population at key Chinese ports that serviced the trade from Southeast Asia and the Indian Ocean littoral was clearly not in decline. In particular, the prosperity of the foreign population of Guangzhou in the early twelfth century is attested to by the *Pingzhou ketan*.[57] All these developments indicate that foreign maritime trade activities in China did not decline despite the lull in diplomatic missions around the turn of the twelfth century.

Srivijaya retained the position of foreign headman in Guangzhou during the early twelfth century. According to the *Pingzhou ketan,* the foreign headman of Guangzhou had organized a religious gathering at the port during this time. The invitation of a Srivijayan Buddhist ascetic by the headman for the event suggests that the latter was a Srivijayan representative,[58] and that Srivijayans remained one of the key groups of foreign traders at Guangzhou. These favorable conditions at the Chinese port enabled Srivijaya to become Guangzhou's most highly regarded trading partner at that time, in particular as a key supplier of camphor, sandalwood incense, and frankincense,[59] and as the main entrepôt at which merchant ships and products from the Indian Ocean littoral and the Middle East met those from China and Southeast Asia.[60] Although Srivijaya's diplomatic relationship with China appears to have reached a plateau by the 1080s, its favorable position in Guangzhou was maintained and later further enhanced during the twelfth century.

Following a brief resumption of tribute missions from Champa, Tonkin, Java, and the Arabs, in 1104, 1107, 1109, and 1116, respectively, the short lull in tribute missions at the turn of the twelfth century was eventually overshadowed by a general lull in tribute missions after 1116.[61] Unlike previous lulls, this decline appears to have had a serious effect on the Northern Song court, resulting in the issuing of a decree in 1123 ordering foreign states to dispatch tribute to the court.[62] Although the decree was addressed to the Southeast Asian states and those of the Middle East and Indian Ocean littoral, it appears that the Northern Song court did not dispatch any missions beyond its borders to convey this decree to the states in question, unlike in 987. The decree would have instead been made known to the local representatives of these foreign states stationed at the ports, with the expectation that the information would then be relayed back to their home states.

The decree of 1123 mentioned no drastic decline in shipping activities in the Chinese ports accompanying the lull in tribute missions, unlike the decree that had been issued a century earlier in 1028, which had clearly been a response to a stagnation in trade.[63] In fact, the foreign population, which had been growing in size and ethnic diversity during the late eleventh century, had by the early twelfth century apparently increased its presence in the Chinese port cities through prolonged sojourns. This is indicated by the decree passed in 1114 declaring that the assets of any foreign household established in China for more than four generations when they were left without any successors would be absorbed and administered by the mercantile shipping superintend-ency.[64] The substantial size of the foreign population in the Chinese port cities in the early twelfth century suggests that there was no dramatic decline in foreign mercantile shipping activities or trade in foreign products at the Chinese ports.

The 1123 decree appears to have addressed the absence of diplomatic exchanges, rather than trade missions. This concern with diplomatic missions was probably the result of the political pressures within China itself, in response to military problems experienced by China from the Jurchens in the north. That conflict, as well as the internal unrest that began to erupt within Song borders in parts of northern China by the beginning of the twelfth century, had already led, in 1106, to a temporary return to the former regulation naming Guangzhou as the only place from which ships could set sail beyond China (to stem the loss of revenue as a result of corruption at the ports).[65] The fact that foreign tribute missions had continued to arrive for ten years after 1106 indicates that diplomatic exchanges continued between China and its trading partners—in particular, Java, Champa, Tonkin, and the Arabs. The 1123 decree appears to have been an attempt on the part of the Northern Song court to bolster its political legitimacy as China's rightful dynasty through the concept of virtue: the virtue whereby the Song emperor's rule would naturally attract the vassalage of border and foreign states. The dispatch of tribute missions to the Northern Song court by foreign states would have served to highlight the point that the court still retained this authority.

The decree was apparently ignored by China's trading partners and their representatives at the Chinese ports.[66] This suggests that these local representatives, who were constantly attuned to the political and administrative changes taking place in China, kept the rulers of their states updated and that by 1117 a wait-and-see attitude had been adopted in their diplomatic relations with the Northern Song court. Given the military and internal pressures on Song China at this time, the Song court was apparently too preoccupied with its own survival to have been able to follow through on its 1123 decree. It was not until 1137, a decade after the establishment of the Southern Song court at Hangzhou, that Srivijayan tribute missions to the Chinese court resumed.

The Twelfth to the Fourteenth Century: The Demise of the Regional Approach

Following the establishment of its capital at Hangzhou, in 1127, the Southern Song court quickly directed its attention to the maritime realms as a source of state revenue, and ultimately as a means of maintaining its political hold over southern China in the face of military pressure north of the Yangtze River. The new Song court's swift recognition of the importance of maritime trade to China led to the reestablishment in 1128 of the mercantile shipping superintendencies of Liangzhe and

Fujian (Quanzhou).[67] Guangzhou's superintendency was reestablished in 1130.[68] This marked the beginning of a continuous policy of reorganizing the administration of maritime trade, which lasted about forty years. By the 1160s the reorganization of mercantile shipping regulations was largely completed, and China's maritime trade climate and administration remained largely the same from then until the end of the Southern Song, in 1279. The restructuring sparked a sustained increase in maritime trade at the Chinese ports that continued through the twelfth century, reflected in the growth in revenue collected by the Song court.

The Malay region, with Srivijaya as the region's chief emporium and the political and economic representative of the Malay port-polities to China, was a key contributor to this sustained growth in trade. Srivijayan missions to China resumed in 1137, after a forty-two year hiatus. Three trade missions, carrying tribute consisting of high-value items, were dispatched during the Southern Song, in 1137,[69] 1156,[70] and 1178.[71] The latter two, which brought with them large quantities of goods, were similar to the trade missions that had been dispatched during the tenth and eleventh centuries. The 1156 mission was rewarded with cash of the exact value of the products presented, indicating that China recognized Srivijaya's intention and reciprocated accordingly. These missions would not have been the only shipments of products dispatched from the Malay region to China during the twelfth century. Malay ships probably plied the maritime route from the Malacca Strait to southern China annually, as they had been doing for the previous century or so. In addition, Srivijaya's request in 1146, via the Guangzhou mercantile shipping superintendency, that the import duty on frankincense and a number of maritime Southeast Asian products be reduced from 40 percent to 10, indicates that it was still actively transshipping high-value foreign products to China in the 1140s.

At the port level, Srivijaya's status and influence continued to rise throughout the twelfth century. This was most apparent at Guangzhou, where in 1156 the Srivijayan foreign headman was appointed foreign official,[72] the highest official position at a Chinese port attainable by a foreigner. The appointment, which included the transfer of five Chinese officials to assist the newly appointed Srivijayan foreign official, suggests that greater administrative responsibilities were at this point given to the Srivijayan representative to facilitate the flow of international trade at Guangzhou, which came largely from Southeast Asia and the Indian Ocean littoral.

Srivijaya's commercial influence extended beyond the administration of port activities, to affecting the shaping of mercantile shipping regulations. In matters pertaining to trade, Srivijaya had access to the state councillor in charge of Song China's foreign affairs, who relayed the administrative dealings with Srivijaya and any requests made by Srivijaya to the Southern Song court. Srivijaya's privileged access was unique among China's trade partners. Presumably, Srivijaya's trade with China was conducted predominantly under the auspices of its ruler,[73] and in that respect its conduct of trade was different from that of China's other major trading partners—such as the Arabs, Java, Japan, and Korea—which was dependent on individuals and private commercial organizations, with little or no direct involvement by the political center. Thus, commercial dealings with Srivijaya were still regarded by the Southern Song court as intercourse between states, and appropriate attention and official access were made available accordingly. In 1144, when the duty on fine products was raised to from 10 percent to 40, foreign traders had complained to the mercantile shipping superintendency, but to no apparent avail.[74] Yet in 1146, when Srivijaya voiced concern over its losses in the frankincense trade as a result of the higher rate, an inquiry was immediately launched and the following year the rate reverted to 10 percent.[75] No other trading partner of China is recorded as having as much influence over China's mercantile shipping regulations.

Srivijaya's continued role as a key player in China's maritime trade was also attested by the nature of the tribute dispatched to the Southern Song court in 1156 and 1178. Almost all the products presented were fine, or high-value, goods from the Middle East, India, and Southeast Asia. The exceptions were pepper, sandalwood incense, and foreign textiles, which for customs purposes were classified by the mercantile shipping superintendency as low-value products.[76] All the products were presented in large quantities. It thus appears that, during the twelfth century, Srivijaya continued to have full access to all types of products from all the regions that were participants in international maritime trade. In particular, its role as a major supplier of frankincense to China, the most important incense for the Song court in terms of revenue generation, continued well into the twelfth century. In addition, Srivijaya had by this time become a major supplier of pepper, camphor, and sandalwood incense, products that had become staples in China's maritime trade and were absorbed by the general Chinese market in great quantities. This is affirmed by Zhou Qufei, who noted in the *Lingwai daida* (1178) that Srivijaya possessed the commodity wealth of the other trading regions because of its naval prowess along the Malacca Strait and its success in forcing almost all mercantile vessels that used the strait to call at its chief port (at this time, Muara Jambi), making it the chief entrepôt of the international maritime trade.[77] The Chinese administration regarded Srivijaya at that time as third, after the Arabs and Java, among the states in the Indian Ocean littoral and Southeast Asia, based on its access to trade products, even though it produced few products of its own.[78]

It was in this context that Srivijaya's first tribute mission to the Southern Song court arrived in 1137. The absence of any evidence indicating that Srivijaya had been suffering from an internal or regional conflict prior to 1137 suggests that the mission was dispatched in response to the partial lifting in 1133 of the ban on the trade of foreign products imposed in 1127. Srivijaya's rationale for conducting tributary relations with China at the beginning of the Southern Song was still completely governed by trade, and there was no fundamental shift in its policy toward China from the position it had adopted in the tenth and eleventh centuries.

Developments on the diplomatic front, however, appear to have taken place by this time. Following the presentation of tribute to the Song court, the Srivijayan king requested that his envoys be accorded the same ceremonial treatment as that which the Song court had accorded the Arab envoys, by using the same type of paper to record the list of reciprocal gifts.[79] This reveals several features of the diplomatic relationship between Srivijaya and the Southern Song court that had developed by this time. First, this was the first time such a request had been made by a Srivijayan king, suggesting that before this either the issue of ceremonial standing had not been considered to be as important as it clearly was by 1137 or Srivijayan envoys were no longer the recipients of ceremonial accord similar to that received by the Arab envoys, as they had been in the past. From the detailed records of the reception and rewards bestowed on Srivijayan envoys throughout the eleventh century, the latter reason appears the more plausible.

There was some ambivalence on the part of the Southern Song court toward the 1137 mission. The Srivijayan envoys were not received by the Song court but were instead given audience at Guangzhou. The mercantile shipping superintendency appears to have regarded this occasion as a trade mission, not a diplomatic one. However, the nature of the gifts the Southern Song court made in return indicates that, in the end, the mission was still treated with significant regard, revealing that the court was eager to reestablish diplomatic relations with Srivijaya. However, the treatment of Srivijaya's missions by the Southern Song court had already been downgraded to a degree, indicating that the renewed relations would not be as elevated as those Srivijaya had enjoyed in the late eleventh century.[80]

In 1156, when Srivijaya dispatched a rich tribute mission carrying large quantities of trade products, the Southern Song court again departed from the Northern Song court's practice of treating diplomatic and commercial relationships as essentially the same. The Southern Song emperor's response to the mission was that only the admiration of the imperial culture by foreign states was to be praised, and therefore rewarded and encouraged, while the dispatch of foreign products to the court was not.[81] State-level overtures, as far as the emperor was concerned, were to be purely diplomatic and were not to include any commercial implications or functions.

The diplomatic status of states like Srivijaya and Champa, which had used their diplomatic relations with China for commercial ends, declined in this altered climate. By the 1160s, Srivijaya had still not regained the title of favored vassal it had previously enjoyed. In 1168, possibly at Srivijaya's instigation, an imperial advisor requested that the court confer the title of favored vassal on Srivijaya again. Although the request was eventually granted, the conferment ceremony and the accompanying presentation of ceremonial gifts did not occur at the capital, Hangzhou,[82] suggesting that it was not an important issue for the Song court. Diplomatically, Srivijaya was no longer as important to China as it had been in the late eleventh century.

In 1178, Srivijaya's mission, which brought with it large quantities of high-value trade products, was redirected to Quanzhou, even though it had already embarked from the port of Guangzhou to the capital. The manner in which the mission was subsequently dealt with at Quanzhou, which was in accordance to instructions issued by the imperial court, was entirely in accordance with the mercantile shipping regulations, with no ceremonial treatment accorded.[83]

This may explain why the 1178 mission was the last mission dispatched by Srivijaya to China during the Southern Song period. Since diplomatic overtures had ceased to be necessary for commercial success in the changed political and commercial climate of the Southern Song, Srivijaya no longer felt tribute missions to be necessary. The missions it sent were mainly commercial. This was particularly so since its trade at Guangzhou was already facilitated by the strong representation at the port that it had painstakingly developed over the previous centuries.

The shift in the Song court's economic orientation southward, and toward the maritime economy, therefore affected its foreign policy perspective in a fundamental way. During the tenth and eleventh centuries, the Song court generally interacted with the countries of Southeast Asia for noncommercial purposes only. Thus, trade was, by default, the basis on which it conducted its foreign policy and diplomatic intercourse. By the early eleventh century, the Song court ranked states according to their commercial potential and contributions to China's import-export economy.[84] The decree of 1123, requesting the states of Southeast Asia, the Middle East, and the Indian Ocean littoral to dispatch tribute to the Song court, issued against the backdrop of uninterrupted foreign trade arriving at the Chinese ports, suggests that toward the end of the Northern Song, there was a shift away from the court's purely commercial rationale for its relations with these states. Political recognition of the moral authority of its dynastic rule was now the prime objective. The military pressure from the Jurchens in the north was the catalyst for this fundamental change.

This new rationale remained in place even after the establishment of the Southern Song court at Hangzhou, in 1126, since the pressure from the north continued despite the court's retreat south of the Yangtze River in 1126. Within four years of the move, Java, Dashi, Jiaozhi, Champa, and Khmer Cambodia had each dispatched at least one tribute mission to the new Song court. Although the customary presentation of high-value trade products took place, the granting of titles and ceremonial articles in return suggests that the Southern Song court regarded these missions as occasions for reinstating its diplomatic relations with these states and not necessarily as opportunities to merely reaffirm economic relations.

With the rationalization of the administration of maritime trade in China in the early decades of Southern Song rule, the court sought to keep the role and functions of commercial and diplomatic missions distinct and dealt with its economic and political relationships with the foreign states separately. Different agencies were established to deal with dignitaries and missions from each of the different foreign regions, namely, Korea and Japan, the central Asian states, the hill tribes of southwestern China, the Southeast Asian polities, and the Indian Ocean littoral states. These agencies were brought under the direct jurisdiction of the Ministry of Rites after 1127, which was in turn under the direction of a state councillor.[85] The mercantile shipping superintendency, formerly responsible for receiving and presenting to the imperial court tribute that was dispatched by foreign states, now merely received tribute missions upon their arrival at the ports. The eventual presentation of foreign tribute to the imperial court was now under the charge of the state councillor. The mercantile shipping superintendency no longer had a hand in China's diplomatic relations with the maritime states of Southeast Asia, the Indian Ocean littoral, and the Middle East.

In 1130 the Song court began establishing diplomatic commanderies in China for Java, Zhenla (Cambodia), and the Dashi (Arabs), all of which were regarded by China, both politically and economically, as first-tier states in their respective spheres of influence. The intention was to maintain permanent diplomatic relations with these states. The towns in which the commanderies were established were responsible for their maintenance and security, and the tithes of a stipulated number of households within the vicinity of these commanderies were allocated for the maintenance of the dignitaries of these states whenever they arrived in China and sojourned at the commanderies.[86] The Song court adopted the position that its diplomatic interaction with those it regarded as first-tier states of Southeast Asia, the Middle East, and the Indian Ocean Littoral was to be centered on periodic visits by dignitaries through the maintenance of a permanent diplomatic presence in China, in place of tribute missions. This was the first time that such a proactive policy had been initiated by China in its relations with the states of the "southern barbarians." Srivijaya, representing the Malay region, was excluded from this list of first-tier states.

Tribute missions, on the other hand, were to be the means by which other states that were attracted to the superiority and benevolence of the imperial culture of the Song dynastic rule were to conduct their diplomatic relations with the Southern Song court. These second-tier states were not regarded as being in the same league as Java, Zhenla, and the Dashi Arabs. The states that dispatched tribute missions to Song China after 1131 were Zhenlifu (a dependent of Zhenla),[87] Cengtai (unidentified), Srivijaya, and Champa.

It is possible to explain the disparity in the fortunes and status of Srivijaya in China at the port and state levels as being the result of the Song court's ability to separate its economic and political interactions with foreign states. This argument, although plausible, is not without its flaws. It is important to assume, for example, that the economic relationship between two states remains a key determinant of their diplomatic importance to each other. Hence, as long as the Malay region continued to be a major contributor to China's maritime economy, Srivijaya's status in the Song court's eyes, at the state level, should have continued to be favorable, rather than in decline. This should be particularly true of the Southern Song, when maritime trade became all the more important after the Song court lost northern China to the Jurchens in 1126 and contributed up to 5 percent of the Southern Song court's total state revenues collected during the twelfth century.[88] Srivijaya's fortunes at the port and state levels therefore appear to contradict the political realities of Song China.

Srivijaya's apparent rise in importance at Guangzhou also appears to contradict the growth of Chinese maritime trade and shipping that was occurring from the late eleventh through the thirteenth century. Srivijaya's increased status at Guangzhou in the twelfth century seems to indicate, at first glance, that the growth of Chinese maritime trade during this period did not pose any competition to Srivijaya's role as the main carrier of China's trade with Southeast Asia and the Indian Ocean littoral, and the purveyor of foreign products that the Chinese market knew about only when they were brought to the Chinese ports. Yet the fact that Chinese traders were, by the eleventh century, able to travel to Southeast Asia to procure products indigenous to the region, as well as obtain products originating from further afield that were being made available at Southeast Asian ports, would have led Chinese traders to pose a serious threat to Srivijaya's hitherto time-honored role as China's economic proxy in its indirect access to Southeast Asian, the Indian Ocean littoral, and the Middle Eastern markets.

It is against the backdrop of the process of enlargement of China's maritime economy, particularly the Chinese sector of the Asian maritime trade, that the seemingly contradictory developments of Srivijaya's standing at the port and state levels in China may be understood. As long as Srivijaya continued to supply China with Middle Eastern and Indian Ocean products, it continued to be able to cater to a niche in China's maritime trade in which the Chinese traders did not appear to have been able to compete successfully. This was particularly so after 1164, when the Song court imposed extremely high compulsory purchase rates in order to control 60 to 70 percent of the inflow of luxury products of Middle Eastern and Indian Ocean origin, which forced Chinese traders to concentrate on low- and high-value products that were not affected by the rate changes. Hence, Srivijaya's status at the port level continued and improved during the late eleventh and the twelfth century. However, China's maritime economy had expanded by the twelfth and thirteenth centuries, fueled largely by the expansion of trade in low- and high-value Southeast Asian products, which had, by the late twelfth century, come to dominate China's import trade. In this respect, Srivijaya's contribution to the Chinese maritime economy appears to have shrunk in relative, if not in absolute, terms. In the process, Srivijaya's importance to China's maritime economy would have decreased through the course of the twelfth century. This appears to have been reflected in its standing in China at the state level, and its diplomatic standing in the Song court's eyes was therefore negatively affected as well.

While Srivijaya continued, throughout the twelfth century, to conduct its trade with China at the Chinese ports, shipping products that it believed the Chinese market was interested in consuming, other ports in the Malay region had, at the same time, begun to directly engage China economically. The Malay ports carried this out by catering to the Chinese traders and shipping that were beginning to operate actively in Southeast Asia and the Malay region. The location of economic interaction in Malay-Chinese trade was beginning to shift to Southeast Asia. That development may be noted from Song period records pertaining to the Southeast Asia–China trade that date to the twelfth and thirteenth centuries. In the early twelfth century, the *Pingzhou ketan* notes that Chinese traders were already going to Jambi, Sumatra, annually to obtain such products as pepper and sandalwood incense. The *Lingwai daida* (1178) notes that by the 1170s the Chinese had begun to rank foreign trading partners according to the range and value of the products being made available at their respective ports, not what their ships could bring to China.

By this time, Srivijaya was apparently painfully aware of this development and attempted to begin shipping Southeast Asian products to China. By doing so, however, it set itself in direct competition against Chinese traders and shipping, which were, by this time, able to operate in larger shipping volumes than Srivijaya could. Srivijaya's role in the region's trade with China was, in the process, critically eroded. The resulting vacuum was filled by the emergence of a number of ports along the Malay coastline.

In such a context, ports in that region no longer needed a regional representative to handle their trade with China collectively. By the early thirteenth century Srivijaya's representative role in the Malay region's trade with China, and therefore its grip on the Malay ports, had begun to unravel. Ports in the northern Malacca Strait, such as Lambri and Semudra, were beginning to emerge as alternative entrepôts in the region, catering to Indian Ocean and Chinese traders. In addition, such minor ports as Kompei, in northeastern Sumatra, and Pahang and Kuala Berang, on the eastern coast of the Malay Peninsula, had apparently established direct trading relations with Quanzhou by this time.[89] These small port-settlements could not replace Srivijaya as a transshipper of Indian Ocean and Middle Eastern goods, but they did export low-value products to China.[90] Such ports began to trade directly with Chinese traders, who were arriving in the region annually. Each port was hawking a few specific products to Chinese traders. Although the range of products made available to the Chinese traders was limited at each port, the products, or their relative quality, were often unique to the specific port.

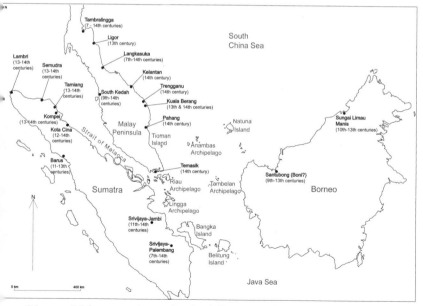

Map 3.1. Malay ports that maintained direct or indirect trade with China before the fifteenth century

There is no evidence that the contact established by these port-settlements was initiated and maintained at the state level. The absence of any textual record of tribute missions dispatched by these settlements to the Chinese court during the Southern Song period suggests that formal state-level involvement in the trade that these settlements developed with Chinese traders was probably minimal. Foreign participation in China's maritime trade was thus no longer confined to a few important trading partners but included an increasing number of minor partners as well, reflecting the broad-based nature of the trade between China and Southeast Asia that had developed by the early thirteenth century. This development was to continue into the fourteenth century, culminating in a trade characterized by the participation of numerous small ports, almost completely replacing key regional ports.

The decline of Srivijaya's hold over the Malay region coincided with the expansion of Chinese maritime trade activities in Southeast Asia from the late eleventh century on, and the expansion of the geographical scope of private Chinese traders continued into the Indian Ocean in the late thirteenth century. These traders appear to have taken over much of the role of shipping products from the ports of southern and eastern India to China, and vice versa, a role that Srivijaya had previously played. Chinese texts note that even in the early thirteenth century, Srivijaya continued to be the key trading partner through which China's supply of frankincense was obtained, as had been the case since the advent of the Song period.[91] However, by the first half of the fourteenth century frankincense was no longer one of the products carried to China from the Sumatran ports of Jambi or Palembang.[92] This although frankincense continued to be imported into Guangzhou during the late thirteenth and the early fourteenth century.[93]

In 1275 the sacking of the Srivijayan capital at Jambi by the East Javanese kingdom of Singhasari precipitated the final breakup of the Malay thalassocracy headed by Srivijaya, leading to the mushrooming of numerous autonomous port-polities in the Malay region and a change in the context of maritime trade in the region. This period, which coincided with the advent of Yuan rule in southern China in

1279, witnessed the further decline of Sino-Malay diplomatic relations. In 1279 officials at the Chinese coastal ports declared that Yuan China was open for maritime trade, prompting a diplomatic response from Java and Kollam (west coast of India). A similar response was not forthcoming from the Malay port-polities that had emerged after Srivijaya's demise. The small competing Malay region polities of the late thirteenth century appear to have lacked both strategy and leadership in their conduct of their relations with Yuan China. Local infighting may have led to instability in the region for some time following the fall of Srivijaya. The encroachment of the Javanese and Siamese in the region may have also contributed to the lack of a prompt response at the regional level.

In 1284, in response to the command of the governor of Fujian, envoys from four northeastern Sumatran port-polities, including Lambri, Perlak, and Deli,[94] presented letters from their rulers as well as tribute.[95] Details of the tribute and the reciprocal gifts were again not recorded. It is apparent that these ports were economically linked to the maritime trade based in Fujian and that their traders conducted business at Quanzhou. The governor's order was probably issued in Fujian, and the consequent presentation of letters and tribute by the four polities, which took place in the same year, was probably made by their respective representatives resident in Quanzhou. This incident suggests that the maintenance of diplomatic relations at the provincial level by polities that desired to continue their trade relations with the coastal ports of China was viewed by the Yuan provincial administrations as important. A similar incident occurred in 1286, when, at the order of the Yuan official Yatingbi, five Malay port-polities, including Lambri, Tamiang, and Samudra, dispatched envoys to present tribute to China.[96] Finally, in 1292 one of the generals leading the Mongol naval expedition against Java dispatched two officers on a diplomatic mission to the Strait of Malacca while the Yuan fleet was still off the coast of Champa. In response to that Yuan mission, four port-polities, including Lambri and Samudra, dispatched tribute missions to the Yuan court that same year.[97] The substantial sum of money carried by the Yuan mission for the purpose of trade and special purchases must have attracted the attention of these port-polities, prompting a swift response to the request that tribute missions be dispatched to China.[98]

These spates of missions, dispatched en mass by several Malay polities, came in response to the demands of Yuan officials, and not at the initiative of the polities' rulers themselves. The economic context that had developed by the late thirteenth century no longer required or favored a concerted regional diplomatic response to China. Trade with China had by the twelfth century begun to be centered increasingly in Southeast Asia, and for the Malay region, it had become fairly well-established by the early thirteenth century. There was no longer a compelling need to interact with the Chinese court in China.

Nor did the Yuan court view tribute missions and diplomatic intercourse as necessary for furthering commercial exchanges. China's maritime commercial activities were, at least until 1323, relegated to the Ortaq clique and their collaborators. Instead, they appear to have been regarded as a means of bolstering the political legitimacy of the ruling dynasty. Furthermore, the Yuan court appears to have been keen to engage the major states of maritime Asia only on the diplomatic front. The missions sent by the Malay port-polities were never regarded by the court as on the same level as those from Java, or from Malabar and Kollam, on the western coast of India. The absence of elaborate ceremony on the part of the mission from Samudra in 1282 was noted by the Yuan court, which commented that the envoys did not present any memorial to the emperor.[99] The 1284, 1286, and 1292 Malay missions appear to have been better received because of their presentation of letters from the Malay rulers, which appear to have been deemed by the Yuan court an important aspect of tribute relations.

This policy was reflected in the court's keen desire to establish some form of patron-client relationship with Kollam, Malabar, and Java, regarded by the court as the most important states in maritime Southeast Asia and the Indian Ocean littoral at that time. To that end, a number of Yuan envoys were sent to the three states during the first thirty years of the Yuan period. In return they dispatched missions to the Yuan court.[100] The Malay region was left out of the diplomatic interaction that was taking place.

There were, however, exceptions to this late-thirteenth- and fourteenth-century pattern of diplomatic interaction. In 1280, a year after the Yuan dynasty had consolidated its control over southern China, a Yuan envoy sent to demand the dispatch of a diplomatic mission from Kollam, stopped at Samudra on his outward journey. The ruler of Samudra seized the occasion to accept vassal status under the Yuan and dispatched envoys to the court as a sign of this acceptance. The Samudra envoys arrived in China in 1282 and were received by the Yuan court.[101] Jambi, the erstwhile capital of Srivijaya, was another Malay port-polity that attempted to seize the upper hand in this diplomatic game. It dispatched diplomatic missions to the Yuan court on its own accord in 1281, 1299, and 1301. It appears that Jambi, drawing on the Srivijayan tradition of seeking to establish tributary relations with China for political and economic benefit, regarded the change in the dynastic rule in China as an opportunity to renew political and economic ties. It may have regarded such overtures with the Yuan court as being important for its reestablishment as a regional power in the Malacca Strait following the sacking of Srivijaya's capital by Singhasari in 1275.[102] The dispatch of successive missions in 1299 and 1301 may be an indication of this urgency. Samudra, on the other hand, appears to have been sufficiently influential in the northern Malacca Strait to attempt several overtures to China, presumably in the hope of being recognized by the Yuan court as the key polity in the Malay region.

The lack of response from the Yuan court to Samudra and Jambi's diplomatic overtures indicates that the port-polities were not successful in achieving their respective objectives. Unlike the Song court, the Yuan court's diplomatic relations with maritime Asia were predominantly politically motivated, with economic motives taking a secondary place. In maritime trade, the Yuan court favored, at least until 1323, direct state involvement in China's maritime economy, over the encouragement of private participation and indirect stewardship of the maritime economy that was favored by the Song court. As a result, no mission was forthcoming from the Malay region after 1301. This lull in state-level exchanges continued to characterize the whole of the fourteenth century.

This state of affairs came to an end only at the beginning of the fifteenth century, when China, under Ming rule, embarked on a proactive and outward projection of its maritime capability by commissioning a series of imperial voyages between southern China and the eastern coast of Africa. In 1405, Malacca, a Malay port-polity established in 1401, seized on this change in Chinese foreign policy and led the Malay region in reestablishing diplomatic relations with China.

Chapter 4

MALAY AND CHINESE FOREIGN REPRESENTATION AND COMMERCIAL PRACTICES ABROAD

Direct engagement in a foreign economic region often resulted in the development of representation at these foreign markets, particularly at the gateways through which foreign products were fed into the domestic economies of the foreign trading partners, and where indigenous products or manufactured items were dispatched abroad in return. Such representation, or agency, at foreign ports was an important channel through which market access and knowledge of the foreign markets' demand could be ascertained and eventually met.

The causes of the development of representation at foreign ports were largely similar for both Chinese and Malay traders. The key difference was that while Chinese maritime trade was driven chiefly by private concerns, the Malay region's trade was driven primarily by state participation. As long as state-level economic exchanges with China remained important to the overall well-being of the maritime economy and political well-being of the Malay region's port-polities, the representation maintained at the key southern Chinese ports, Guangzhou and Quanzhou, would continue to be indispensable. However, when the Malay maritime economy was no longer dependent on such state-level exchanges, such representation in China would no longer be imperative.

For the Chinese, as direct trade in the Malay region became increasingly important, the need to establish some form of representation at the Malay ports became increasingly pressing. In addition, as maritime trade between China and the Malay region became increasingly diffuse, of lower unit value, and controlled by private parties, important commercial practices were developed by Chinese traders to exploit the evolving context of the trade, as well as the opportunities as they presented themselves, to maximize profits.

Malay Agency at Chinese Ports
The Northern Song Period

The presence of foreign agents at the Chinese ports started well before the tenth century, following the establishment of the mercantile shipping superintendency at Guangzhou during the late Tang,[1] and building on the trade that consequently developed at this port. Following the advent of Song rule in Guangdong in 970, foreign commercial presence quickly extended beyond Guangzhou. By the end of the tenth century, foreign traders had extended their commercial operations north along the Chinese coast. With the establishment of a superintendency at Mingzhou sometime between 990 and 994, a number of foreign traders, including those from such maritime Southeast Asia polities as Java, appear to have begun to establish commercial links at that port as well.[2]

Initially, foreign traders had to conduct their trade with China through the mercantile shipping superintendencies. Song mercantile shipping regulations permitted foreign ships to call only at designated international ports. This limited foreign commerce mainly to the ports of Guangzhou, Hangzhou, and Mingzhou. Access to the domestic Chinese market was thus virtually nonexistent. Nonetheless, from the outset, foreign traders had been keen to gain access to the domestic market and to connect with the Chinese economy outside of the purview of the superintendencies. As early as the third decade of the eleventh century, small numbers of Southeast Asian and Indian Ocean littoral traders had been calling regularly at prefectures along the southern Chinese coast and trading directly with the local Chinese population and officials there. The coastal prefectures of Fujian, due to their location between the international ports of Guangzhou and Dinghai, were particularly active in this clandestine trade. Ports designated for domestic maritime trade, such as Zhongmen harbor and Fuzhou, were used as illegal access points to these localized markets, with foreign merchant ships arriving at these harbors every year.[3] The trade apparently involved both high- and low-value foreign products, since both relatively low value Chinese products, such as silks and ceramics, and such high-value items as gold, were used in these exchanges.[4] Coastal trade and access to at least the coastal economy of Fujian province had thus been established by foreign traders by the early eleventh century.

This illegal trade with coastal Fujian, which continued through the eleventh century, apparently involved maritime Southeast Asian traders. By the first half of the reign of the emperor Shenzong, Southeast Asian and Indian Ocean littoral traders were regularly arriving at the coastal prefectures of the Fujian circuit, without first clearing customs at an international port.[5] Contemporary accounts abound of Quanzhou harbor being visited by a fair number of foreign ships annually, of the ready availability of foreign products at the port of Quanzhou, and of the frequent participation of the port's officials in this illicit maritime trade.[6]

While tax evasion may have been a likely motivation for this practice, an additional reason appears to have been the desire for access to the domestic market beyond the international ports. As more foreign traders participated in trade with China, and as the Northern Song court shifted away from regarding foreign trade as the preserve of state-level relations, the pressure for greater access to the Chinese domestic market gradually increased as well. While the Chinese domestic trade in foreign products was gradually being liberalized by the Song court to encourage participation by Chinese private traders, foreign access to the Chinese domestic economy continued to be confined to commercial operations at Guangzhou, Hangzhou, and Mingzhou. The trade at these ports would have been dominated by the state-sponsored trade of China's foreign trading partners. The foreign traders attempting to trade beyond the designated ports were therefore most likely not operating under the auspices of their polity's state-sponsored trade. Those Malay traders operating under the auspices of Srivijaya would not have needed to proceed to any location other than Guangzhou, where Srivijaya's commercial presence was well established.

By the late eleventh century, in an attempt to reach a compromise with foreign traders over access to the domestic market, the Song court extended the market access that foreign traders had hitherto enjoyed from the boundaries of the port cities to the boundaries of the prefectures in which the ports were located.[7] By doing so, the court hoped to reduce the clandestine trade along the southern Chinese coast. Access to the Chinese domestic trade had become an important commercial issue for the foreign traders engaged in China's maritime trade, including those from the Malay region, who after 1028 had begun to rely much less on state-level trade missions and increasingly on trade conducted at the port level.

By the end of the eleventh century a significant foreign population had developed in Guangzhou. Several key foreign groups were present at the port, and they were governed by their respective foreign headmen, who were in turn appointed by the mercantile shipping superintendencies. Foreign quarters, or areas within a city, were established in the ports to accommodate foreigners whose chief purpose for residing in China was to participate in or facilitate maritime trade.

The mercantile shipping superintendencies were ultimately responsible for all the foreign residents at the ports. Their responsibilities included seeing to the nonmaterial needs of the foreign population. Although the foreign population was accorded a large degree of autonomy in matters of religion within the confines of the ports, the provision of adequate facilities for the religious needs of the resident foreign community was facilitated by the superintendencies. Parcels of land were allotted or sold to the various foreign ethnic groups so that cemeteries and places of worship could be established near the cities. These places of worship, including mosques and Buddhist and Hindu temples,[8] became increasingly important as the foreign population increased, their sojourn in China lengthened, and the number of locally born foreigners grew. These religious centers became the social and spiritual focal points of the various foreign groups sojourning at the Chinese ports. They also most likely served as institutionalized means of enforcing accountability in business transactions between traders who shared a common religion but who would otherwise not have known each other, and therefore could not be held accountable through kin-based means.

The foreign population was not isolated from the Chinese population of the ports. The Chinese literati of Guangzhou, for example, were known to have attended the religious events periodically organized by the city's foreign headman.[9] Although the Song court distinguished between people of Chinese and non-Chinese stock resident in China, by the early twelfth century, locally born foreign residents were allowed greater freedom of movement and commercial access to the Chinese domestic market than temporary sojourners. In 1104, following appeals by foreign traders, the Song court allowed locally born foreign traders to operate beyond the prefectural boundaries of the international ports, subject to first obtaining an official permit from the mercantile shipping superintendency. Market access was granted even to the markets at the Song capital of Kaifeng.[10] The success of this petition indicates that foreign residents were by this time exerting a greater influence at the ports than before.

In addition to their commercial influence, the increasing number of locally born foreigners had a significant impact on the Chinese social elite by the late eleventh century. The issue of marriages between such foreigners and members of the Song imperial clan arose during the Zhezong Yuanxiao era (1086–94). A dispute highlighted in the *Pingzhou ketan* involved a female member of the Song imperial clan and the estate of her deceased husband, who had resided in the foreign quarter of Guangzhou and was most likely a foreigner.[11] Both families were thus from a highly affluent background, reflecting the extent of the social and business alliances built between foreign traders and the social elite of Song China, as well as the social and economic standing that foreign residents could attain at the Chinese ports by the late eleventh century.

The case led the Song court to prohibit intermarriage between foreign residents and members of the imperial clan, unless the foreign family had been resident in China for at least three generations and had had a family member receive an official appointment within one of those generations.[12] The restriction was consonant with the general regulations promulgated by the Song court to govern the marriage of Song imperial clanswomen.[13] However, it would have had the unintended effect of preventing foreign groups that had recently arrived and were residing in China from advancing their interests through marriage with the Song social elite. The policy unwittingly favored long-established foreign groups, thereby according them the opportunity to further advance their already well-established interests.

In 1114 an edict was passed ordering that the estate of foreigners whose families had resided in China for more than five generations be absorbed and administered by the local mercantile shipping superintendency if there was no business partner to inherit the estate or the estate was not bequeathed to any kin upon death.[14] While this was an extension of the superintendency's earlier practice of taking charge of the cargo and property of any foreign trader who was critically ill or dead upon arrival at a Chinese port, selling off the cargo in the official markets on behalf of the trader, and safekeeping the sale proceeds until a claim was made,[15] the 1114 edict was an official recognition of the growing presence of foreign communities that had settled in China for a long period and were thus subjected to the same administrative procedures as Chinese households. However, the use of the superintendencies as the civil government's arm in implementing this procedure suggests that the Northern Song court still associated these locally born foreign residents with China's maritime trade, and that they were not naturalized as citizens of China.

In order to facilitate its trade with China, the Malay region established and maintained a presence at the key ports of Guangzhou and Quanzhou, the most readily accessible from the South China Sea. Srivijaya's agents were no doubt planted at the Chinese ports to facilitate the conduct of trade between the Malay port-polities and China, to receive both the ships and cargo that arrived from the Malay region, as well as to source for and provision ships returning to the region with Chinese products.

The presence of Malay agents in China began as early as the late Tang, culminating in the appointment of a Srivijayan as foreign official at Guangzhou in 905. For states whose relationship with Song China was ultimately based on trade, establishing their influence at the ports through the presence of long-term residents was an essential course of action. As the region's trade with China gradually shifted from state-level trade exchanges conducted at the court level to state-sponsored trade conducted at the Chinese ports, the role that the Malay agents played gained in importance. Srivijayan agents were installed to facilitate the trade that was arriving from the Malay region. Similar agents were installed at the Chola port of Nagapattinam, in southern India, by the beginning of the eleventh century,[16] and their functions included the championing of the commercial interests of the Srivijayan ruler and traders, maintaining and improving Srivijaya's influence among the officials of the ports' administration, and furthering Srivijaya's status at the respective foreign courts.

Such agency was not confined to traders operating under the common auspices of a ruler but also extended to a larger network of individual traders, often from the same region, and over time extended through marriage alliances with certain groups of Chinese at these ports. As the Malay region's trade with China had begun to shift from largely the transshipment of high-value Middle Eastern and Indian Ocean products to one that also included increasingly large quantities of both low- and high-value maritime Southeast Asian products by the first half of the twelfth century, and as the Wang Anshi reforms resulted in international maritime trade being conducted solely at the port level, it became necessary for a permanent presence of commercial contacts at the Chinese ports for the facilitation of the trade conducted not just by Srivijaya but by large-scale Malay traders or collectives of smaller-scale trading concerns that operated outside Srivijaya's state-sponsored trade.

The presence and effectiveness of this community sojourning in China enabled Srivijaya to maintain continuous state-level overtures toward the Song court since the latter's inception, as well as to make concerted efforts at building up its influence at the port of Guangzhou during the eleventh century through such undertakings as the restoration of the Taoist temple at Guangzhou, between 1064 and 1070, and its subsequent maintenance, all of which were carried out at great expense.[17] These actions reaped for Srivijaya favorable regard both in the eyes of the Song court as well as the Guangzhou administration during the eleventh and twelfth centuries.

By the late eleventh century the Malays, under the auspices of Srivijaya, formed one of the most prominent groups of foreigners residing at Guangzhou. The Srivijayan headman was capable of organizing notable religious events, to which the foreign population of Guangzhou, as well as eminent members of the Guangzhou administration and literati, was invited. On one such occasion, recorded in the *Pingzhou ketan,* the Srivijayan headman invited a Srivijayan religious expert to Guangzhou to recite a Buddhist canon.[18] The successful invitation of a Srivijayan expert for the event, which would have been possible to organize only if the Srivijayan headman was able to undertake the significant costs involved, as well as to possess the influence to successfully invite such a religious expert to Guangzhou, reflects the headman's, and in turn Srivijaya's, high social and financial standing at the Chinese port.

As the Song court's policies governing foreign residents were amended in favor of locally born foreigners at the beginning of the twelfth century, Malay residents apparently benefited from these changes as well. The 1104 edict allowing locally born foreigners complete access to the Chinese domestic market would have particularly benefited foreign traders who had commercial concerns already established at the Chinese ports for a long time, and thus had locally born representatives. While the *Songhuiyao* mentions the Arabs as a key group in this petitioning process, other groups, in particular those from the Malay region such as the Srivijayans, certainly benefited from this change as well.

The restrictions placed on marriages between foreigners and members of the Song imperial clan at the end of the eleventh century also played to the advantage of Malay residents in China, in particular the Srivijayans. The requirement that foreign families intending to enter into a marriage alliance with an imperial clan family have an official appointment in the Chinese bureaucracy would have had the unintended result of limiting such marriages with foreigners from maritime Asia to the Srivijayans, Javanese, and Arabs—the only foreign groups at the ports that had individuals who bore the title of foreign headman or foreign official, as well as honorary official titles conferred while conducting state-level exchanges during the eleventh and early twelfth centuries. As a result, the commercial and social influence of these groups would have been enhanced. For Srivijaya, the standing and activities of its representatives at the Chinese ports increased in importance and intensity during the early decades of the Southern Song.

The Southern Song Period

Malay representation at the Chinese ports continued initially under the auspices of Srivijaya in the early decades following the advent of Southern Song rule, in 1127. The status of Srivijaya's representation, particularly at Guangzhou, the chief international port of Song China, continued to increase in importance and appears to have reached a peak during the mid-twelfth century. In 1156 a Srivijayan envoy who had been resident in Guangzhou for some time was appointed the foreign official of that port, the highest appointment attainable by a foreigner. The increased influence the Srivijayan residents wielded at Guangzhou does not appear to have been due to numerical superiority alone but, more important, to their economic influence at the port. This suggests that by this time, the importance of Srivijaya's economic role at Guangzhou superseded those of other foreign groups.

Srivijayans were by this time not only present at Guangzhou. According to the *Zhuozhai wenji* by Lin Zhiqi (ca. 1160s), a cemetery for Quanzhou's foreign residents was built by a Srivijayan merchant named Shi Nowei, who was based at that port,[19] presumably at his own expense. The establishment of the cemetery was not Shi Nowei's only act of philanthropy toward the needs of the foreign community at Quanzhou,[20] and it would not have been Srivijaya's only one as well. There were other wealthy Srivijayan merchants residing at Quanzhou, a number of whom probably acted as Srivijaya's agents.[21] The presence of locally born Srivijayans at Quanzhou indicates that Srivijaya must have established a presence here sometime before the mid-twelfth century, possibly since 1087, when a mercantile shipping superintendency was established at this port. The building of a foreigners' cemetery by the prominent Srivijayan merchant Shi Nowei suggests that a significant number of Srivijayans had taken up long-term residency at Quanzhou by the mid-twelfth century.

Nonetheless, despite the proliferating presence of Srivijayans along the southern Chinese coast, Srivijaya concentrated its official efforts mainly at Guangzhou. Srivijayan contributions to the conduct of public works at Guangzhou, such as the restoration of the Taoist temple in the mid-eleventh century, are recorded by the Chinese as official overtures instigated and sustained by the political elite of Srivijaya. In contrast, no text mentions that the contributions made by Srivijayans at Quanzhou occurred at the instigation of, or with the financial support of, the Srivijayan ruler himself. Official overtures at Quanzhou were therefore not conducted at the same level of intensity nor accorded a similar level of support by the Srivijayan court. The activities of Srivijayans at Quanzhou may instead have been those of private traders from Srivijaya or the Malay region, many of whom would have most likely operated commercially in their own capacities.

The presence of individuals from the Malay region at Quanzhou in a private capacity appears to have been part of larger developments in the nature of Malay representation in China that was developing from the mid-twelfth century on. Foreign traders and residents at the southern Chinese ports who conducted commercial activities outside the purview of state-sponsored trade were gradually increasing in number and importance through the twelfth and thirteenth centuries. The advent of Southern Song rule in 1127, which saw a broadening and diffusion in China's maritime trade, and a dramatic shift in the court's handling of its trade and diplomatic relations, resulted in traders operating outside of the purview of state-sponsored trade beginning to rise in importance in China's maritime economy. The annual farewell feast provided by the mercantile shipping superintendencies to send foreign traders off at the start of the northeast monsoon, which had begun at Guangzhou as a prefecture-level initiative and was later extended to Quanzhou in 1144, was clearly intended for the general assembly of foreign traders from Southeast Asia and the Indian Ocean littoral. This was not purely a state-level event, and thus not solely intended for traders operating under the purview of state-sponsored trade, but for those operating under private concerns as well.

By the thirteenth century the decline in state-sponsored exchanges to China, the growing commercial presence of Chinese maritime traders in Southeast Asia, and the increasingly diffuse nature of China–Southeast Asian trade, saw state-sponsored representation at the Chinese ports eclipsed by a more informal and general representation from the Malay region. The *Yunlu manchao,* for example, notes that traders from such minor Malay ports as Pahang, Kuala Berang, and Kompei were present at the port of Quanzhou.[22] Malay representation at the southern Chinese ports was no longer under the auspices of Srivijaya alone.

At the same time, the nature of commercial activities of locally born foreigners in China was making significant strides. These sojourners had moved beyond attempting to extend their commercial activities into the Chinese domestic market, to the use of China as the base for their maritime trade activities. Foreign access to the Chinese domestic economy worked in both directions. Not only did foreign traders sell foreign products directly in the Chinese market, they also exported Chinese products that were in demand abroad. A tag recovered from the Quanzhou wreck, inscribed with the characters *ya li,*[23] denoting a Muslim name, suggests that Muslim traders were basing their maritime trade operations in China by the second half of the thirteenth century. Nonetheless, the presence of only one such tag at the Quanzhou wreck site suggests that this development was then still in its infancy. More important, it appears that these China-based foreign traders were Muslim, and therefore likely of Middle Eastern or Persian origin, not from Southeast Asia. Malay representation at the Chinese ports may have begun to wane by this time, a decline that would become apparent during the Yuan.

The Yuan Period

The decline of Malay representation at the Chinese ports came to a head with the advent of Yuan rule over southern China. Between 1284 and 1323, during which time Yuan maritime policy oscillated between favoring either official or private Chinese overseas trade ventures, the importance of certain groups of foreign sojourners who had come to base their commercial maritime operations in China by the late thirteenth century, and who were privileged by the Yuan court despite the vagaries of Yuan maritime trade policies, gained significantly. The prohibitions imposed on private Chinese maritime trade would have extended to include foreign traders resident at the Chinese ports. All wealthy households, not just Chinese ones, were forbidden from sponsoring or participating in overseas trading ventures whenever these prohibitions were in force.[24] Only those China-based foreign traders who were able to collaborate with the Ortaq clique were unaffected by these prohibitions.

It appears that this was a calculated policy to make China's maritime trade the preserve of a select group of China-based foreign traders. China-based foreign commercial interests were in competition with local Chinese interests in China's maritime trade. Such conditions would have had the effect of limiting the establishment of advantageous alliances to a select group of foreign traders who were already well established in China and were probably economically powerful as well. The key collaborators with the Ortaq clique were the Muslim Middle Eastern and Persian traders, based mainly at Quanzhou. It is clear that by the late thirteenth century, they were emerging as the clear winners in this prolonged competition between the different groups of locally born foreigners in China. The growing influence of Islam as the religion of the favored foreigners in China, as well as its spread among the trading communities of the Indian Ocean littoral, clearly had an impact on the trading communities of the Malay region.

The absence of textual reference to the Malay region's involvement in these developments in China, coupled with the critical decline in the political importance of the region's polities in the eyes of the Yuan court, suggests that the region's polities were unable to capitalize on these critical changes in China. Malay traders were apparently bypassed. The emergence of Middle Eastern and Persian traders as the beneficiaries of the change in China's maritime trade context in the Yuan period contributed to the establishment of Muslim traders as a powerful commercial force in Southeast Asia and the Indian Ocean from the late thirteenth century on. At the same time, the active participation of Chinese shipping in Southeast Asia made the Malay traders' role in bringing foreign products to China less vital. This in turn led to the decline in importance of Malay region representatives at the southern Chinese ports. The location of economic exchange, which had until the thirteenth century been carried out at the Chinese ports, had by this time shifted to Southeast Asia and the Malay region.

Chinese Maritime Trade Practices in Southeast Asia and the Malay Region

The Chinese commercial presence in Southeast Asia differed significantly from the Malay presence at the southern Chinese ports. The development of commercial networks in China's maritime trade with the Malay region in the tenth to the fourteenth century depended on the permitting of Chinese private participation in maritime trade in Southeast Asia. As long as trade remained a state monopoly, commercial networks through which private trade could be conducted could not be established or developed. State-level trade remained rigid. However, with private participation, trade could develop into a sophisticated complex of networks and practices, with market access based on linkages at both the individual and group levels.

All these developments hinged on the existence and flourishing of private trade. The connecting of private networks in the domestic Chinese economy to the international maritime shipping trade appears to have been vital to the commercial viability of private participation in Chinese maritime trade from the late tenth through the fourteenth century. The permission accorded by the Song court from the tenth century on to Chinese private traders to exploit their domestic networks, and to distribute their foreign imports directly into the Chinese market, rather than having to depend on the bureaucracy's official markets to absorb their imports, provided the impetus for the growth and development of China's maritime trade in private hands.

These changes in the state policies governing China's maritime trade were crucial factors in determining the way in which Chinese maritime commercial activities developed. As a result, the late eleventh through the fourteenth century witnessed private traders develop their maritime trade activities into a complex yet coherent system. China's trade with Southeast Asia was characterized by the conduct of both small-scale peddling trade and large-scale direct trade between the two regions. Intraregional trade, in particular that of Southeast Asia, was developed as a viable secondary commercial activity by Chinese maritime traders, and led to participation at various levels as Chinese maritime shipping regulations permitted. As their commercial contact with Southeast Asia increased in intensity, Chinese traders also progressively accrued a high level of knowledge of the Southeast Asian markets. This led to the development of other commercial practices, such as product quality grading and regional and product specialization, which were developed in the context of an increasingly sophisticated maritime economy and in response to the changing manner in which maritime trade was conducted by the Chinese. The system of trade, and the mode of operation of Chinese traders in Southeast Asia, was further supported by the establishment of access to the domestic and foreign markets through social linkages.

Trade at the Various Levels:
Regional Exchanges, Port-to-Port Peddling, and Intraregional Trade

Chinese private trade operated at a number of levels from the late tenth through the fourteenth century. At the macro level, trade was characterized by the import of island Southeast Asian raw materials into China, and the export of Chinese manufactured and processed goods in the reverse direction. However, this general exchange pattern was made up of different patterns of exchange, with a large number of ports woven together with overlapping layers of trading networks.

At the macro level, the China–Southeast Asia trade was direct. This was due to the time constraint imposed by the Song court on Chinese shipping that registered to sail abroad. While there is no record of this restriction in the late tenth and the eleventh century, the *Songhuiyao* notes in an 1164 memorial that Chinese mercantile vessels were expected to return to their original port of departure within nine months, failing which the Song court would investigate the cause of a vessel's late return, and would mete out punishment if the late return was not due to unforeseen circumstances or difficulties. The memorial notes that this restriction had been put in place before 1164 and appears to have dated to the Northern Song,[25] possibly when Chinese ships were permitted to sail abroad to trade, in the late tenth and the eleventh century.

Chinese shipping operating in Southeast Asia was dispersed due to this restriction. It resulted in Chinese shippers establishing direct links with key economic areas of Southeast Asia, instead of a singular route from southern China along the coast of mainland Southeast Asia to maritime Southeast Asia. By the late eleventh and the early twelfth century, multiple shipping routes emanated from the southern Chinese ports, branching out into the various economic zones in Southeast Asia. According to the *Pingzhou ketan,* Chinese ships would disperse in different directions upon entering open waters after leaving the port of Guangzhou.[26] Chinese ships were, for example, already maintaining direct links with the Malay region through the key port of the Strait of Malacca—Jambi, Sumatra, under the rule of the Malay region's chief polity: Srivijaya. Such direct links would also have been maintained with the key port of the other subregions in Southeast Asia, including Java and Champa.

This practice of maintaining dispersed shipping networks at the interregional level of trade is also evident from archaeological data of shipwrecks surveyed in island Southeast Asian waters. The Pulau Buaya wreck, most likely a Chinese vessel of the late eleventh or early twelfth century, appears to have been sailing from China to Sumatra when it foundered. Its cargo comprised predominantly Chinese products, with a few products of mainland Southeast Asian origin. The latter group was most likely picked up incidentally by the ship's crew while the vessels were stopping over at a mainland Southeast Asian port for supplies, and consisted of a small number of Cham earthenware *kendis* (drinking vessels).[27] The same pattern is evident of the trade in the reverse direction. The Quanzhou wreck, another Chinese vessel dated to the 1270s, was returning to China from island Southeast Asia when it foundered at Quanzhou Bay. Its cargo comprised predominantly Malay products, with only a small amount of the cargo from the Middle East and India, and no mainland Southeast Asian products,[28] indicating that the vessel had picked up the bulk of its return cargo at a Malay port before sailing for China, and did not call at any mainland Southeast Asian port to conduct any significant amount of trade before arriving at Quanzhou.

At the individual level, commercial activities were much more complex. The Chinese participants of maritime trade were not limited to traders or entrepreneurs with vast amounts of capital. The liberalization of Chinese maritime shipping and the progressive lowering of the level of Chinese state participation in the maritime trade economy throughout the eleventh and twelfth centuries resulted in an increasingly complex mix of individuals and groups participating in maritime trade. Along with large-scale commercial activities, the activities of small-scale traders flourished as well.[29]

By the late eleventh century small spaces in a ship's hull were rented out by the foot run to traders, who packed large quantities of Chinese products, obtained mainly on credit, to be sold at Southeast Asian ports.[30] The development of small-scale trade was due to the flexibility of the length of time individuals could remain abroad. There was no time restriction imposed on individual travel by Chinese traders. The *Pingzhou ketan* notes that by the late eleventh century Chinese traders remained abroad for as long as ten years.[31] The fact that the credit extended by entrepreneurs to these traders was structured so that the owed interest remained unchanged regardless of the time traders spent abroad indicates that prolonged trading voyages were the norm and that the institutions that financed such voyages had developed by the late eleventh century with this practice factored in.[32] The absence of restrictions on the length of time Chinese traders could remain abroad continued into the twelfth century. An 1159 memorial recorded in the *Songhuiyao* notes that the Song court was not able to keep track of the number of Chinese citizens abroad, where they were headed or currently residing, and the length of time they were abroad or the purpose for their travel.[33] Similarly, during the Yuan period, there is no record of any restriction on the length of time Chinese individuals could remain abroad.

These developments resulted, by the thirteenth century, in small-scale trade developing into a sophisticated mode of operation. Among the ninety-six ownership tags recovered from the Quanzhou wreck,[34] dated to the 1270s, seventeen have the characters *kan shui ji* written on them, while one has the characters *kan ji*. The character *kan* denotes a managerial or administrative position or role, while the character *ji* denotes a business concern. Another four tags with only the characters *shui ji* written on them and two other preceding characters missing were also recovered, and probably have similar denotation as those by the eighteen tags.[35] The tags most likely belonged to various private business concerns. These businesses either appointed traders for trading voyages or the business owners personally took part in the voyages. While these traders would no doubt have carried out their own trading activities using their personal capital, the character *kan* implies that they would also have acted as agents, accepting funds at the ports as investments in the maritime trade voyages they were participating in.[36] The sophistication of maritime trade could only have developed in the absence of excessive bureaucratic or fiscal burdens. Such agency trade continued into the fourteenth century.

Chinese traders operating on a small scale would also have been able to conduct peddling trade. Governmental restrictions did not hamper such traders. Unlike Chinese shippers, they were not weighed down by issues of vessel ownership or the cost of renting a ship and were thus in a good position to participate in a segmented trade. Individual traders would seek short passages from port to port along the international trade routes, thereby segmenting and prolonging their trading voyages. The prolonged trading trip and peddling trade that small-scale traders conducted would have allowed them to increase the value of their initial investments over time, making a round trip from China much more profitable than if they made a direct return trip to and from a single port in island Southeast Asia.

The prolonged stay of Chinese traders in a region also led to their participation in intraregional trade. This became a logical and important complementary commercial activity to their main China–Southeast Asia trade during their sojourn abroad. Intraregional trade would have enabled Chinese traders to further insure the profitability of a trading voyage.

Chinese traders catered to the specific market demands of island Southeast Asian ports. The increasing knowledge about minor island Southeast Asian economic regions and ports among Chinese traders is evident from information recorded in Chinese texts such as the *Zhufanzhi* and the *Dade nanhaizhi*. Information in *Daoyi zhilue* suggests that by the mid-fourteenth century, Chinese traders were aware of and able to cater to very specific and diverse market demands. This is evident, for example, from the textiles trade of the ports in the northeastern Malay Peninsula that Wang Dayuan apparently participated in. One of the types of textiles noted by Wang to have been imported by these ports was textiles from Champa and Hainan Island. The specific types of textiles demanded by these ports—both where they came from and their decorative patterns and dye colors—were noted in detail.[37] This even though they were minor ports with small populations and small markets. The information in the *Daoyi zhilue* is therefore most likely a reflection of Wang's personal participation in this intraregional textile trade. The level of knowledge that Wang Dayuan possessed about such a minor economic area was possible only if he had remained there for a long time—in this case, approximately twenty years. An extended sojourn in an economic area was therefore vital to a trader's accruing the commercial knowledge necessary for successful participation in localized trade.

By the fourteenth century Chinese shipping appears to have begun to participate in intraregional trade in island Southeast Asia as well.

With the advent of Yuan rule in 1279, the restriction on the length of stay abroad imposed on Chinese shipping during the Song appears to have been revoked. Under such conditions, Chinese shipping could now remain outside China for extended periods, and a number of Chinese shippers began to base their operations in island Southeast Asia. This provided a further boost to Chinese participation in intraregional Southeast Asian trade.

Archaeological research provides crucial evidence in place of the absence of textual references to this commercial development. The cargo recovered from the *Turiang* wreck, a Chinese vessel dated to the late fourteenth century, or early Ming, comprised predominantly ceramics, of which 57 percent were of Thai origin, 8 percent from Vietnam, and 35 percent from southern China.[38] The predominance of Thai ceramics indicates that Chinese shipping participated vigorously in Southeast Asian intraregional trade by the end of the fourteenth century. This participation was not confined to ceramics. The presence of fish bones and eggshells in several large Thai storage jars found in the hull of the vessel suggests that this trade involved Southeast Asian foodstuffs as well. The Southeast Asian products were stacked at the bottom of the ship's hold,[39] indicating that the ship began its trading voyage from a Southeast Asian port, not a Chinese one.

The participation of Chinese shipping in Southeast Asian intraregional trade in the fourteenth century was apparently not confined to the immediate areas through which the major trade routes traversed. The final position of the *Turiang* wreck, around one hundred nautical miles from the east coast of Johor, Malaysia, suggests that it was heading for southwestern Borneo or southern Sulawesi before it foundered.[40] This suggests that Chinese shipping was servicing Southeast Asian economic areas that lay outside the international maritime trunk routes.

Data from the *Turiang* wreck reflect the intraregional trade conducted by Chinese traders in the early Ming, when the Ming court's ban on Chinese maritime trade was being instituted. However, the apparent ease with which Chinese shippers compensated for the restrictions imposed by the court by immediately increasing their participation in Southeast Asian intraregional shipping reflects the knowledge and experience in this aspect of trade that Chinese traders possessed by this time, and the relative ease with which they could substitute operating between China and Southeast Asia with operating within Southeast Asia itself. It also suggests that by this time Chinese traders had begun to use Southeast Asian ports as the base of operations, instead of just operating out of China. In order for that to happen, these traders would have had to establish a more permanent status at these ports.

Social Linkages and Market Access

In order to successfully participate in the maritime trade of island Southeast Asia, Chinese traders needed to obtain access, directly or indirectly, to the markets in this region. Among the means were available to Chinese traders to establish such links were commercial, social, and political alliances with foreign trading groups, and aligning their commercial interests with those of the commercial groups that were present in both the Chinese and Southeast Asian ports. Textual records from as early as the tenth century note the presence of Chinese individuals at island Southeast Asian courts. The *Songhuiyao*, for example, records that the first Javanese mission to the Song court, which arrived in 991, was guided by a Chinese trader who had been resident at the Javanese court for quite some time before his eventual return to China.[41]

However, it is on the establishment of economic linkages by Chinese traders with foreign trading groups through intermarriage that we have the most information. Intermarriage was an important means of establishing or reinforcing such linkages both within China and in Southeast Asia. The *Pingzhou ketan*'s record of the feud between certain members of the imperial clan of the Song court at Guangzhou and members of a foreign family resident at Guangzhou, over the estate of a deceased prominent male foreign resident who had married a female member of the Song imperial clan, provides some information on such efforts conducted at the higher levels during the latter half of the eleventh century.[42] Such high-level alliances took place at the port level, apparently with the Song court completely unaware of them, suggesting that such social linkages were organic and not officially sanctioned.

Intermarriages in China, until the late eleventh century, do not appear to have been based on equal social backgrounds. As long as there was no official directive governing such marriages issued by the Chinese court, economic benefits would have been the key determinant of such social alliances. Complementary commercial functions, possibly for the best commercial synergy, would have determined the selection of marriage partners. The nature of the linkages between the domestic and foreign commercial networks they were then able to establish would have differed from trader to trader, or group to group.

However, once the Song court passed, in the late eleventh century, official directives governing intermarriages, such unions, in particular those involving members of the Song imperial clan, became restricted to foreign groups of equal social status. The *Pingzhou ketan* notes that the high-profile feud over the deceased foreigner's estate, mentioned earlier in this chapter, brought these social networking efforts to the attention of the Song court in the Zhezong Yuanyou era (1086–93).[43] The feud resulted in the Song court subsequently reiterating the prohibition against intermarriage between foreigners and members of the Song imperial clan, unless the family to which the foreigner belonged had been resident in China for at least three generations and had had at least one family member receive an official appointment during his residency in China.[44] Such a requirement was resonant with the general regulations regarding the marriage of clanswomen, which appears, at least until the late eleventh century, to have been ignored by the clansmen residing at China's southern ports.

While the strict regulation governing the marriage of imperial clanswomen was not, in its language, specifically prejudiced or favorable to of any foreign group at the Chinese ports, the requirement of an official appointment in the Chinese bureaucracy effectively limited such marriages to Southeast Asian and Indian Ocean littoral groups at the southern Chinese ports to the Srivijayans, Chams, Javanese, and Arabs—China's first-tier trading partners during the eleventh and twelfth centuries.[45] These were the only foreign groups at the Chinese ports that had individuals with official appointments or honorary official titles conferred upon them by the Song court.[46] The policy would have had the unintended effect of reinforcing the commercial and social influence of these groups as well as that of the Song imperial clansmen. It would have also restricted the extent to which the imperial clansmen were able to establish proxy links abroad. For them, links could be formed, after the late eleventh century, only with foreign traders operating at the highest levels of trade, such as state-level or state-sponsored trade.

Unlike the imperial clansmen, traders lower in the hierarchy of Chinese society do not appear to have been hampered by restrictions placed on the foreign groups with which they could form social alliances. The establishment of social and economic networks through intermarriage between Chinese traders and foreigners no doubt took place at the lower levels as well. Links could, and were most likely, established between Chinese and foreign traders who were operating at the levels of trade below state-sponsored exchanges.

Establishing social linkages with foreign trading groups operating at the Chinese ports appears to have been a crucial step for Chinese traders in expanding their business, since, even as Chinese private participation in the domestic sector of China's maritime trade increased throughout the eleventh century, the scale of Chinese shipping remained, during this time, fairly limited. China continued to rely heavily, at least until the late eleventh century, on foreign shipping to carry its trade, both into China and abroad. Chinese traders would have attempted to surmount their limited shipping capabilities by establishing social links with foreigners who were resident at the Chinese ports, who acted as agents for the foreign shipping that called at the Chinese ports each year. Chinese private participation in the domestic economy would have thus been linked with international shipping. Indirect access to foreign markets that were unfamiliar to Chinese traders based in China would have thus been obtained. Such alliances would have not merely benefited Chinese traders but foreign traders as well. Foreign traders were not permitted, during the Song period, to conduct their commercial activities beyond the prefectural boundaries of the ports at which they were based.[47] Foreign traders would thus in turn have also secured access to the Chinese market indirectly, through social alliances with Chinese families.

As Chinese shipping developed from the late eleventh century on, and as more Chinese traders ventured into Southeast Asia, the need to attain direct access into the various markets of the region became imperative. As Chinese traders attempted to cater to the needs of the Southeast Asian markets at the regional and port levels, coupled with the need to procure the region's products for the Chinese market, intermarriage abroad between Chinese traders and the local residents of Southeast Asian trading ports began to occur.

One of the earliest records of intermarriage occurring at Southeast Asian ports can be found in the *Daoyi zhilue*. In the entry on Champa, the text notes that Chinese traders were known to marry local women at the Cham ports.[48] Such marriages did not appear to have been short-term arrangements of convenience, since these traders returned to their Cham wives regularly. The text also notes that these wives were often able and willing to provide financial support for their Chinese husbands' maritime trade activities.[49] Thus, these intermarriages were most likely long-term commitments.

Such marriages appear to have occurred in island Southeast Asia as well. In the entry on Longyamen (Keppel Straits, Singapore), the *Daoyi zhilue* notes that Chinese were residing among the indigenous population of that settlement.[50] It is highly likely that, given the close physical proximity between the Chinese and local residents, intermarriage occurred at that port-settlement as well. Such marriages would no doubt have facilitated the Chinese commercial activities centered on that settlement.

The scale of such overseas marriages, even by the fourteenth century, appears to have been fairly limited. Such marriages appear to have been initiated only by Chinese traders operating at the lower levels of the China–Southeast Asia maritime trade. Their extended presence at the Southeast Asian ports was a result of the peddling trade they conducted, reflecting their lack of a permanent base of operations due to their small capitalization. It is also likely that these traders were, by the fourteenth century, substantially involved in the intraregional trade of Southeast Asia and had begun to use Southeast Asian ports, rather than Chinese ports, as the launching points of their trading trips. The lack of economies of scale in their trading activities, and the often small size of the Southeast Asian markets they were operating in, made it necessary for them to possess local knowledge and networks in order to maximize their profits. An intimate knowledge was necessary in order to be aware of the minute differences in the demand of the various markets within the economic area that they were catering for, as well as to successfully gain access to these markets. The port-settlement at the Keppel Straits, for example, was one of two on the island of Singapore and catered to the Riau–southern Johor economic area at the southern end of the Malacca Strait.[51] From the archaeological data gathered so far from contemporaneous sites in this area, the market was most likely fairly small and would thus have lacked any highly organized structure for the conduct of trade. Local linkages and personal connections would thus have been important for foreign traders to successfully operate from the port-settlements in this area.

Commercial Practices: Economic Area Concentration, Product Specialization, and Product Quality Grading

During the Song period, restricting Chinese vessels' stay abroad to one full monsoon cycle limited the furthest geographical extent of Chinese mercantile shipping activities to Java and Sumatra on the western trunk route, and the Philippines and northeastern Borneo on the eastern route.[52] Individual vessels were thus unable to cover the whole of Southeast Asia during the Song. In addition, the need for Chinese ships to register their intended destinations with the mercantile shipping superintendencies before a voyage restricted them to one Southeast Asian economic area per round trip. These structures inevitably led to Chinese traders specializing in specific economic areas.

Archaeological data indicate that such specialization was well established by the late thirteenth century. The cargo of the Quanzhou wreck, for example, comprised predominantly Malay region products, indicating that the trading activities of the merchants onboard was confined to the Malay Peninsula, the east coast of Sumatra, the Riau-Lingga Archipelago and the western coast of Borneo. The sizeable amounts of pepper and betel nuts found on the wreck, along with the minute quantities of Middle Eastern products,[53] suggests that the ship's destination had most likely been a Malay-region entrepôt where at least some products from economic areas further west and east were made available to foreign traders.

Chinese shippers apparently specialized in a particular Southeast Asian economic area for considerable lengths of time. The Quanzhou wreck exhibited examples of dowel pegging and cord lashing—island Southeast Asian techniques employed in the construction of a ship's hull—even though the vessel was of Chinese construct and made predominantly of Chinese pine.[54] The substantial repairs undertaken on the ship in the Malay region suggest that its operators must have been sending the vessel to the region for a considerable time before it foundered.[55] Area specialization, and the accompanying increase in knowledge of the ports and products of a given area, inevitably led to the practice of product specialization by Chinese traders.

Although individual travel abroad was not hampered by time restrictions similar to those on Chinese shipping, Chinese traders generally had their commercial activities limited to the economic areas covered by Chinese shipping networks and thus generally specialized in a small number of products. To be successful, individual traders needed to know the products they specialized in. Area specialization, however, most likely limited the range of products available for export to China, so the eventual number of products in which individual traders could specialize would have been even smaller. This is borne out by data from the Quanzhou wreck. Of the eight types of products recovered from the wreck site, four, which constituted the overwhelming proportion of the cargo recovered, were Malay-region products.[56] Chinese traders were, by the early thirteenth century, aware of the many products available for export by the ports of this subregion. The few products that the traders of the Quanzhou wreck specialized in were therefore apparently drawn from the limited range of products available at the particular port the vessel had called at, in accordance with the declaration made prior to its departure from China and the limited time it had abroad. In addition, given the high number of diverse business concerns represented on the ship, as indicated by the range of wooden product-ownership tags recovered, it would appear that specialization in an economic area and its products occurred at a number of levels and was practiced by both large-scale Chinese entrepreneurs as well as small-scale traders and trading agencies by the late thirteenth century.

The increase in the knowledge of the ports, markets, and products of Southeast Asia, and the practice of area and product specialization, led to the development of another complementary practice by Chinese traders by the twelfth century—product quality grading. When the quality of a given product could be quantified, the value could be assigned to a given shipment of that product entering the Chinese market. Such a practice required three key conditions. First, sufficiently large quantities of a product had to be imported so that a diversity of quality was apparent. Differing quality grades could not be applied arbitrarily, since all participants of the trade would generally accept the benchmarks. Second, those who developed the grading system had to be active participants in the shipping trade, involved in obtaining a product from its source, and have a fairly detailed knowledge of its geographical origins. Access to a wide enough geographical range of sources was necessary so that knowledge of the differing qualities of that product could be accrued. Third, there appears to have to have been a central agency where knowledge of foreign products could be collated. Extensive, carefully gathered knowledge was thus crucial to the development and implementation of a quality-grading system on which Chinese maritime traders could agree.

As long as the importation of foreign goods was largely carried out by China's foreign trading partners, or the Chinese state was the dominant player in the domestic trade in foreign products, the Chinese market lacked the sophistication needed for quality grading. Chinese traders also lacked the knowledge and ability to develop such a commercial practice. In the context of Chinese maritime trade, the three conditions necessary for quality grading came together only from the late eleventh century on. It is not surprising, therefore, that the first Chinese official reference to quality grading appears in 1133.[57]

Nonetheless, a comprehensive grading system was already in use by Chinese traders by that date. Only three grades were used in this system—top, middle, and low,[58] and its application in the procurement of foreign products appears to have been fairly limited. By the mid-twelfth century, a handful of Southeast Asian aromatics were graded in this manner, reflecting the increasing intensity of commercial contact that Chinese traders had developed with Southeast Asia. The demand in China appears to have been strong enough and their price band sufficiently broad for quality grading to be applied only to these products.

The product grades used by Chinese traders were quickly adopted by the Song court in 1141; the mercantile shipping superintendencies relied heavily on quality grading to determine the rate of duty levied on a product.[59] The adoption of quality grading was the Song court's reaction to, and acceptance of, a Chinese commercial practice that had come to characterize the way in which Chinese private maritime trade was conducted. Texts such as the *Lingwai daida, Yunlu manchao,* and *Zhufanzhi* reflect an increasingly intimate knowledge of the products of the various Southeast Asian economic subregions that were being made available by their respective key ports to Chinese traders throughout the twelfth and the early thirteenth century.

By the early thirteenth century, quality grading, hitherto confined to high-value Southeast Asian aromatic products, was also extended to many low-value products from the region. Such texts as the *Yunlu manchao* and the *Zhufanzhi* note that low-value products like beeswax and coconut-fiber mats were by this time subjected to quality grading. The grading system developed for such products, which was a simplified system, was different from that adopted in the twelfth century for aromatics. Only the foreign source of the best grade of a particular low-value product was noted. The system was thus most likely employed by Chinese traders only during the procurement stage in Southeast Asia. These low-value products acted as substitutes for certain products produced in China, but only the best foreign sub-stitutes would have been able to compete successfully in the Chinese market. Such low-value products would have been imported into China in very large quantities, since a high turnover would have been needed to make them to be profitable.

By the early fourteenth century the economic subregions in South-east Asia in which Chinese traders operated had become well defined. This is evident from the Chinese vision of the maritime world of that time. According to the *Dade nanhaizhi,* maritime Southeast Asia was divided into three regions—the Small Western Ocean, the Large East-ern Ocean, and the Small Eastern Ocean. The Small Western Ocean encompassed the Malay region, the Small Eastern Ocean the Sea of Borneo and the Sulu zone, and the Large Eastern Ocean the Java Sea region. Each of these geographical regions was in turn divided into subregions based on the geographical extent of political entities, real or imagined.[60] The Small Western Ocean encompassed the two politi-cal entities of Srivijaya and Tambralingga believed to have been located along the eastern coast of the Isthmus of Kra. Srivijaya was represented by the geographical extent of the Malacca Strait region and Sri Lanka, while Tambralingga was represented by the Gulf of Siam and the northeastern tracts of the Malay Peninsula and present-day southern Thailand.[61] The Small Eastern Ocean comprised the kingdom of Bor-neo, which included the Sulu zone and southern Philippines within its borders, while the Large Eastern Ocean comprised the kingdom of Tanjungpura, which encompassed the southwestern and southeastern coast of Borneo, Sulawesi, and Maluku, and the kingdom of Majapa-hit, which encompassed the islands of Java and Bali, and the islands further east.[62]

The geographical framework in the *Dade nanhaizhi* was most likely based on information supplied by Chinese traders operating from the port of Guangzhou at the end of the thirteenth century and reflected the geographical knowledge of maritime Southeast Asia that these traders possessed, based on their respective specialization. It is clear that the three key economic subregions in which Chinese traders con-centrated their operations were the Malacca Strait region and the Bay of Bengal, the Java Sea region, and the Sulu zone and northern Borneo. The rise of Quanzhou as a port from the late eleventh century, which led to the development of the eastern route to Southeast Asia via Taiwan Island and the northern Philippines by the fourteenth century, gave rise to vibrant Chinese trading activities in the Sulu zone and northern Borneo by the thirteenth century.[63]

The polities noted in the *Dade nanhaizhi* were not necessarily in existence by the early fourteenth century. In the case of Srivijaya in the Malacca Strait, its role as a regional polity ended with the sacking of the capital, Jambi, by Singhasari in 1275. Official texts of the Yuan period mention no foreign state by the name of Sanfoji, the name used during the Song for the polity of Srivijaya. Nonetheless, in Yuan texts written by or based on information provided by Chinese maritime traders, the term Sanfoji continued to be used for the port of Jambi as well as the Malacca Strait region. The same appears to have been true for Tambralingga, which, by the fourteenth century, had declined into a minor port-polity.[64] The use of such polity names was a reflection of the geopolitical and commercial knowledge of maritime Southeast Asia that had developed among Chinese traders over the course of the previous centuries and had lingered on in the consciousness of Chinese traders in the early fourteenth century, even after these polities had declined or disappeared.

Chinese knowledge of Southeast Asian markets, and the products available from them, continued to increase through the course of the fourteenth century. Southeast Asian products had by this time become the main products imported by Chinese traders operating from southern Chinese ports. Of the list of sixty-nine foreign products noted in the *Dade nanhaizhi* to have been imported by Chinese traders based at the port of Guangzhou, forty were sourced from Southeast Asia.[65] By the mid-fourteenth century Chinese traders possessed detailed knowledge of the products that were being made available by almost all the ports in Southeast Asia that were known to the Chinese, as is evident in the *Daoyi zhilue.*

In the practice of product quality grading, both the comprehensive and simplified systems were used by Chinese traders in their procurement of products from the economic areas in which they specialized. Information in the *Daoyi zhilue* suggests that by this time Chinese traders were applying the comprehensive grading system to any product that would eventually have a sufficiently wide price band upon being imported into China. For example, Wang Dayuan, author of the *Daoyi zhilue,* himself a Chinese trader operating in the Malay region and Bay of Bengal, comprehensively graded lakawood incense, *chen* and *su* gharuwood incense (two different classes of gharuwood that were officially recognized by the Chinese market and the mercantile shipping superintendencies), and *jiangzhen* (most likely a type of construction timber).[66] Chen and su gharuwood incense were already subjected to comprehensive quality grading by the twelfth century,[67] while lakawood incense, a low-value product during the Song period and subjected only to simplified grading, appears to have increased sufficiently in price in the Chinese market through the thirteenth and fourteenth centuries for it to develop a wider price band by the fourteenth and consequently be subjected to comprehensive grading.[68]

The simplified grading system, on the other hand, was applied to a larger number of products than was the comprehensive system. Wang Dayuan noted at least one port as the source of the best quality of each of eight products. For important products, more than one best-quality source was noted. For example, Wang noted that the best-quality crane's crest (the crest of hornbills, used by the Chinese for carving objets d'art) and pepper were available from two sources each.[69] A differentiation of quality was made between the two sources, with one supplying the top quality of the product, and the other supplying a quality merely superior to that available from any other foreign port. It is probable that as far as possible, Chinese traders would travel to the source from which the best quality of a specific product was available.

Product quality grading went hand in hand with area and product specialization and by the mid-fourteenth century reflected the degree of knowledge Chinese traders possessed about their respective geographical areas of specialization. Wang Dayuan's commercial activities provide some insight into how Chinese traders operated. He appears to have had very detailed knowledge of twelve products: chen and su gharuwood,

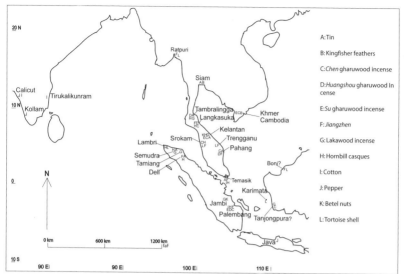

Map 4.1. Geographical distribution of the twelve products graded by Wang Dayuan

lakawood incense, jiangzhen, tin, feathers, crane's crests, cotton, pepper, tortoise shells, betel nuts, and beeswax. This knowledge was reflected by his application of the comprehensive and simplified quality grading systems on them. The ports from which these products were made available for export were located mainly on the Malay Peninsula and in the Malacca Strait region, as well as a few along the coast of the Bay of Bengal and the Gulf of Siam. In addition, Wang's knowledge of the other ungraded products from these places, such as turtle carapaces, sappanwood, tin, gold, and ivory, was also comprehensive. It is therefore evident that his commercial activities were centered primarily in the Malay region, extending occasionally into the Bay of Bengal.

The average number of products a Chinese trader specialized in also appears to have increased by the mid-fourteenth century. Wang Dayuan most likely specialized in all twelve products he graded. It appears that by this time, Chinese trade, at least at the individual level, had become more diffuse than before. This was the result of less restrictive regulations imposed on Chinese traders and shipping by the Yuan court after the second decade of the fourteenth century.

The commercial practices of Chinese traders in the Malay region, as well as the nature of Malay representation in China, indeed evolved in response to the larger developments in the economic and diplomatic contexts of Sino-Malay relations, as well as the political and administrative developments in China, through the tenth to the fourteenth centuries. In turn, the changing patterns of trade affected the types of products eventually traded between the two regions. A study of the nature of the economic interaction between China and the Malay region would therefore not be complete without a detailed study of the products traded between the two.

Plate 1. (*top*) Chinese bronze mirror; recovered from the Intan wreck. *Courtesy of Michael Flecker*

Plate 2. (*left*) Chinese silver ingots with incised Chinese characters, cast during the interregnum (904–71); recovered from the Intan wreck. *Courtesy of Michael Flecker*

Plate 3. Chinese copper coins of one cash value, Northern Song; recovered from the St. Andrew's Cathedral site, Singapore

Plate 4. Shards from a Longquan platter; recovered from the St. Andrew's Cathedral site, Singapore

Plate 5. Cross-sectional profile of a Zhejiang greenware bowl; recovered from the Fort Canning Hill site, Singapore

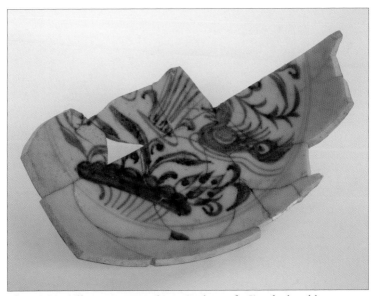

Plate 6. Partially reconstructed interior base of a Jingdezhen blue-and-white porcelain bowl; recovered from the Fort Canning Hill Site, Singapore

Plate 7. Qingbai shards with incised decoration; recovered from the Fort Canning Hill site, Singapore

Plate 8. Shard from a qingbai jarlet molded in the form of a star fruit; recovered from the St. Andrew's Cathedral site, Singapore

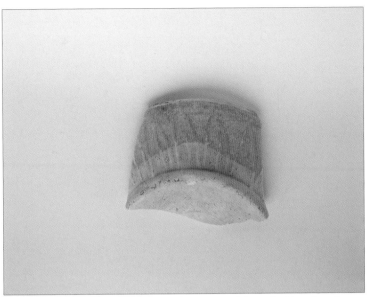

Plate 9. Shard from a Dehua ware dish; recovered from the Fort Canning Hill site, Singapore

Plate 10. Shards from a Guangdong-type storage jar; recovered from the Fort Canning Hill site, Singapore

Plate 11. Cizao small-mouth bottle (mercury jar); recovered from the Parliament House site, Singapore

Chapter 5

CHINA AS A SOURCE OF MANUFACTURED PRODUCTS FOR THE MALAY REGION

China, with its superior manufacturing technology, developed, from the tenth to the fourteenth century, into a vital source from which the Malay region could import a wide variety of manufactured products. These were items that the people of the Malay region could not produce, and while many were initially regarded during the early first millennium AD as status symbols that represented the respective abilities of the rulers of the Malay ports in tapping into the lucrative Chinese market, by the late tenth century, most Chinese manufactured goods had become the staple trade items that the Chinese used to procure the foreign products they desired.

The development of the export trade in Chinese products to the Malay region in these centuries depended on three key factors—changes in regulations pertaining to maritime trade and fiscal policies in China, changes in the manner in which maritime trade was carried both by China and Southeast Asia, and changes in the volume and unit value of that trade. Such changes occurred in two phases. The first phase, which began with the advent of the Song dynasty and lasted until around the twelfth century, was characterized by exchanges normally carried out at Chinese coastal ports, with traders from the Malay region taking the active role in shipping foreign products to China. To begin with, the mode of payment for goods that arrived in China was largely dependent on the mercantile shipping regulations and fiscal policies in place at the time of exchange. Changes in the regulations, as well as the fiscal policies implemented by the Song government, therefore had a profound impact on the nature of these reciprocal exchanges. Moreover, payment for the products arriving at the ports was made both in Chinese currency and bullion and in Chinese products. The use of the former was fairly straightforward. For tribute presented in kind, however, specific items, and their respective qualities, were used by the Song court to reflect not only the value of the products brought to China but also the status accorded to the foreign missions. Goods used for this purpose included silk and articles of silver and gold. The items that foreign envoys received were thus not necessarily in demand back home. Other items, such as bullion and currency, which often formed part of the reciprocal payment for tribute items presented, were used at the Chinese ports to pay for products saleable at home and at other intended markets further down the chain of maritime trade.

The second phase was initiated by the permission given, in the early eleventh century, to Chinese traders and ships to go abroad to trade, and brought into full swing by the 1090 liberalization of Chinese maritime shipping, which opened the Chinese coastline to maritime trade. As a result of the consequent increase in the volume of Chinese shipping between China and maritime Southeast Asia, particularly from the late eleventh century on, trade moved from being exclusive to being more commonplace. In addition, trade moved from having to be funneled into China through the three designated international ports—Guangzhou, Hangzhou, and Mingzhou—to being on a much larger scale and diffuse along the Chinese coastline. Finally, the location of exchange gradually shifted from China to Southeast Asia. A greater range of such products as ceramics, metals, and textiles was made available to the foreign markets, as the economic hinterlands just behind the Chinese coastline became increasingly integrated into the Chinese maritime economy and their economic production became increasingly geared toward meeting the demands of these overseas markets.

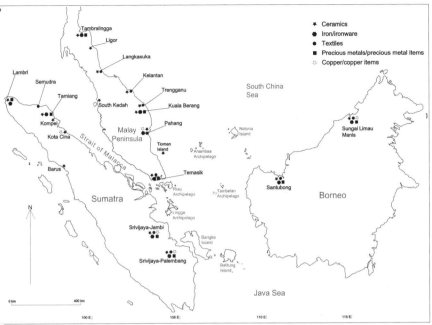

Map 5.1. Distribution of Chinese products imported by Malay ports, tenth through fourteenth century

Five key categories of products were exported to the region from the tenth to the fourteenth century—metals, currency, textiles, foodstuffs, and ceramics.[1] These remained the main categories in China's export trade to the region throughout this period, although, as patterns of trade changed, the relative importance of specific products also changed.

Metalware

China's use of metals in its conduct of international maritime trade had become well established by the late Tang and continued through the Song and Yuan periods. Following the establishment of the mercantile shipping superintendencies in the first decades of Song rule, such metals as gold, silver, lead, tin, and iron were traded for foreign products.[2] The range of value of these metals allowed the Chinese to meet the changing nature of trade, in particular with maritime Southeast Asia, as it developed from a select trade based predominantly on the import of luxury products, to one dominated by lower-value products.

By the late tenth century, metals were exported to maritime Southeast Asia as bullion, workable forms, and finished articles. Finished articles were a major form of metals exported to the Malay region. Articles made of precious metals played a significant role in diplomatic exchanges between China and her foreign trading partners, and were a key feature of the Song court's reciprocation for the tribute brought by the missions of foreign states to China. Other metal articles, including copper and iron items in finished and workable forms, were used in the general maritime trade. The export of metal in bullion form was fairly rare, although, at times when the maritime trade regulations in China permitted such exports, bullion in the form of ingots and even coins was shipped to the Malay region in specific instances and periods during the tenth to the fourteenth century.

Precious-Metal Articles and Bullion

As with other metals, China's use of gold and silver in international maritime trade, both in article and bullion form, had become well established as early as the late Tang. Articles made of precious metal were among the important categories of Chinese gifts in state-level exchanges during the late tenth and the early eleventh century. The Song court regarded such items as indicators of the status of a foreign state and confined their use to dealings with important state-level trade missions. The use of precious-metal bullion, on the other hand, was linked to China's general maritime trade. As early as 971, gold and silver were used to barter for foreign products brought to the port of Guangzhou.[3] Precious metals were presumably used to trade for such high-value foreign products as rhinoceros horns, elephant tusks, pearls, camphor, and frankincense. For instance, the Song mission of 987 to China's major foreign trading partners in Southeast Asia and the Indian Ocean littoral used gold to purchase high-value aromatics and other precious products.[4] Bullion provided an important way of conducting high-value trade without contravening Song regulations, which stipulated that gold and silver articles were to be used only in ceremonial exchanges.

The Malay region was a recipient of both forms of precious metals. Srivijaya received precious-metal articles in return for the tribute it presented to the Song court in 975.[5] Within maritime Southeast Asia, Srivijaya and Java were the only two polities noted in Song texts to have received such items during this period, attesting to the status of Srivijaya as the dominant port in the Malay region, paralleling that of Java within island Southeast Asia. The region also received precious-metal bullion through its trade with China in the tenth century. Ninety-four silver ingots of Chinese origin have been recovered from the Intan wreck site. These ingots were apparently used in the payment of official taxes, including the salt tax, in China during the early tenth century, when southern China, including such ports as Guangzhou and Quanzhou, were under the control of the southern kingdoms of Min and Han.[6] These ingots, which were highly valuable due to their function in Chinese fiscal transactions as well as their bullion value, were probably reexports on their way from Srivijaya-Palembang to Java, where silver would have been used in the minting of local coinage.

However, a substantial portion of the Chinese precious metals received by Srivijaya in the late tenth and the early eleventh century does not appear to have been used locally. Although gold was highly prized and had a ceremonial function in the region's religious practices,[7] the Malay region's gold needs were met locally, since Sumatra and the Malay Peninsula were major exporters of gold.[8] At the same time, there is little evidence to suggest that silver bullion was ever used in the Malay region in the same quantities as in other maritime Southeast Asian regions, such as Java. Instead, Chinese gold and silver articles were obtained and used by Srivijaya to advertise to trading partners in the Indian Ocean its ability to provide valuable goods from China. To this end, two gifts of Chinese gold, most likely in manufactured form, were made to the Karonasvamin temple at Nagapattinam by a Srivijayan agent stationed at that Indian port early in the eleventh century.[9]

The use of precious-metal bullion in maritime trade increased throughout the tenth and eleventh centuries. In 1015 the Song court blamed the outflow of silver to Southeast Asian, Indian Ocean littoral, and Middle Eastern states for the rise in the price of silver in China. The use of precious-metal bullion also spread beyond the officially sanctioned international ports by the early eleventh century. A memorial submitted to the Song court in 1025 noted that the officials of Zhongmen harbor in Fuzhou, which was not a designated international maritime port at that time, had been ordering the local citizens to barter for high-value Middle Eastern, Indian, and Southeast Asian products with precious metals.[10]

While precious-metal articles and bullion were used during the tenth century in state and nonstate trade respectively, by the mid-eleventh century, their use had begun to overlap. After 1030, apart from three instances, precious-metal articles ceased to be listed in state-level diplomatic and trade exchanges between China and her trading partners. Instead, precious-metal bullion was used. This shift may have been the result of the increasing monetization of China's maritime trade, a process that had begun during the reign of Renzong (1023–63). This practice continued into the 1070s. The reforms of the trade and barter regulations implemented by Wang Anshi in 1072 led to the use of precious-metal bullion instead of articles in the high-value transactions of state-level exchanges, and during the fifteen-year period of the Wang Anshi reforms, no precious-metal articles were given to any tribute missions. The Malay region was a recipient of such payments of bullion. The 1078 Srivijayan mission, for example, received 10,500 taels of silver as partial payment for the tribute it presented to the Guangzhou mercantile shipping superintendency.[11]

Although the use of gold and silver articles declined in state-level exchanges, the Malay region, in particular Srivijaya, was still keen to import these items, possibly for reexport, but also as prestige items, for use by its own ruling elite. Thus, the Srivijayan envoy of the 1078 mission requested permission from the Song court to purchase a gold belt and silverware with the silver bullion and copper cash the Song court had given in return for the tribute presented.[12] The export of precious-metal items to the region, however, continued to be limited to state-level trade exchanges. The absence of Chinese precious-metal articles in the known shipwrecks of the period in maritime Southeast Asian waters suggests that these did not feature as part of the general trade that took place between China and the region.

The use of precious-metal articles in state-level trade exchanges was revived for a short time in the late decades of the Northern Song. However, during the Southern Song, the rationalization of the Song court's foreign policy perspective from the 1130s on led to a decline in the use of silver and gold articles in China's maritime trade with Southeast Asia and the Malay region. The last time a Srivijayan tribute mission was rewarded by the Song court with silverware was in 1137.[13] After that, only silver bullion was used as payment in state-sponsored trade. The value of the silver bullion awarded by the Song court to its major trading partners was carefully calculated to match the value of the tribute presented.[14]

In the latter half of the twelfth century, China's position on the export of precious metals started to become increasingly prohibitive. In 1175 a memorial was issued lamenting the severe outflow of valuable metals via international trade.[15] While copper was the main concern of the memorial, the viability of the continued use of gold and silver in China's maritime trade was also questioned.[16] Consequently, an edict was issued that all subsequent state-level trade arriving in China was to be reciprocated with such manufactured products as silk and ceramics. By 1219 this prohibition was extended to the use of precious-metal bullion in all of China's maritime trade transactions. A memorial submitted in that year strongly discouraged mercantile shipping superintendencies from using silver and gold in the purchase of high-value foreign products, in particular frankincense.[17]

Despite these developments, the export of gold and silver to maritime Southeast Asia during the early thirteenth century did not cease completely. In fact, the *Zhufanzhi* (1225) notes that the major Malay region ports, including Srivijaya-Jambi, Tambralingga, and Kuala Berang, were importing both silver and gold from China. The volume of this trade is not known, although it was likely to have been fairly small.

Nevertheless, the decline in the role of tribute and state-sponsored exchanges as a channel of trade and diplomatic intercourse in the Southern Song period resulted in the decline in the export of precious metals to the Malay region during the thirteenth century. In addition, China's import of high-value Middle Eastern and Indian Ocean products, which were the most expensive foreign products, had begun to decline in relative importance by the early thirteenth century, eclipsed by the trade in Southeast Asian products, many of which were of lower value. The need for precious-metal bullion as a barter item to match the value of the foreign products imported by China was thus not as great as before. Most of these lower-value imports were paid for with Chinese manufactured products, such as ceramics, metalware, textiles, and foodstuffs. The volume of the trade in gold and silver bullion and articles from China declined in tandem with these changes.

Following the advent of Yuan rule in China, edicts were issued in 1283, 1294, and 1322 prohibiting the use of gold, silver, and copper in maritime trade.[18] It is apparent from these edicts that precious metals continued to be exported from China during the Yuan period. However, whatever little demand for precious metals the Malay region maintained with China was, by this time, limited only to workable forms.[19] Tamiang and Temasik imported silver and pure gold, while Lambri imported ungraded silver and gold.[20] While Sumatran and Malay peninsular sources no doubt satisfied most of the demand for gold in raw or workable form, it is unclear where the main exporters of silver were located. It is therefore possible that Chinese silver continued to be imported by the region's ports.

In general, Chinese articles of precious metal were more in demand in the Malay region than was bullion. Since access to such articles was largely restricted to participants in tribute exchanges with China, when the role of such exchanges diminished and eventually ceased by the twelfth century, the export of precious metals to the region also declined. Instead, it was China's export trade in low-value metals and metalware that gained in prominence from the tenth through the fourteenth century.

Iron

Sources of iron ore were numerous in maritime Southeast Asia. Historically, only Java and Bali were so deficient in iron that they needed to rely on imported sources. Indeed, the quality of Southeast Asian low-carbon iron and ironware, like the iron from the Indian subcontinent, was higher than that of iron from China. However, the chief advantage enjoyed by the Chinese iron industry was economies of scale, particularly in the production of cast iron. Throughout the tenth to the fourteenth century, China exported cast-iron objects, such as woks and cauldrons, and wrought-iron ingots "refined" from cast iron. Chinese ingot iron was high in sulfur and therefore low in quality. It must therefore have been sold very cheaply in order to have competed successfully in the maritime Southeast Asian market.[21]

Maritime Southeast Asia's demand for Chinese iron products developed, from the mid-tenth century, as a minor part of the region's trade in Chinese products. This early export of iron to the Malay region is reflected both in Chinese textual accounts, which indicate that the metal was used in China's trade with the region by 971, as well as in the archaeological data from the Malay region. Cylindrical bars and iron pieces in the form of long blades have been recovered from the Intan wreck. Chemical analysis has revealed a high level of sulfur content in them, indicating a Chinese origin.[22] The presence of only these two types of iron products, apart from three iron woks and a few composite-metal implements, suggests that the range of iron products imported by the Malay region, to be reexported to Java, was confined to partially worked iron. In addition, the modest quantity of iron products, amid a very mixed cargo recovered from the wreck site, suggests that the volume of trade in Chinese iron was fairly modest during the tenth century.

By the late eleventh century, export of Chinese iron to the Malay region appears to have increased significantly. Archaeological information from the region sheds light on this matter. Several concretions at the Pulau Buaya wreck site have been identified as piles of iron woks, suggesting that the market for iron cooking vessels had expanded, many of them probably reexported to Java. Partially worked wrought iron continued to be an important form of iron imported as well, reflected by the presence of at least one bundle of iron pieces in the form of long blades at the wreck site.

By the twelfth century, iron appears to have become an important Chinese export commodity. The 1141 list of high and low value products involved in China's maritime trade included workable iron, iron articles, and such cookware as cauldrons. An 1175 memorial lamenting the outflow of metals via China's maritime trade mentions iron as one of the key metals exported out of China.[23] Iron exports were sufficiently large by the second half of the twelfth century to be mentioned by Song officials, along with gold, silver, and copper, in relation to China's maritime export trade.

Explicit textual references to the export of Chinese iron to the Malay region do not occur until the early thirteenth century. According to the *Zhufanzhi,* Srivijaya-Jambi was the only port in the region, aside from Kuala Berang,[24] noted to have imported Chinese iron. Java was the only other direct importer of Chinese iron, aside from the Philippines, in island Southeast Asia. Srivijaya-Jambi probably remained a source through which some Chinese iron products were reexported to Java.[25]

There was a progressive increase in the volume of maritime Southeast Asia's trade in ironware from China throughout the twelfth and thirteenth centuries. By the second half of the thirteenth century, Chinese iron was becoming the most important product exported from China to maritime Southeast Asia, surpassing even ceramics in volume and value of trade. Direct trade with China was carried not just by Chinese traders but by Southeast Asian traders as well. The quantity of iron products identified at the Java Sea wreck site totaled some 190 tons, with Java as the probable destination. Substantial quantities of workable circular and trapezoidal iron ingots were being shipped by the Java Sea vessel, suggesting that partially processed iron remained a major import to the region. The presence of stacks of iron woks at the wreck site, however, indicates that the large-scale export of manufactured ironware to maritime Southeast Asia was already taking place by the thirteenth century, a significant development from the iron trade that characterized the tenth and eleventh centuries. While the product range had not expanded dramatically, workable and usable iron products had become equally important in China's export trade to the region by this time.

The increase in China's export of iron products to the Malay region in the twelfth and thirteenth centuries appears to have occurred in response to the key developments in the China–maritime Southeast Asian trade. The rising importance of maritime Southeast Asian low-value products from the late eleventh century on was key to the rise in the volume of the reciprocal trade in Chinese iron products to the Malay region. The peak of China's export of iron products to the region appears to have coincided with the broadening and diffusion, as well as the lowering of the unit value, of China's maritime trade during this time. The shift in the region's trade with China from high-value Middle Eastern and Indian Ocean products to high- and low-value Southeast Asian and Malay products led to the need for a Chinese product that was of sufficiently low value for the unit value and volume of exchange to be well matched. Ironware suited this purpose very well.

The advent of Yuan rule in southern China, in 1279, saw iron remaining as the only metal officially permitted for exchange in China's trade with maritime Southeast Asia.[26] By 1323, however, the trade in iron was also prohibited.[27] Nonetheless, the ban does not appear to have affected the export of iron to the Malay region.[28]

The iron trade, however, appears to have declined during the late thirteenth and the fourteenth century, as suggested by the archaeological data from Malay settlement sites. The Temasik-period sites in Singapore are characterized by the absence of any other type of Chinese ironware, such as cauldrons, and small amounts of iron slag. It appears that the volume of Temasik's imports of Chinese ironware was negligible in comparison to other Chinese products, such as ceramics. As the China–maritime Southeast Asia trade ebbed somewhat during the late thirteenth and the fourteenth century, the volume of the iron trade to the Malay region declined correspondingly.

Copper

The intrinsic value of copper made it an important measure of value in China throughout the Song and Yuan periods.[29] Given its high price in China, it is unsurprising that little has been recorded concerning the international trade in Chinese copper other than as copper cash during the tenth to the fourteenth century. The Malay region's consistently limited import of Chinese copper and bronze items, aside from coins, was confined to such items as gongs, mirrors, and religious building material (e.g., roof tiles).

Since there were many sources of cheaper copper ore within Southeast Asia—such as western Sumatra, Timor, Thailand, the Philippines, and Burma—the Malay region had little incentive to import unworked Chinese copper.[30] The reliance of the region on Southeast Asian and possibly Indian Ocean sources for workable copper in the tenth to the thirteenth century is reflected in data from the Intan and Pulau Buaya wrecks. Large quantities of bronze scrap of non-Chinese origin have been recovered from the Intan wreck, while a significant number of copper ingots of non-Chinese origin have been recovered from the Pulau Buaya wreck. No workable copper from China has so far been recovered.

There was nonetheless some trade in selected Chinese copper and bronze items in the tenth century and later.[31] Ninety-five fragments of Chinese bronze mirrors were recovered from the Intan wreck.[32] These mirrors, however, constituted only a small fraction of the total number of copper articles retrieved from the site. Most were Southeast Asian items, which were both more numerous and varied than the Chinese bronze articles. However. the Malay region imported Chinese copper-alloy articles because of their superior quality and workmanship, as is apparent from the Chinese mirrors recovered from the Intan wreck. Several bronze gongs have also been recovered from the Pulau Buaya wreck, suggesting that a minor trade in cast-bronze ceremonial items continued until the early twelfth century.[33]

In 1172 the only recorded import of copper-based items by the Malay region from China occurred. That year, the Srivijayan ruler purchased a large quantity of copper in China and requested permission from the Song court to cast it into thirty thousand roof tiles, to be exported, along with a number of Chinese artisans, for installation on a temple in Srivijaya.[34] The request must have been submitted in spite of the Srivijayan agents in China being fully aware of the ban on copper exports, a ban consistently reiterated through the twelfth and the early thirteenth century through at least six edicts. Permission was eventually granted, and the tiles most likely were shipped.

The 1172 incident, like the other instances of Malay importation of Chinese copper, was a sporadic occurrence, and by the thirteenth century it appears to have disappeared. This state of affairs is reflected in the *Zhufanzhi,* which notes no imports of Chinese copper items by any maritime Southeast Asian port. The general absence of copper as a Chinese export commodity, except in the form of cash, to the region continued into the fourteenth century. At such settlement sites as Temasik, for example, no Chinese copper-based artifact has been recovered.

Currency: Copper Cash

From the tenth to the fourteenth century Chinese copper coins, or cash, played an important role in maritime trade between China and her foreign trading partners. The divisibility of copper cash (due to its low value compared to silver or gold bullion) made it a common medium of exchange in the trade in both low- and high-value products at the Chinese ports, and it was in high demand among China's foreign trading partners.

Given its scarcity in China and its vital role in the functioning of the Chinese economy, the Chinese court guarded against the export of copper cash from the tenth to the fourteenth century. Before 1041 anyone caught exporting more than two thousand coins would be banished, or executed if the amount was more than three thousand. After 1041 the regulations became more stringent, and anyone caught exporting more than one thousand coins would have been executed,[35] even though the annual value of China's maritime trade was growing steadily throughout the eleventh century.

Even as China's international maritime trade expanded and underwent monetization during the late tenth and the eleventh century, it is not apparent, either from textual records or archaeological information, that the volume of copper cash traded abroad increased in tandem during this period. In the Taizong Chunhua era (990–95), for example, when the maritime trade of China was on the increase, the disbursements of copper cash from the imperial coffers to facilitate trade at the Chinese ports were insignificant,[36] suggesting that the outflow of copper cash was minimal. Even when China's maritime economy began to be monetized, during the reign of the emperor Renzong (1023–63), with trade being valued in currency terms,[37] the intention of the move was to affect only the domestic sector of China's international trade. Although China was already exporting silver and gold, the Song court vigilantly guarded against the outflow of Chinese copper cash. In China, copper cash was paid to foreign traders with the intention that the coins would be used to purchase Chinese products at the coastal ports before the traders left China. Compulsory purchases by the Song court's mercantile shipping superintendencies using currency, and the increase in the production of copper cash during the reign of Renzong,[38] does not appear to have led to any significant increases in the outflow of copper cash to the Malay region. Archaeological excavations conducted at settlement sites in Jambi and Palembang, the key ports of the Malacca Strait in the tenth to the thirteenth century, have so far uncovered relatively few Chinese copper coins.[39]

Nonetheless, some Chinese copper cash did find its way into the Malay region. Although there is no known textual record of the export of copper cash to the region in the tenth century, archaeological data indicate that these coins were in fact represented, though on a very limited scale. For example, 137 Chinese copper coins were recovered from the Intan wreck,[40] indicating that they were already a Chinese export item to the Malay region by this time.

In 1074, to further encourage an increase in foreign trade, the embargo on the export of copper cash from China, which had been instituted at the advent of Song rule, in 960, was lifted.[41] Increases in the production of copper cash were officially sanctioned to facilitate the smooth implementation of this new trade policy. The annual production of copper cash was increased from 1.3 million strings in the early eleventh century to around 6 million by 1078.[42]

The 1074 lifting of the embargo led to massive quantities of Chinese copper cash being shipped to the Malay region. The export of copper cash during this time occurred at all levels. At the state level, there was a shift in the nature of the reciprocal gifts presented by the Song court to state-level trade missions arriving in China, away from the presentation of prestige articles of gold, silver, or copper, to the disbursement of only copper cash and silver bullion to match the value of the foreign products presented. The recipients of such cash disbursements included the Cham missions of 1072 and 1086, the Dashi Arab mission of 1073, and the Chola mission of 1077.[43] The Malay region was also a recipient of such currency payments. In 1078, Srivijaya dispatched a trading mission to China. In return for the white gold, camphor, frankincense, and other foreign products it presented to the port authorities at Guangzhou, it received 64,000 strings of copper cash as well as 10,500 taels of silver.[44] The 1078 mission would not have been the only time during this period that the Malay region obtained copper cash through state-sponsored trade.

Chinese copper cash would also have been obtained through non-state-sponsored trade facilitated by Malay traders and agents stationed at the Chinese port of Guangzhou, and from 1086 on, at Quanzhou, in southern Fujian, as well.[45] The buoyant state of the China–maritime Southeast Asian trade in the second half of the eleventh century—which resulted in a significant growth in the latter's transshipment of Southeast Asian, Indian Ocean, and Middle Eastern products to China—would have led to a significant export trade in copper cash through unofficial means to the Malay region.

Malay use of Chinese copper cash is largely unknown. It did not appear to have been adopted as a currency by the ports of the region. Metal pieces, or alloys, were the means of exchange employed by the ports from the tenth to the fourteenth century, as attested by the *Quanzhi,* an 1149 Chinese text containing information on the forms of money used in China as well as by China's foreign trading partners.[46] On the other hand, the ports at the northern tracts of the Malacca Strait, which were orientated toward the Bay of Bengal and the Indian Ocean, appear to have preferred to adopt currencies from Indian Ocean littoral states or to mint local currencies modeled after such Indian Ocean currencies.[47]

Nor did copper cash appear to have been imported by the Malay region to be smelted for its metal content. There is very little archaeological evidence in the region, from either settlement sites or shipwrecks, to suggest that Chinese copper cash was a source of the region's imports of workable copper, since there were cheaper sources of copper ore in Southeast Asia.

The role of Chinese copper cash in the Sino-Malay trade appears, instead, to have been linked with monetary developments in Java. Javanese epigraphy indicates that by the thirteenth century Java had officially adopted Chinese copper cash as the currency to be used in low-value official transactions such as the tabulation and payment of taxes. This official move was most likely preceded by the adoption of these coins in ordinary market transactions in the late eleventh and the twelfth century, as attested to by the archaeological data from East Java.[48] The period during which Java began to restructure its lower-denomination currency coincided with the lifting of the export ban of Chinese copper cash by the Song court in 1074. The large-scale export of Chinese copper cash in the late eleventh and the early twelfth century appears to have provided Java with a suitable form of coinage to replace the awkward small-denomination silver-alloy coinage used until the eleventh century.[49] Java's high demand for copper cash was most likely based on its awareness of this Chinese item over a prolonged period.[50] For this purpose, one-cash value coins were adopted for the domestic Javanese economy.

While direct trade between Java and China undoubtedly served as a key source of copper cash to fuel this currency development in Java, the Malay region would most likely have been another important source of copper cash. The region maintained trade with Java during this time and acted as an economic interface between Java and China. In particular, such key Malay ports as Palembang and Jambi, which conducted intense economic exchanges with China through both state-sponsored and private trade, would likely have been an important source of Chinese copper cash to Java in the second half of the eleventh and the early twelfth century. The large payments of copper cash by the Song court in return for the shipments of foreign products brought by Srivijaya to the Chinese ports in the late eleventh and the early twelfth century, and their absence at the key port-settlement sites of the Malay region, suggest they were not intended for use in the region but appear to have been reexported to Java.

Malay transshipment of Chinese copper cash to Java was relatively short lived. The Malay ports' ability to play this transshipment role was apparently fully dependent on the Song court's lifting of the export embargo on Chinese copper. Once the embargo was reinstated, the ability of Malay-region ports to act as conduits in the copper cash trade appears to have been severely curtailed. Following the advent of Southern Song rule, in 1127, the export of copper cash was banned. This ban was reiterated in 1133.[51] China still paid for the import of foreign products in copper cash. The 1156 Srivijayan trade mission, for example, was repaid at Guangzhou with coins equal in value to the products it had presented to the Song court.[52] However, traders were now expected to use the currency to purchase Chinese products before leaving China.[53] However, by the late twelfth century copper cash was no longer used in China's official maritime transactions. An 1175 memorial, which lamented the massive outflow of copper cash via international trade, ordered that silks, ceramics, and lacquerware were to be used instead in the exchange for foreign products brought via state-sponsored missions.[54] All subsequent state-level missions to China were consequently reciprocated with gifts only of nonmetal Chinese products.

With the instituting of the export ban on Chinese copper cash and the adherence to the ban by China's Southeast Asian trading partners, Chinese traders became the only channel through which these coins could be exported from China. The direct commercial contact between Chinese traders and Java appears to have led to the continued export of copper cash to the latter. The *Zhufanzhi* notes that Chinese traders were surreptitiously shipping Chinese copper cash to Java in the early thirteenth century.[55]

By the fourteenth century maritime Southeast Asia's trade in Chinese copper cash had nearly vanished. The small-scale minting of copper cash by the Yuan court, following the adoption of paper currency as the chief medium of exchange in China during its rule, culminated in China ceasing to be a major source of copper cash by the late thirteenth century. By the fourteenth century Chinese texts no longer note copper cash as an item demanded or used by any maritime Southeast

Asian port. In Java copper coins modeled after the Tang-period *Kai-yuan tongbao* were instead minted from the mid-fourteenth century on to meet the currency demands of the Javanese economy.[56] It was only in the late fourteenth century, when the minting of copper cash resumed under the Ming court, that these coins were once again made available to Java and imported in significant quantities.

While the export of Chinese copper cash as a trade item to the Malay region took place between 1074 and 1126, they were present at a number of Malay port-settlements. The amount of copper cash recovered from the settlement sites varies significantly. At Palembang and Jambi, archaeological finds of these coins remain sporadic,[57] while at Sungai Mas,[58] Pengkalan Bujang,[59] and Kompei,[60] only a few of these coins have been recovered. Conversely, at Kota Cina,[61] Sungai Limau Manis, and Temasik,[62] significant numbers have been recovered.

The relative profusion of Chinese copper cash at Kota Cina, Sungai Limau Manis (present-day Brunei), and Temasik—which comprised one-, two-, and ten-cash-value coins—may be linked to the extent to which the port-settlements maintained trade links with states whose economies relied on such coinage. These included Java and its trading sphere in central and eastern Indonesia and China. Despite the general use of barter and metal bullion at the Malay ports for conducting international transactions, foreign currencies brought by traders from such key Asian economies as China were apparently accepted by Kota Cina, Sungai Limau Manis, and Temasik as well. In the case of Kota Cina, which was active from the twelfth to the early fourteenth century, the possible presence of a sizable community of Chinese settlers[63] may have facilitated the acceptance of copper cash at the port-settlement. In the case of Sungai Limau Manis and Temasik, both of which were active during the late thirteenth and the fourteenth century, their proximity to, and possible dependence on, Java as a major external market for which they catered, may have led to their adoption of copper cash as a means of facilitating their economic exchanges with Java.[64] This would also have enabled these coins to be used by other traders, such as the Chinese, arriving at these ports with them.

The use of copper cash by Chinese traders in the Malay region during the late thirteenth and the fourteenth century is substantiated by archaeological data obtained from the Quanzhou wreck. Five hundred and four Chinese copper coins and five iron coins, dating from the Tang and Song periods, with the most recent minted in 1272, were recovered, some from the vessel's twelve cargo holds, although most were found scattered on the hull floor of holds three, six, and seven. They were of all three coin denominations used in China: one-, two-, and ten-cash value.[65] Unlike the copper cash recovered from the Sinan wreck, which were stored in ceramic containers,[66] those from the Quanzhou wreck appear to have been carried by the Chinese traders on the vessel on its outward journey and subsequently traded into the Malay region for indigenous and transshipment products. The acceptance and use of Chinese copper cash by Malay ports as a means of exchange from the tenth to the fourteenth century was, however, limited. This is reflected by the large amount of copper cash that had remained unused at the end of the trading voyage of the traders on the Quanzhou wreck vessel. Chinese copper cash was simply not widely accepted by Malay ports as an external currency in the conduct of trade, nor widely adopted as a form of local currency for local use by Malay port-settlements.

Textiles

Silk was a key Chinese export during the Song and Yuan periods. At the outset, the value of Chinese silk used in maritime trade was fairly high, given its importance in state-level trade. The earliest record of its use in Song China's international trade dates to 966, when silk garments, along with cash and wares, were given to the envoys of Champa in return for ivory and aromatic products.[67] The 987 mission dispatched by the Song court to Southeast Asia and the Indian Ocean littoral carried with them silk as one of the two products (the other being gold) to be used both as courtly gifts and as items of barter for high-value foreign products at the ports of call.[68] By the late tenth century silk was used as a barter item and traded for high-value goods brought by state-level trade missions,[69] and by the beginning of the eleventh century, refined silk was recognized by the mercantile shipping superintendencies as one of the five categories of goods used in China's international maritime trade.[70] Despite the limited textual record of silk as a trade product, it is clear from the reciprocal gifts made by China to state-level trade and diplomatic missions from foreign states that refined silk was highly valued. During the tenth and the early eleventh century, recipients of silk in state-level exchanges included Champa, the Dashi Arabs, India, and Java. While there is no direct reference to the use of silks as reciprocal gifts in state-level exchanges with Srivijaya during this period, the very rich gifts given to the mission of 1008 almost certainly included silk[71].

Despite its importance in state-level trade exchanges, the only reference to the use of silks in China's exchanges with the Malay region dates to 1082, when a daughter of the king of Srivijaya submitted tribute consisting of camphor and textiles, along with a memorial, to the mercantile shipping superintendency of Guangzhou.[72] It is interesting to note that while the products presented at Guangzhou were sold by the Guangzhou superintendency before the receipt of the reciprocal gift from China, the gift made to the mission was neither cash nor bullion, which was normally presented by the Song court in its state-level exchanges during the 1070s and 1080s. Instead, the proceeds of the sale were used to purchase silks, which were in turn used as the reciprocal gift.[73] Presumably, it was imperative to present sufficiently prestigious gifts. Since articles of gold and silver could not be used in this context, high-value silks, whose status was below that of articles of precious metals, were presented.

By the early twelfth century, following the Song court's opening of the Chinese coastline to Chinese maritime shipping in 1090, lower-value silk became a key product carried by Chinese private traders to maritime Southeast Asia. The *Pingzhou ketan* notes that Chinese traders would amass silks, along with other manufactured items, on credit before embarking on a trading trip to that region. The value of the Chinese products carried by individual traders was not normally very high. Although small-scale traders were by this time carrying silks abroad, probably in small batches per individual trader, the overall volume was probably larger than in previous centuries.

The late-eleventh- and twelfth-century expansion and diffusion of China's maritime trade also led, by the early thirteenth century, to a tremendous increase in the range of silk products exported to maritime Southeast Asia. In a 1219 memorial recorded in the *Songhuiyao,* it was recommended that the use of metals in China's maritime trade cease and that silk be used instead as a key commodity to barter for the foreign products coming into Chinese ports. Three types of silk were specifically mentioned—silk cloth, presumably plain dyed; silks with decorative patterns applied through dyeing; and silks with printed decorative patterns.[74] The recommendation of the use of different types of silk cloth in 1219 is an indication of the Song administration's awareness of the breadth of the taste for silk that had developed among China's trading partners.

The range of silks exported to maritime Southeast Asia was, in fact, much wider than the three types listed in the 1219 memorial. According to the *Zhufanzhi,* Srivijaya-Jambi imported silk brocade, damask, and tie-dyed cloths; Tambralingga, Langkasuka, and Java imported tie-dyed silk cloths; and Borneo imported brocades.[75] In addition, silk umbrellas were imported by Tambralingga. The Chinese were clearly aware that while lower-value silk products were generally imported by some ports in the Malay region, higher-value silks continued to be key products in the trade of wealthier maritime Southeast Asian ports.

The introduction of new Chinese textiles to maritime Southeast Asia continued into the fourteenth century. By that time the tastes of specific ports were catered to by Chinese traders operating in the Malay region. According to the *Daoyi zhilue,* Kelantan imported

Table 5.1. Chinese textiles imported by maritime Southeast Asian ports, early thirteenth century					
	Langkasuka	Tambralingga	Srivijaya-Jambi	Java	Borneo
Silk and cotton umbrellas		•		•	
Black silk				•	
Rouge silk				•	
Multicolored woven silk				•	
Tough-woven silk	•	•		•	
Silk brocades			•	•	•
Multicolored silk brocades				•	
Jianyang silk brocades				•	•
Multicolored downy textiles				•	
Source: ZFZ 1:5b–8b, 10b–14a, and 34b–36b.					

	Checkered handkerchiefs	Woven silk	Patterned cloth	Printed cloth	Multicolored cloth	Red cloth	Blue cloth	Blue satin	Colored satin
Tambralingga						•			
Malilu							•		
Pahang		dyed							
Kelantan	•								
Trengganu		red							
Langkasuka				•					
Borneo									•
Tanjongpura								•	
Java		dyed						•	
Deli			•		•				
Jambi			•						
Palembang					•				
Semudra							•		•
Longyamena[a]			•					•	
Banzub[b]				•					

Source: DYZL 5a–7a, 8a, 10a–b, 11b, 13a–14b, 16a–b, and 18a–b.
[a] Temasik, Keppel Strait.
[b] Temasik, Fort Canning Hill.

checkered handkerchiefs; Langkasuka and Banzu (the Temasik settlement on the north bank of the Singapore River) imported Chinese printed cloth; Linggabodhi imported cloth with printed blue-and-white decorative patterns; and Semudra and Longyamen (the Temasik settlement at Keppel Straits, Singapore) imported multicolored and blue satins respectively.[76] The *Daoyi zhilue* also notes that Tambralingga and Srivijaya-Jambi continued to import silk cloth, plain-dyed and decorated with patterns respectively; while Pahang, Trengganu, Langkasuka, Deli, Palembang, Longyamen, and Semudra were noted to be importers of dyed silks or silk decorated with patterns.[77] By the mid-fourteenth century Chinese silk was in demand in most Malay ports.

Two distinct subregional preferences were apparent to the Chinese traders. The ports along the Malacca Strait preferred blue and multicolored cloths to other dye colors, as well as patterned and printed cloths. Ports on the eastern coast of the Malay Peninsula and northern Borneo, on the other hand, preferred only plain-dyed Chinese textiles. The somewhat limited interest in Chinese textiles with decorative patterns may be accounted for by the Malay Peninsular and northern Bornean ports' demand for textiles produced in Java, Champa, and Calicut, which were predominantly decorated with patterns achieved through resist-dyeing, wood-block printing and tie-dye methods. This intraregional trade in Southeast Asian and Indian decorated textiles would have been evident to Chinese traders trading in the Malay region. The detailed knowledge of the preferences of specific Malay ports embodied in the *Daoyi zhilue* suggests that Chinese traders adjusted their offerings with cloths from competing sources in mind.

Given that Indian, Southeast Asian, and Chinese sources of textiles would have been made available to ports of the Malay region, the subregional preferences reflected by the patterns of the textile import trade was more likely the result of different market demand dictate and tastes, rather than merely a reaction to different degrees of accessibility to textile sources in Asia. Demand for Chinese textiles still came chiefly from ports on the eastern coast of the Malay Peninsula and the southeastern coast of Sumatra. While a certain proportion of the textiles imported into the region would have been redistributed to the other ports in the Malay region, ports in the northern parts of the Malacca Strait must have maintained a more vibrant import trade in textiles with markets in the Indian Ocean littoral than with China, thereby accounting for the general absence of demand for Chinese textiles.

Ceramics

Ceramics loomed large in Sino-Malay trade. Archaeological data from maritime Southeast Asia indicate that by the late Tang, there was already a considerable trade in Chinese ceramics. A large proportion of the late Tang ceramics found at the Ko Kho Khao and Laem Pho sites off the Isthmus of Kra, in what must have been Tambralingga's territory, was from the Guangdong region. In the Malacca Strait, Changsha dishes also constituted an important type of Chinese ceramics traded there, a large number of which have been recovered from the Belitung wreck, off the northern coast of Belitung Island.[78]

Maritime Southeast Asian demand for Chinese ceramics increased with the advent of the Song. There is consistent mention of ceramics as a key Chinese export throughout the Song and Yuan texts. However, specific textual information on this trade to the Malay region is fragmentary. The only one currently known is a singular reference dated to 962, when white stoneware was listed among the items the Song court gave in return for tribute presented by Srivijaya.[79] Apart from that, ceramics were not recorded among the reciprocal gifts used by China in its tribute exchanges with Srivijaya or any maritime Southeast Asian polity, nor in any other context of interaction between China and that region.

Nonetheless, ceramics must have grown increasingly important in the trade between China and maritime Southeast Asia. According to the *Songhuiyao* and the *Songshi*, ceramics were among China's most important maritime exports at the turn of the eleventh century.[80] The *Pingzhou ketan* notes that ceramics was one of the key exports shipped by Chinese traders from Guangzhou to maritime Southeast Asia annually during the late eleventh and the early twelfth century. The *Zhufanzhi* notes that by the early thirteenth century, Chinese ceramics were exported to several key maritime Southeast Asian ports, including Langkasuka, Tambralingga, Srivijaya-Jambi, Java, Borneo, and Kedah, from whence they would no doubt have been redistributed to other ports within their respective economic spheres. The *Zhufanzhi* also notes that *qingbai* wares (whitewares with a clear, light-blue glaze) were imported by Java,[81] green-glazed stoneware by Borneo, and platters and earthenware bowls by Srivijaya-Jambi.[82] The *Daoyi zhilue* notes that by the mid-fourteenth century, both green- and blue-and-white wares were the predominant types of ceramics imported by ports on the Malay Peninsula, while green- and qingbai wares were imported by ports in the Malacca Strait region. Palembang and the Keppel Straits (present-day Singapore) were also noted to have imported ceramics from Chuzhou (southern Fujian).[83]

The information in the Chinese texts is nonetheless incomplete. Archaeological data provide a more comprehensive picture of this trade. Two main types of ceramics were imported by maritime Southeast Asia—fine and coarse stoneware. The former included bowls, dishes, and even spoons and ladles, while the latter included storage jars, bottles, and mortars. The ceramic shards recovered from settlement and shipwreck sites in the region also indicate that a wide range of ceramics was imported in large volumes during the tenth to the fourteenth century. The cargoes of the shipwrecks indicate that ceramics constituted one of the largest groups of nonperishable products exported by China to the Malay region throughout this period. Despite the relatively low unit value of ceramics, the export trade as a whole was valuable.

The Malay region's import trade in ceramics already existed by the tenth century. The Intan wreck, for example, was carrying significant quantities of Chinese ceramics, indicating that these items were imported into the Malay region by that time. While the Malay market would have consumed some of these products, a portion would have been redistributed to other Asian markets. The Malay region was an indirect source of Chinese products for such further regions as the Indian Ocean littoral and the Middle East, as well as the less directly accessible islands of the Indonesian Archipelago.

The Malay import trade in ceramics appears to have hit an initial peak as early as the late eleventh and the twelfth century. The *Ping-zhou ketan* notes that by the late eleventh century, the cargo holds of the trading vessels leaving Guangzhou were mainly loaded with large and small ceramics of matching sets before their departure for Southeast Asia.[84] By the early twelfth century ceramics had become the main product by volume exported by China to the Malay region. Ceramics were the largest group of Chinese products recovered from the Pulau Buaya wreck site, for example. Shipments of Chinese ceramics to the region, and the Malacca Strait in particular, not only catered to the region's own demand but also that of the other regions that the Malay ports serviced. The surge in ceramics exports to the Malay region thus had already occurred even before a ban was placed on the export of copper cash by the Song court in China in 1175, an act that has often been cited by historians as the major impetus for the boom in the export trade in Chinese ceramics during the Song.[85]

Chinese ceramic exports to the Malay region were given a further boost, in the late twelfth and the thirteenth century, by several maritime trade restrictions by the Song and Yuan courts. Two restrictions were of particular importance to the ceramics trade. The 1175 ban on the export of Chinese copper cash, an official attempt to stem to outflow of valuable metals, was reinforced by a ban in 1219 on the use of gold and silver in official maritime trade transactions. The 1219 ban specifically named ceramics as one of the Chinese products to be used in place of gold and silver.[86] The resulting need for substitutes for gold, silver, and copper led to an increase in the volume of the ceramics exported out of China by the thirteenth century. From then until the mid-fifteenth century, when a maritime ban imposed by the Ming court led to a massive decline in the export of Chinese ceramics to Southeast Asia, ceramics remained the main Chinese product exported to the Malay region.

The Malay region's trade in Chinese ceramics from the tenth to the fourteenth century reflected two general developments in southern China. The first was the development of the ceramics industry. At the beginning of the Northern Song, the southern Chinese ceramics industry produced predominantly white-, Yue-type, and qingbai-type wares. By the late twelfth century, however, greenware (celadon-glazed ware) had overtaken white- and qingbai wares as the main type of ceramics produced in southern China, including products of the southern Fujian and Longquan in Zhejiang provinces. By the fourteenth century, while greenware continued to be the main type of ceramics produced in southern China, other important ceramics were being produced as well. These included blue-and-white ware produced at Jingdezhen in Jiangxi Province, and Dehua ware, produced at Dehua in southern Fujian. Many of these types of ceramics were eventually exported to the Malay region.

The second development was the shift in the China–maritime Southeast Asia trade. In the late tenth century it was funneled through the international Chinese ports of Hangzhou, Mingzhou, and Guangzhou, but by the twelfth century it was a more diffuse trade along the Chinese coast. Before the establishment of the mercantile shipping superintendency at Quanzhou in 1087 and the liberalization of maritime shipping in 1090, Guangzhou was the chief port of call for traders from Southeast Asia, as it was furthest south along the Chinese coast and was thus most accessible to traders coming from or via Southeast Asia. During this time, most of China's export trade to Southeast Asia, the Middle East, and the Indian Ocean littoral was supported by Guangdong. The Guangdong kilns were therefore the key suppliers of ceramics in China's export trade to Southeast Asia. The designation

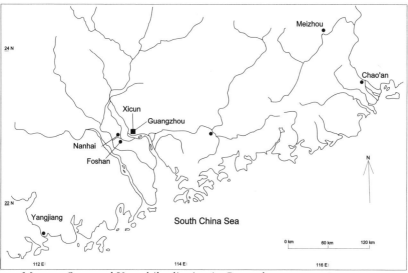

Map 5.2. Song and Yuan kiln districts in Guangdong

of Quanzhou as an international port in 1087 and the shipping liberalization, however, caused the economic hinterland along the southern Chinese coast to gear a significant part of its economic production to cater to the demands of China's export trade.[87] This was followed, from the late eleventh century on, by the development of kiln districts in southern Fujian to cater to China's southbound ceramics export trade.

These two developments determined to a large extent the types of ceramics exported by China to the Malay region from the tenth to the fourteenth century. In the late Tang and early Song, Yue-type ware, along with white- and qingbai wares, were the key types of ceramics produced by the kilns in southern China. Yue-type ware was produced mainly in Zhejiang Province, while kilns in Jingdezhen as well as in Guangdong produced white- and qingbai wares. Export ceramics from other regions were funneled through Guangzhou during the tenth and most of the eleventh century. That these were exported to the Malay region is indicated both by finds at the Malay ports and by the ceramic cargoes of shipwrecks. The Intan wreck's cargo comprised substantial quantities of white-, qingbai, and Yue-type ceramics, as well as brown- and green-glazed coarse ceramics.[88] At the Sungai Mas sites in Kedah, dated to the tenth through the twelfth century, the main types of ceramics recovered are whiteware, followed by Yaozhou-type greenware. Both types of ceramics may be attributed to kiln districts in Guangdong. In addition, the only Chinese coarse stoneware recovered from Sungai Mas were Guangdong-type shards. The Malay region's ceramics import trade in the late tenth and the eleventh century mirrored the general production of the southern Chinese ceramics industry.

By the twelfth century qingbai-type ceramics began to be exported to the Malay region in large quantities. Chronologically, the profusion of this type of ceramics in the Malay region lies between the profusion of Yue-type and whitewares characteristic of the tenth century, and the subsequent dominance of greenware in the thirteenth century. And in southern China Yue-type wares were the main type produced for much of the second half of the first millennium AD. These were eventually overtaken by the qingbai and greenwares during the Northern Song, with the green and celadon traditions then dominating the kilns' production during the Southern Song.[89]

The shift in emphasis from whiteware to greenware in the export trade to the Malay region is also apparent from the difference in the cargoes of the Intan, Pulau Buaya and Java Sea wrecks. Unlike the tenth-century Intan wreck, which carried only Guangdong wares, the late-eleventh-to-early-twelfth-century Pulau Buaya wreck carried a ceramics cargo of more mixed origin. The greenware recovered from the wreck site appears to have been of southern Fujian origin, while much of the whiteware may be from the Zhangpu kilns in southern Fujian and Jingdezhen, in Jiangxi. The storage jars were from Guangdong.[90]

By the early thirteenth century, greenware had become the main type of ceramics produced and exported by southern China. At the same time, the rise of Quanzhou as a center of China's maritime trade with Southeast Asia had an impact on the types of ceramics exported to the Malay region. While celadon-glazed ceramics, most of which were from Longquan in Zhejiang province, were exported to the region by the thirteenth century, the majority of the greenware recovered from settlement sites as well as shipwreck sites of this period remained

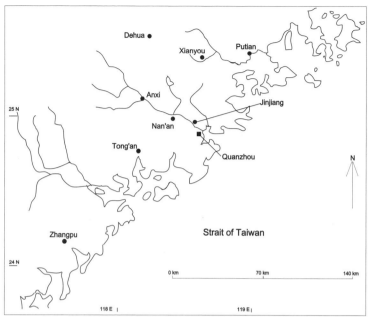

Map 5.3. Song and Yuan kiln districts in southern Fujian

southern Fujian products. Although Guangzhou continued to be an important gateway for the ceramics export trade, the gradual shift of the center of this trade from Guangzhou to Quanzhou during the twelfth and thirteenth centuries led to a corresponding northward shift in the catchment area of the ceramics exported to maritime Southeast Asia. This shift can be seen in the cargo of the Java Sea wreck, which comprised largely southern Fujian greenware and a small quantity of southern Fujian whiteware.[91]

These twelfth- and thirteenth-century developments are discernible from the ceramics assemblages recovered from Sungai Limau Manis (present-day Brunei), a settlement dated between the tenth and the thirteenth century, and from Pengkalan Bujang, in Kedah, dated between the twelfth and the early fourteenth century. At Sungai Limau Manis, the majority of the fine stoneware shards recovered from this site originate from greenware, indicating that the peak of the settlement phase occurred between the eleventh and the thirteenth century. At Pengkalan Bujang, the ceramics in the assemblage were made in both

Guangdong and southern Fujian, with the latter forming the bulk. Greenware from both southern Fujian and Zhejiang form the majority of the shards in the assemblage, including greenware of the Tong'an type, and lead-glazed ware from the Cizao kilns at Jinjiang district. In contrast, whiteware shards, the main products of the Guangdong kilns, constitute a very small proportion of the ceramic finds.[92] Coarse stoneware from southern Fujian kilns have also been recovered, in contrast to the nature of the coarse stoneware recovered from the earlier Sungai Mas settlement site, which were solely from Guangdong kilns.

A similar pattern is observed in the ceramic finds of Kota Cina, a northeastern Sumatran port-settlement active from the twelfth to the early fourteenth century. Once again, the greenware shards, most of which were from ceramics of southern Fujian and Longquan origin, represent the largest group of ceramics imported by the settlement. A significant number of white and qingbai shards, many of which may have originated from southern Fujian, have also been recovered.[93] The increasing importance of Quanzhou, by the thirteenth century, as the point from which Chinese ceramics were shipped to the Malay region is reflected in the ceramics recovered at this settlement site. However, Guangzhou also continued to be an export gateway for China's ceramics trade. Some of the white and qingbai shards and Guangdong coarse stoneware that may be attributed to the Guangdong kilns have also been recovered. Nonetheless, there are far fewer Guangdong shards than southern Fujian shards.

After Quanzhou was designated the chief international port of Yuan China, at the end of the thirteenth century, China's ceramics trade with maritime Southeast Asia became largely centered at that port. Southern Fujian and its neighboring provinces to the north, such as Jiangxi, Jiangsu, and Zhejiang, became established as the region of ceramics industry catering for the region's ceramics demand. The proliferation of kiln areas in Zhejiang, the consolidation of the southern Fujian ceramics industry centered at Dehua, Anxi, and Jinjiang, and the rising importance of both Dehua and Jingdezhen as national centers of ceramics production, meant that the main ceramic wares exported to the Malay region during the late thirteenth and the fourteenth century were products of these kiln centers.

This development is reflected by the ceramics recovered from the archaeological sites of Temasik, a late-thirteenth-to-fourteenth-century port-settlement in Singapore. Greenware shards of southern Fujian and Longquan origin form the majority of the ceramic shards that have been recovered there, followed by Dehua ware shards, and *shufu* (whiteware coated with an opaque white glaze), qingbai, and blue-and-white ware shards of Jingdezhen origin. The presence of southern Fujian, Dehua, Longquan, and Jingdezhen ceramics, which together form the bulk of the fine stoneware finds at Temasik, reflect the importance of Quanzhou as the chief gateway of China's ceramics export trade to the Malay region by this time.[94]

From the tenth through the fourteenth centuries, China's ceramics export trade to the Malay region essentially occurred at two levels. At the first level were the kiln districts in the immediate hinterlands of Guangzhou and Quanzhou. Most of these provincial kiln districts had easy waterway access to the two ports, and their production was largely in response to the demands of the export trade centered at these ports. These ceramics exhibited much lower level of craftsmanship, and thus generally lower unit value, than ceramics originating from such well-known national kiln centers as Longquan and Jingdezhen.

At the second level of the trade were higher-quality ceramics sourced from national kiln centers in southern China renowned for specific wares. Most of these centers, with the exception of the Dehua kilns, were located outside Guangdong and southern Fujian. These ceramics included qingbai, shufu, and blue-and-white ceramics from Jingdezhen (Jiangxi), brown- or black-glazed ceramics from Jizhou (Jiangxi), celadon ceramics from Longquan (Zhejiang), and whiteware from Dehua. The products of these kiln centers were relayed to the ports of Quanzhou and Guangzhou through domestic trade networks before eventually being exported to maritime Southeast Asia. Their higher quality, the need to transport them to the Chinese international ports, and the number of hands they passed through before eventually being exported abroad, made the unit value of these ceramics higher than those obtained from the ports' immediate hinterlands.

As is evident from archaeological data, there was a shift in the export trade in ceramics from the tenth through the fourteenth century—from predominantly provincial products to products mainly from the national kiln centers. The ceramics recovered from the tenth-to-twelfth-century settlement of Sungai Mas in Kedah were predominantly from Guangdong. The fact that ceramic trade links appear not to have extended beyond Guangdong was probably due to the absence of any international ports along the southern Chinese coast between Guangzhou and Liangzhe circuit before 1087. However, by the twelfth century the pattern of trade had begun to change. Ceramic products of national kiln centers were beginning to be imported by the Malay region. At Kota Cina, these higher-value ceramics account for almost half the fine stoneware ceramics by quantity recovered during excavations in the 1970s.[95] This is characteristic of the ceramics assemblages of settlements of the fourteenth century as well. Data from the Temasik settlement sites in Singapore indicate that such shards account for slightly less than half the fine stoneware ceramics assemblage.[96] The ceramics trade maintained by the Malay settlements was thus not predominantly of low unit value, as one would expect from contemporaneous shipwreck data, but one in which higher-unit-value ceramics were almost as common.

It is possible, however, that high-quality Chinese stoneware have been overrepresented at these sites. The data available from Sungai Limau Manis, Pengkalan Bujang, Kota Cina, and Temasik reflect the ceramic consumption patterns of key port-settlements of the Malay region. These sites were the chief ports of their respective economic spheres of influence—northeastern Borneo, the northwestern tracts of the Malay Peninsula, southern Kedah, northeastern Sumatra, and the Johor-Riau archipelago—and functioned as subregional collection and distribution centers and gateways to the regional and international maritime economies. A large portion of the low-unit-value ceramics coming into these ports would have been redistributed to the peripheral settlements in their respective economic spheres.[97]

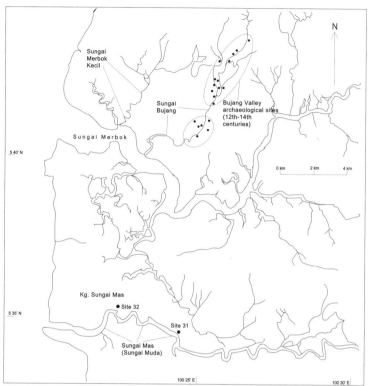

Map 5.4. Archaeological and settlement sites in southern Kedah, tenth through fourteenth century

This distribution pattern is evident by the tenth century and is reflected by the data from Sungai Mas, in southern Kedah. The ceramics assemblage from Sungai Mas site 31, Kampong Sireh, a satellite settlement approximately six kilometers upriver from the main port-settlement, has yielded only a fraction of the range of wares represented in the assemblage from Kampong Sungai Mas (Sungai Mas site 32). A portion of the imported ceramics was apparently sent upstream to the satellite settlement. These ceramics were largely of low value, being products of Guangdong kilns. In contrast, the Kampong Sungai Mas settlement kept for itself the more valuable ceramics, such as Zhejiang ceramics, and the Yaozhou-type greenware from the Xicun kilns.

This uneven distribution of fine ceramics is also characteristic of ceramics assemblages from the fourteenth-century Temasik-period sites in Singapore and Riau. Temasik imported large quantities of low-unit-value ceramics to be redistributed to its economic dependencies. Green- and whitewares, as well as utilitarian stoneware, similar to those excavated in Singapore, albeit with simpler decorative styles and techniques, have been found in the nearby Riau Islands.[98] These were peripheral settlements dependent on the main port of Temasik.

The settlements at the periphery would have been less affluent than the main port-settlement. This difference also existed within the key settlements of a port-polity, as evidenced by the data on blue-and-white ceramics recovered from the Temasik-period sites in Singapore. Larger proportions of blue-and-white ceramics have been recovered from the Fort Canning Hill sites than from the plain area sites.[99] Thus, even within a port-settlement, there were clear disparities in the ceramics that the residents could afford. In the case of Temasik, it appears that the residents on Fort Canning Hill were the most affluent, followed by those who occupied the plain area, and finally those of the Riau Islands.

The different status of the ports in the Malay region, and the roles they played, determined the ceramics consumption pattern that their settlements developed. Port-settlements in the Malay region that were collection centers had noticeably different ceramic import patterns from those that were not. Pulau Tioman (Tioman Island), for example, which functioned solely as a navigational marker and a stopping point where ships' crews could obtain water and supplies along the China–maritime Southeast Asia route, imported insignificant quantities of ceramics sourced from the Chinese national kiln centers.

The ceramics import pattern at stopping-off places was entirely dependent on external factors. In the case of Pulau Tioman, the ceramic finds indicate that the island's ceramic imports were determined purely by developments in the pattern of shipping between southern China and maritime Southeast Asia, the shift in the center of that trade, and developments in the southern Chinese ceramics industry. This is reflected in the changes in the volume and type of ceramics imported from the tenth to the fourteenth century. Guangdong shards of the tenth to the twelfth century form the bulk of the ceramics assemblage. The best-quality Guangdong wares, such as the Yaozhou-type ceramics from Xicun and the high-quality qingbai-glazed wares from Chao'an, Guangdong, are absent. This suggests that the general quality of the imported Guangdong wares was low. By the mid-twelfth century, Tioman Island's import of Chinese ceramics had declined significantly. Among ceramics of the Song and Yuan periods, southern Fujian and Longquan celadon shards each account for 3 percent of the total ceramics assemblage, while the Yixing-ware shard is statistically negligible.[100]

The lack of a discernible pattern in Tioman Island's import trade in ceramics from southern China, apart from the fact that the forms were the most common ones produced by the respective kiln districts in China, strongly suggests that Tioman Island relied exclusively on the incidental calling of trading vessels at the island and was not able to exert any influence over the types of ceramics it received. One possible reason for this pattern may have been the role Tioman Island played in the China–maritime Southeast Asia trade. Before the thirteenth century, apart from Tioman Island, there does not appear to have been any port of interest to Chinese shippers along the eastern coast of the lower Malay Peninsula. However, by the early thirteenth century Pahang was noted by the Chinese as a trading port.[101] By the fourteenth century, following the disintegration of Srivijaya in 1275, other minor ports along the eastern coast of the Malay Peninsula, such as Kelantan and Trengganu, had emerged and begun to serve as stopping points for ships heading for island Southeast Asia or the Indian Ocean littoral.[102] In addition to food and water, these ports also made available a small range of products for export. Tioman Island, however, does not appear to have been able to offer any products for export. Thus, from the early thirteenth century on, increasing competition from ports with more to offer appears to have led to the dramatic decline in the number of ships calling at Tioman Island. The ceramics made available to the settlements on the island would have declined accordingly.

While the average unit value of the fine stoneware imported by the key port-settlements in the region was relatively high, the real value of that trade was modest. At Kota Cina, fine stoneware shards account for only 13 percent of the total ceramics assemblage,[103] with shards of ceramics from national kiln centers in China accounting for less than half of that proportion. A similar pattern characterizes the fourteenth-century sites of Temasik.[104] The volume of Chinese fine stoneware imported by individual port-settlements in the region was therefore relatively small.

Although the numbers and types of fine stoneware imported by collection centers in the Malay region appear to have been fairly uniform, the overall ceramics trade that each port maintained differed. in terms of numbers and origin of coarse ceramics imported. At the settlement sites in the northern tracts of the Malacca Strait, Chinese ceramic shards constitute a minor proportion of all ceramic shards recovered. At Kota Cina, for instance, Chinese ceramic shards account for only around one-third of the total ceramics assemblage by weight,[105] with coarse stoneware from China accounting for only 22 percent of the total ceramics assemblage.[106] Similarly, only between one-quarter and one-third of the ceramic shards recovered from the Pengkalan Bujang sites are from Chinese stoneware.[107] The small proportion of Chinese coarse stoneware is in contrast to the large quantities of earthenware in the assemblages of these settlements, some of which may have been imported from India.

The opposite pattern holds true for settlements in the southern tracts of the Malacca Strait. These settlements imported large quantities of Chinese coarse stoneware. At Temasik, for instance, shards originating from such ceramics account for nearly three-quarters of the total ceramics assemblage recovered from sites along the Singapore River,[108] and slightly more than half the total ceramics assemblage from the Fort Canning Hill sites.[109]

China was the main source of fine stoneware for the Malay region between the tenth and the fourteenth century, although Middle Eastern industries also exported attractive, though lower-fired, glazed wares. Thus, regardless of the geographic orientation of the external economies of the Malacca Strait settlements, Chinese fine stoneware were in demand. This reflects the general pattern of demand for these ceramics in the Malay region. Utilitarian ceramics, on the other hand, such as storage jars, bottles, and basins, were produced all over Asia, the main difference being that between earthenware and coarse stoneware. The importation of utilitarian ceramics would instead have been determined by such causes as price, which was affected by the proximity of the ceramic sources, and other factors, such as the trade in the products that were carried in ceramics intended for storage.

The geographic location of the Malay port-settlements determined, to a large extent, the import pattern of the utilitarian ceramics. Settlements in the northern tracts of the Malacca Strait obtained their utilitarian ceramics from regional and Indian sources. The proliferation of fragments of glassware and sgraffito ceramic wares of Middle Eastern origin, and of what appears to be Indian utilitarian pottery,[110] are characteristics not reflected in the assemblages recovered from settlements in the southern tracts of the strait. This difference highlights the importance of the Indian Ocean littoral trade links to the settlements in the northern Malacca Strait. Settlements in the southern tract of the strait were, instead, oriented toward the South China Sea, and obtained most of their utilitarian ceramics from southern China and mainland Southeast Asia.

The range of Chinese coarse stoneware forms imported by the Malay port-settlements, although limited, did expand somewhat over time. At the Sungai Mas settlements, only storage jar shards were present, suggesting that this was the main form imported by southern Kedah in the tenth and eleventh centuries. However, by the twelfth century, other forms, such as bottles, basins, and mortars, were also imported by such settlements in the area as Pengkalan Bujang.[111] This expansion in the range of forms is apparent at Kota Cina and the Santubong sites (present-day Sarawak, in northern Borneo) as well, where shards of storage jars, basins, mortars, and bottles have also been recovered. This range did not change during the fourteenth century. The forms imported by Temasik were the same as those imported by the port-settlements at Pengkalan Bujang, Santubong, and Kota Cina, although they were imported in greater numbers. Thus, apart from storage items and basins, the coarse Chinese stoneware imported by Malay settlements were mortars, for which a high degree of hardness in the fired clay body was an asset.

The trade in Chinese utilitarian ceramics was confined almost entirely to the products of Guangdong and southern Fujian. The main sources of this coarse stoneware were the Xicun, Foshan, and Qishi kilns, near Guangzhou, and the Jinjiang and Cizao kilns, near Quanzhou. These ceramics were obtained from sources most accessible to these two ports, since cost was very important. Only one type of coarse ceramics originated from outside the immediate Guangzhou or Quanzhou catchment region: storage bottles produced by the Yixing kilns of Jiangsu Province. Shards of this ware have been recovered at both Pulau Tioman[112] and Temasik.

While the trade in coarse stoneware was an important aspect of China's export trade to the Malay region in its own right, these space-consuming items, in particular storage jars and bottles, were unlikely to have been exported from China empty. Data from the Intan and *Turiang* wrecks indicate that foodstuffs were an important group of products carried in these jars.[113] Finds in the wreck of the *Turiang* suggest that large storage jars were used to transport such moisture-laden solid foodstuffs as pickled vegetables, preserved fish, or shrimp paste.[114] Large jars were also used to carry such small items as fine ceramics. Smaller jars and bottles were used to carry liquids, such as wines and sauces. Storage jars were used in the foodstuffs trade both between China and Southeast Asia and within Southeast Asia itself.

The predominance of Guangdong and southern Fujian storage-jar shards at Malay region sites suggests that most of the Chinese foodstuffs imported by the region came from these two areas. Whereas the shards originating from southern Fujian are those of small, thinly potted vessels, those of Guangdong wares are from larger, thickly potted vessels. The types of products transported in the Fujian jars were therefore likely to have been different from those shipped in Guangdong jars.

In the tenth to the early twelfth centuries, Guangzhou was the main supplier of Chinese foodstuffs to the Malay region. The settlements at

Sungai Mas appear to have imported Chinese foodstuffs only from Guangzhou, since only Guangdong-type storage-jar shards have been recovered from the sites in that region. Foodstuffs from the hinterland of Guangzhou were most likely the contents of the imported jars. However, by the latter half of the twelfth century the Chinese foodstuffs imported by the region's settlements had clearly expanded to include those from southern Fujian. At Pengkalan Bujang, Santubong, Sungai Limau Manis, and Kota Cina, shards of both Guangdong and southern Fujian jars and southern Fujian bottles have been found.

By the fourteenth century the Malay region's import trade in Chinese foodstuffs from southern Fujian and Guangdong, and in particular from the southern Malacca Strait area, appears to have become fairly broad based. The number of types of coarse stoneware shards represented in the Empress Place site and Old Parliament House site assemblages (sites of the Temasik period, Singapore) is much greater than in the assemblages from the slightly earlier sites of Kota Cina and

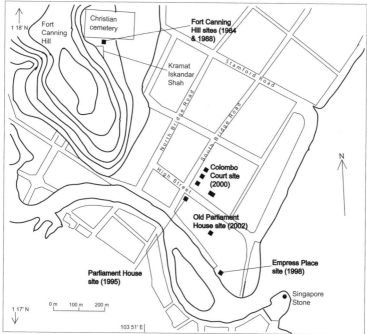

Map 5.5. Temasik-period archaeological sites in Singapore

Pengkalan Bujang, which also lie further to the north. This suggests that a wider range of foodstuffs was being shipped to Temasik's port by this time. Nor was the port's importation of foodstuffs confined by this time to products from Guangdong and southern Fujian. The consistent occurrence of significant quantities of shards in the assemblages that originated from a specific type of ceramic bottle produced in Yixing, Jiangsu, suggests that Temasik maintained a consistent demand for a specific foodstuff from that part of southern China.

Despite Quanzhou's rising importance in trade after the end of the eleventh century, and its eventual replacement of Guangzhou as the most important port in southern China by the late thirteenth century, Guangzhou appears to have remained the more important export gateway for Chinese foodstuffs to the Malay region from the tenth through the fourteenth century. This was probably due to Guangdong's superior agricultural base, which in turn supplied its production of foodstuffs. Southern Fujian's landscape was less conducive to agricultural production, which limited the range of foodstuffs that could be produced. Guangzhou was thus in a better position to cater to the Malay settlements' demands for a diversity of food than was Quanzhou. However, while Guangzhou's foodstuffs trade appears to have encompassed a greater range of products, as reflected by the wide range of sizes of storage jars that may be reconstructed from the shards recovered from Malay settlement sites, the ceramics data also suggest that Quanzhou did conduct a specialized foodstuffs trade with the Malay region.

One such example is the small-mouth bottle, known in Southeast Asian archaeological circles as a mercury jar.[115] Large quantities of shards from these bottles have been recovered from Temasik sites. Chinese archaeologists have identified these bottles as wine bottles.[116] The clay body has been attributed to the Cizao kilns in Quanzhou. Southern Fujian was known, during the Song and Yuan periods, as a major producer of glutinous rice, which was used to produce rice wine. This rice wine was undoubtedly bottled in locally produced ceramic containers. The substantial quantities of small-mouth-bottle shards recovered from sites in the region dated to between the twelfth and the fourteenth century suggest that the demand for southern Fujian rice wine was consistently high during the Southern Song and Yuan periods. The widespread distribution of these bottles suggests that almost all levels of society of the port polities consumed this wine. At Temasik, for example, where such shards have been recovered at Fort Canning Hill, the riverbank sites, and sites in the Riau Archipelago, all levels of society appear to have consumed this particular beverage.

The Malay settlements were apparently not mere passive recipients of foodstuffs and other consumables brought incidentally by trading vessels. At Sungai Limau Manis, eight types of coarse-storage-jar shards have been discerned from the ceramics assemblage that has been recovered through archaeological surveys at the site. This suggests that the import trade in the Chinese products carried in these storages jars, and the range of products that were involved, was fairly consistent. At Temasik, the consistency of the proportions of fifteen identifiable types of coarse-stoneware shards in the Old Parliament House site and Empress Place site assemblages suggests that this port-polity, throughout the span of its existence, maintained a consistent demand for certain foodstuff products from Guangdong and southern Fujian, and for a much more limited range of products sourced from areas further afield and exported via the ports of Guangzhou and Quanzhou.

China remained the chief source of stoneware imported by maritime Southeast Asia throughout the tenth to the fourteenth century. However, toward the end of the fourteenth century the region's source of stoneware ceramics shifted from southern China to mainland Southeast Asia, as Chinese maritime trade was severely curtailed following the advent of Ming rule, in 1368. The result was a temporary but dramatic decline in the volume of the ceramics trade from China that had lasting effects. Chinese ceramics accounted for only one-third of the stoneware recovered from the *Turiang* wreck. The remainder of the ceramics cargo was made up of mainland Southeast Asian stoneware from Thai kilns. The value of the Chinese ceramics trade had also declined significantly. Almost all the Chinese ceramics recovered from the wreck were from Guangdong. No higher-value ceramics were recovered.

This apparent "Ming gap" has been noted at a number of sites in maritime Southeast Asia.[117] This gap was not confined to the export of Chinese ceramics alone; there was a general decline in the export of Chinese products to the Malay region during the early Ming. It was not until the sixteenth century, when the maritime ban eventually was lifted, that that export trade was restored.

The types of Chinese products, and the volume in which they were imported by the Malay region between the tenth and the fourteenth century, changed as the nature, value, and volume of Sino-Malay trade evolved from a relatively small-volume, high-unit-value trade carried mainly by Southeast Asian shipping, to a high-volume and low-unit-value trade carried mainly by Chinese shipping. These changes were also evident in the reverse flow of trade products from the Malay region to China.

Chapter 6

CHINA'S EVOLVING
TRADE IN MALAY
PRODUCTS

From the tenth to the fourteenth century, the Malay region, due to the sheer richness and diversity of its natural resources, developed as a source of primary products to cater to the evolving tastes and needs of the Chinese market. As a source of foreign products to the Chinese market, the Malay region experienced two critical stages. The first, in essence a continuation of the trade that had developed by late in the first millennium AD, saw the region continue as a source of exotic products of predominantly high value, products that could be purchased only by the highest socioeconomic levels of Chinese society. The second stage, which appears to have begun during the twelfth century, saw the Malay region develop as a source of low-value products imported by China in large quantities.

The Malay Region as a Growing Source of Trade Products

China had, during the Tang period, already begun importing products from the Malay region. That trade resumed soon after the establishment of the Song dynasty. Foreign products began to arrive in China via tribute missions as early as 960, and the reestablishment of the mercantile shipping superintendencies at Guangzhou, Hangzhou, and Mingzhou by the Song court allowed the import trade to fully resume by 976.[1] China's importation of Malay products at this time was very much a continuation of the trade that had been established by the late Tang, by which time a number of Southeast Asian products were regularly shipped to China by foreign traders.

No new products were introduced at this time. According to a 976 memorial, following the establishment of superintendencies at Guangzhou and Mingzhou, a number of foreign states were trading with China.[2] Of the products listed in the memorial that could have been sourced from the region were high-value products like coral, pearls, turtle carapaces, tortoise shells,[3] and low-value goods like foreign textiles, ebony, and sappanwood.

Over the next six years, China's trade in Malay products appears to have expanded. In 982, the Song court published a list of state-monopoly items and another list of thirty-seven foreign products that were henceforth permitted to be freely traded among the Chinese so that the domestic demand for them would be adequately met.[4] This latter list reflected the development of Chinese demand for an increasing array of foreign products in the six years following the resumption of maritime trade. Among the fifteen products that could have been sourced from the Malay region were such state-monopoly items as tortoise shells, turtle carapaces, coral, and lac. The deregulated imports included such aromatic products as camphor, gharuwood incense of the chen and huangshou varieties, fragrant aloes and lakawood incense, and medicinal products such as betel nuts and cardamoms.

After 982 there was a gap of approximately one hundred and fifty years before another list of products imported by China was recorded. This gap in information is, however, partially filled by the lists of tribute items presented by the missions of foreign states to the Song court during the Northern Song, recorded in such texts as the *Songhuiyao, Songshi,* and *Wenxian tongkao,* which provide an impression of the trade in high-value Southeast Asian products during the late tenth and the eleventh century. Between 961 and 1011 camphor was a regular tribute item presented by Champa to the Song court.[5] The Cham missions also presented jian gharuwood incense on eight occasions between 966 and 1053, while su gharuwood incense was consistently presented between 986 and 1053. Betel nuts, the only low-value product presented as a tribute item, were brought to China on four occasions between 966 and 1018. Tortoise shells were presented between 992 and 1053. These items were available in the Malay region, and Champa was not the only state that presented products that could have been obtained from the Malay region. In 1077, Tianzhu (the Coromandel coast) presented camphor, among other items, as tribute to the Song court.[6] The Dashi Arabs also presented camphor in 984, 995, 1070, 1072, and 1073.[7] During this period camphor may have come from the Malay Peninsula or Borneo, that from the northwestern coast of Sumatra being considered to be of superior quality.

It appears at first glance that Malay products were making significant headway in China in the early decades of the Song. By 982, Malay imports included five new aromatic and two new medicinal products that had not been noted only six years earlier. Of particular importance were the reappearance of such aromatics as gharuwood and the introduction of lakawood incense,[8] which became key imports during the Song and Yuan. This trade was almost entirely confined to high-value products, with Malay products riding on the transshipment trade in Middle Eastern and Indian Ocean products conducted by Middle Eastern, Indian Ocean and Southeast Asian traders.

However, it is difficult to be certain that all these products came from the Malay region. Chinese textual sources do not mention where they came from. In fact, all fifteen products were not available exclusively from the Malay region but from mainland Southeast Asia as well. Sappanwood, a forest product, was also exported by such mainland Southeast Asian states as Khmer (present-day Cambodia) and Champa, as well as Hainan Island. Betel nuts were widely available from Southeast Asia, India, and Hainan Island,[9] while huangshou gharuwood incense was also found in mainland Southeast Asia and the northern tracts of the Malay Peninsula.[10] Chen gharuwood incense was available both from mainland Southeast Asia and the Malay region, although that obtained from Khmer and Champa was regarded as the highest quality by the Chinese during the late twelfth century.[11] Textiles exported by the Malay region, on the other hand, may have largely been reexports from Java and India. Even lakawood incense was also available from the northern tracts of the Malay Peninsula.[12] This area fell under the influence of such mainland Southeast Asian polities as Tambralingga and Langkasuka (present-day Nakhon Si Thammarat, Thailand), in the northeastern Malay Peninsula, and may have been the source of the lakawood incense that had found its way to China by 982.

A portion of these products, however, almost certainly came from the Malay region. Mercantile shipping between the Indian Ocean and the South China Sea was mediated by Srivijaya in the Malacca Strait, and Southeast Asian products were clearly added to transshipped goods from the Indian Ocean littoral that were heading for China. In addition, traders from the Middle East and India would have had to pass through the Strait of Malacca in order to reach China, and by the early eleventh century that route appears to have become increasingly important in the flow of communications between the Indian Ocean littoral and the South China Sea. The central Asian overland route had by this time become increasingly unsafe; in 1023 the Song court cautioned Arab envoys against using this route. Consequently, Middle Eastern and Indian Ocean mercantile traffic plying the Strait of Malacca and passing through the Malay region would have increased substantially. Malay products may have been picked up by this increased maritime traffic en route to China, and the trade in Malay products to China would have been boosted.

Intraregional Southeast Asian trade could have acted as a second channel through which products from the Malay region reached the Chinese market. By 976 such Southeast Asian states as Java, Champa, Srivijaya, Borneo, and Ligor (present-day Nakhon Si Thammarat) had begun to trade with China,[13] with the Chams and Javanese presenting island Southeast Asian products as tribute to the Song court. Trade appears to have been particularly active during the late tenth and the early eleventh century, during which time Champa presented products from Javanese dependencies, such as pepper and cloves,[14] as well as products that could have originated from the region, such as camphor, tortoise shells, and jian and su gharuwood incense. This suggests that a regional trade in maritime Southeast Asian products existed, with China as an important end market.

However, the promotion of Malay products during the tenth and eleventh centuries was not undertaken by the Malay ports themselves. Certain Malay products, including camphor, were already known to Indian and Middle Eastern traders since the late first millennium AD. However, Malay polities, namely Srivijaya, in the Malacca Strait, focused largely on the transshipment of Indian Ocean and Middle Eastern products to China, leaving out indigenous products in the process. Nor was China actively seeking new products from the Malay region during this time. While China remained a passive recipient of trade that was dominated by products from the Middle East and Indian Ocean littoral, potential exports from the Malay region remained largely unexplored.

It was not until 1078 that the Malay region, under the auspices of Srivijaya, actively sought to promote a Malay product in the Chinese market. That year a Srivijayan mission presented camphor to the Song court as part of a larger tribute presentation that consisted wholly of luxury goods.[15] The court's reciprocal gift of a large amount of silver and copper cash suggests that the quantity of the items presented, including the camphor, must have been fairly substantial.

The promotion of camphor as a product made available by Srivijaya continued for the next ten years, including Srivijayan missions in 1082 and 1088.[16] Although the quantities of camphor presented to the Song court at both occasions were merely a token, the intention appears to have been the reinforcement of commercial signals sent by the 1078 mission that Srivijaya was to be regarded as an important supplier of camphor. In 1082 a Srivijayan princess presented a shipment of camphor, along with textiles, to the Guangzhou mercantile shipping superintendency through a Srivijayan representative stationed at Guangzhou.[17] The Song court's confining of commercial exchanges to the ports did not stop Srivijaya from promoting its camphor at both the port and court levels. This concerted effort was also complemented by Srivijaya's attempts to introduce other camphor products into China. Between 1078 and 1086 camphor oil was presented as tribute to the Song court.[18]

China's import trade in Malay products was, through the tenth and eleventh centuries, conducted mainly in the context of state-sponsored trade carried out by China's trading partners. This trade saw the development of mainly high-value products. The lack of direct contact between foreign traders and the Chinese market tended to restrict the range of products imported to those already known to be in demand. The range of products imported from the Malay region therefore increased slowly during this period.

This changed with the liberalization of Chinese mercantile shipping in 1090, which consequently led to an increase in the commercial activities of Chinese traders in Southeast Asia in the twelfth and thirteenth centuries. As the Chinese market developed, it no longer depended on foreign shipping to bring in foreign products. This change introduced a new element to the trade between China and Southeast Asia—China could now shop abroad. As more capital was invested in Chinese shipping trade, and as the Chinese coastal hinterland began to be drawn into the maritime economy, the nature of China's trade with Southeast Asia, and the Malay region, began to alter.

The 1090 liberalization of Chinese shipping opened Southeast Asia to the Chinese market as a source for new products. The increased direct contact of Chinese traders with Southeast Asian ports, which inevitably led to an increase in the knowledge of the products that were available from these ports, was apparently crucial to the introduction of new products to the Chinese market. The impact of the increasing Chinese commercial presence in Southeast Asia began with an expansion in the categories of products already imported by China, particularly in the category of aromatics. By 1141 China imported such high-value products as civet (a type of musk) and damar incense and such low-value products as clove bark and *zan* and *zheng* gharuwood incense.[19]

The increase in Chinese knowledge of products available from the region also led to the importation of a wider range of types and grades of key products by the mid-twelfth century. In 1133 a memorial containing a list of more than one hundred maritime trade products permitted to be freely traded within China was published and recorded in the *Songhuiyao*.[20] At least sixteen of them probably originated from the Malay region, including such high-value aromatics and medicines as several varieties of camphor and camphor oil, gharuwood incense (of the jian, chen, and su varieties), cardamoms, and lac, and such low-value aromatics as huangshou gharuwood incense, lakawood incense, and muskwood. Other products included rattan, timber coated with camphor paste, coconut-fiber mats, sappanwood, sea turtle carapaces, and beeswax. Textile products such as blankets and woven mats may also have been obtained from Malay sources.

By 1141 the range of products had expanded even further. A memorial from that year found in the *Songhuiyao* records approximately 340 maritime trade products grouped into fine (high-value) and coarse (low-value) categories.[21] The list was intended to standardize customs duties and compulsory purchases of the mercantile shipping superintendencies. This is the first and only record of the categorization of maritime trade products imported by China according to their import-tax rates, reflecting their relative value on the Chinese market. About twenty-five products on this new list may have come from the Malay region. Among the ten types of products noted in the fine category were gharuwood incense (jian, su, and chen varieties), tortoise shells, lac, turtle skins, coral, aloes, damar products (damar bark, damar incense, and black damar) and nine varieties of camphor (ripened, plum-flower, grain, pale white, oily, pale red, *lusu, mula,* and camphor paste). Fourteen coarse-category products were noted. These include compressed gharuwood incense (jian, huangshou, sheng, and zan varieties), lakawood incense, betel nuts, camphor oil, muskwood, sappanwood, beeswax, coconut mats, three different varieties of rattan, turtle carapaces, and various cotton textile products.

The knowledge that Chinese traders and the Chinese mercantile shipping superintendencies possessed about products from the Malay region, and their involvement in the trade in these products, had increased by this time. In 1133 seven types of camphor and camphor products were being traded; within a decade that number had increased to nine. This increased level of knowledge is reflected in the detailed listing of each final product derived from certain raw materials (as in the case of camphor), rather than labeling them under one generic name, as was the practice in the tenth and eleventh centuries.

Despite this increase in the trade in maritime Southeast Asian products, Chinese records provide little detail concerning the sources of products imported in the mid-twelfth century. The volume and value of the trade in Malay products is also not known. However, the range of products imported provides a rough indication of the relative significance of this trade to China's overall maritime import trade. Ten out of sixty-four fine-category products listed in 1141 could have come from the Malay region. Together with other fine category products that probably came from Southeast Asia as a whole, they accounted for slightly more than a third of the total of fine-category products imported by China by 1141. The remainder consisted of Middle Eastern and Indian Ocean products. The increase in trade in high-value products may still have been largely dependent on Chinese demand for products from the Middle East and Indian Ocean littoral. While Southeast Asia and the Malay region were becoming a significant source of high-value products, there was no fundamental change in the nature of China's import trade in fine-quality products.

Despite this state of affairs, high-value Southeast Asian products grew in importance in the mid-twelfth century. In 1147, following an increase in the customs duties levied on fine category products in 1144, the customs duty rate for camphor, cloves, cardamoms, and chen gharuwood incense was again reduced to 10 percent.[22] This administrative action suggests that the volume of trade in these four products had become significant enough for traders to complain about the 1144 rate increase.[23] The importance of the trade in these products is reflected in the tribute offered by such Southeast Asian states as Champa and Srivijaya in the 1150s, which included large quantities of high-value Malay products, such as jian, chen, and su gharuwood incense and camphor.[24] The trade in high-value Malay products was further boosted in the second half of the twelfth century by the dramatic increases in 1164 in the rate of compulsory purchases imposed on luxury products.[25] The resulting unprofitability of the trade in these products effectively excluded Chinese traders, who consequently concentrated on the trade in other high-value products, mainly from Southeast Asia. The lack of mention of well-established high-value foreign products in the *Lingwai daida,* with the exception of chen, su, and jian gharuwood incense, suggests that Chinese traders had by the 1170s concentrated on the trade in high-value Southeast Asian products, rather than the traditional high-value products from the Middle East and the Indian Ocean.

Changes to China's maritime shipping trade in the late eleventh and the twelfth century also boosted China's import trade in low-value products from Southeast Asia. The low value of these products meant that larger volumes were needed to be imported for sufficient profits to be generated. A significant increase in the volume of shipping along the Southeast Asia–China route was therefore a precondition for the growth in China's import trade in low-value Southeast Asian products. The dramatic increase in the importance of low-value imports following the 1090 liberalization of Chinese shipping suggests that the volume of shipping increased significantly during the late eleventh and the twelfth century.

The constraints on profitability in the trade of low-value products, where the profit margin was most likely fairly narrow and a high turnover was essential to produce a profit, meant that foreign traders did not attempt to introduce new products of this type unless they were confident that the products would be accepted by the Chinese market. Thus, it was only with the knowledge possessed by Chinese traders of their home market, coupled with an increase in Chinese shipping in Southeast Asian waters, that the trade in low-value Southeast Asian products began to develop into a significant aspect of the region's maritime trade with China. Chinese traders with connections in China's domestic market would have been able to exploit the demands of that market and introduce low-value Southeast Asian products to it.

Products from Southeast Asia that could serve as superior substitutes for items from domestic Chinese sources began to be imported. Foreign products consumed by China had previously been confined largely to luxury items, aromatics, medicinals, and a small range of miscellaneous products, such as sappanwood and textiles. However, by 1133 that trade had expanded to include furniture-making materials, a category of products not previously imported by China, as well as a significant number of previously unknown low-value products. These included muskwood, rattan, and camphor-coated timber, all of which were used in furniture making. Other low-value consumables included beeswax, coconut mats, and sea turtle carapaces. All these products were apparently substitutes for products that had previously been supplied by domestic sources in China. This development continued into the early 1140s. Rattan, in particular, became an important trade product, culminating in the demand for three types of rattan by 1141.[26]

The trade in low-value Southeast Asian products was further boosted in the second half of the twelfth century by dramatic increases in 1164 in the rate of compulsory purchases levied by the Song court on luxury products. The resulting unprofitability of the trade in these products led Chinese traders to redirect their attention to the trade in low-value products.[27] As that trade developed substantially, the range of products involved broadened significantly by the late twelfth and the early thirteenth century.

The shift in the focus of Chinese traders, from luxury products of the Middle East and the Indian Ocean littoral to both high- and low-value products from Southeast Asia, continued into the 1170s. This change in China's trading pattern with Southeast Asia resulted in China's trading partners, such as Srivijaya, having to redefine their role in China's maritime trade. Srivijaya's 1156 mission reflected a fundamental shift in the Malay region in two respects. First, there was a shift in Srivijaya's transshipment trade, from one confined largely to Middle Eastern and Indian Ocean products to one in which Southeast Asian products were now an important element. Second, this shift in emphasis toward Southeast Asia products included only maritime products of high value.[28] No low-value products from maritime Southeast Asia appear in the list of tribute items presented to the Song court in 1156, even though Srivijaya had managed to obtain access to the sources of pepper and sandalwood incense from Java and its dependencies by the mid-twelfth century. Within the next two decades, the region had to redefine its role in China's maritime trade, this time with respect to low-value products. Information on the 1178 Srivijayan tribute mission to China indicates that low-value products formed the bulk of the tribute items brought to China by this time. High-value Southeast Asian products formed the next significant part of this shipment.[29]

The shipment was clearly different from those presented by Srivijayan missions of the eleventh century and 1156. Srivijaya was apparently attempting to redefine its position and role in China's maritime trade context of the 1170s, away from that which it had painstakingly developed by the late eleventh century.

It appears that by the 1170s the Malay region, under the auspices of Srivijaya, was trying to shift its focus from transshipping only high-value products of Middle Eastern and Indian Ocean origin, to transshipping both high- and low-value products from maritime Southeast Asia. Low-value Malay products were still, however, absent from the tribute presented by the Srivijayan missions in 1156 and 1178. Srivijaya clearly sidelined products from the Malay region in its bid to redefine itself in China's maritime trade context. The display of its ability to supply China with products obtained from Java's sphere of influence, such as pepper and sandalwood incense, may have been the result of Srivijaya's attempts at adapting to the circumstance of an ascendant Java in maritime Southeast Asia, which had become increasingly important to China diplomatically and economically from 1130 on.

At the state level Srivijaya was still the major entrepôt for goods imported from the Indian Ocean region. This situation is reflected in the *Lingwai daida* (1178), which notes that the only product imported by China to originate from the Malay region was chen gharuwood incense of the lowest quality. Furthermore, in the entry on Srivijaya, the polity was not listed as the producer of any local product. Srivijaya's position as the third most prosperous foreign trading partner of China, as noted by the *Lingwai daida,* thus continued to be based on its lucrative transshipment trade in products from places beyond the Malay region.

By the early decades of the thirteenth century, however, the Malay region's trade with China was once again undergoing significant changes. The *Zhufanzhi* (1225) provides a detailed impression of this shift. Ports along the Malacca Strait that maintained economic contact with China by this time included not only Srivijaya but also Barus, Kompei, and Lambri, at the northern end of Sumatra. Barus exported camphor; Kompei, tin and pearls; Lambri, sappanwood and white rattan.

Srivijaya, which continued to be an important collection center in the Malacca Strait and the Malay region and a major trading partner to China, had also begun to make indigenous products available to foreign traders. These included tortoise shells, camphor, chen, su, chan, mature, and green gharuwood incense, lakawood incense, imitation dragon's blood, and the best-quality beeswax and coconut mats. Apart from camphor, pearls, chen and su gharuwood incense, the rest were low-value products. Imitation dragon's blood, an aromatic product similar in appearance to Middle Eastern *Dracaena schizantha* and *D. cinnabari,* was available only from Srivijaya.

A new pattern of trade, however, had begun to emerge in the Malay region. Ports at the northern end of Sumatra had begun to specialize in making one or two high quality products available, the equivalent of which could not be obtained elsewhere. Lambri, for example, was the only port listed by the *Zhufanzhi* as a source of rattan imported by Quanzhou,[30] while Kompei was the only port listed where tin was available for export.[31] The exception was Srivijaya, which continued to be a regional entrepôt and the primary collection center of the region. It collected products available from its dependencies, exporting not only goods from beyond the Malacca Strait, but also the best quality of such Malay products as beeswax, coconut mats, and lakawood incense.[32]

The focus of the ports at the northern end of Sumatra, which appear to have begun to pull away from Srivijaya's control, was on the trade in low-value products. This practice of product specialization, which began in the late twelfth and the early thirteenth century, was to characterize the trade of Southeast Asian, and in particular the Malay region ports, by the mid-fourteenth century. By the early thirteenth century, the Malay region had begun to stand out as a significant supplier of low-value products to the Chinese market. Twenty-two products from the region were noted in the *Zhufanzhi* to have been exported to China. Apart from such products as tortoise shells, camphor, and gharuwood incense, trade in which had been established by the mid-eleventh century at the latest, most products were of low value. The range of these low-value products had clearly expanded beyond those listed in 1133 and 1141.

While high-value products continued to be important in China's maritime import trade, the trade in low-value products imported through Quanzhou had become sufficiently important by the early thirteenth century for the Quanzhou mercantile shipping superintendent at that time, Zhao Ruguo, to record which ports maintained trade relations with Quanzhou. While the key Malay port, Srivijaya, continued to ship high-value Middle Eastern, Indian Ocean, and Southeast Asian products to China, indigenous low-value products had become an important aspect of the Malay region's overall trade with China.

By the end of the Southern Song period, low-value Malay products loomed large in the trade between the Malay region and China. Archaeological remains provide a glimpse of this development. The bulk of the cargo of the Quanzhou wreck, which sank in the 1270s, was low-value products from the Malay region—as evidenced by the finding of gharuwood, sandalwood, and lakawood incense, substantial amounts of peppercorns, and over fifty betel nuts.[33] The trade in maritime Southeast Asian aromatics continued to be the most important feature of the Sino-Malay trade, followed closely by low-value medicinal products. This emphasis of China's import trade on aromatic and medicinal products had not essentially changed since the late tenth century, although the sources had now shifted from the Middle East, Indian Ocean, and mainland Southeast Asia primarily to maritime Southeast Asia. The traditional transshipment trade in high-value Middle Eastern and Indian Ocean products, for which the key ports of the Malacca Strait had been so well known from the tenth century on, had been eclipsed by the import trade in maritime Southeast Asian low-value products by Chinese traders. This development, the culmination of a process lasting almost two hundred years, had transformed the Sino-Malay trade by the end of the Song. The change in the pattern of Sino-Malay trade that began in the late eleventh century, with Chinese traders and maritime shipping increasingly competing with Southeast Asian traders and shipping in sourcing and transporting foreign products to China, appears to have reached its peak by the thirteenth century.

Participation in the trade in low-value products was not confined to traders with lower operating capital. The wooden tags recovered from the Quanzhou wreck, most of which indicate ownership of the cargo by important imperial clan families residing in the Quanzhou area,[34] reflects significant participation by important and wealthy Chinese investors in the low-value products trade with the Malay region. The wreck data suggest that at that time, a group of Song imperial clansmen based at Quanzhou were specializing in the trade in aromatic woods and stimulants from the Malay region, as well as spices from Java and its dependencies. This specialization may have been necessary for profit maximization in bulk trade.

These developments were clearly not one sided. While there was an increase in Chinese commercial operations and shipping throughout the twelfth and thirteenth centuries, ports in Southeast Asia were reacting to the changing commercial environment and repositioning themselves to remain relevant to China's maritime trade. The new trading patterns favored minor port-polities in the Malay region, which in turn undermined the economy and authority of such regional port-polities as Srivijaya. While the *Yunlu manchao* reflects the continued importance of Southeast Asian shipping in China's import trade even as late as the early thirteenth century, by the late 1270s it is apparent that the Chinese had become important shippers in the China–Southeast Asia trade. The Javanese sack of Srivijaya's capital, Jambi, in 1275, finalized the breakup of the old economic and political order in the Malacca Strait, and to an extent in the Malay region itself. Each port-polity in the region was now on its own and dealt directly with the Chinese traders plying the region.

Thus, by the thirteenth century a fundamental shift had occurred in the orientation of the Sino-Malay trade pertaining to the import of products from the latter region to the former had occurred. From being essentially determined by the commercial initiatives of Srivijaya, during the tenth to the twelfth century, trade was now increasingly dictated by Chinese market demand, mercantile shipping, and commercial practices. This was the pattern that was to characterize Sino-Malay trade during the Yuan period.

The Development of Trade in Raw Materials from the Malay Region

The Southern Song dynasty finally collapsed under Mongol pressure, and by 1279 the southern coastal provinces of Fujian and Guangdong came under Yuan administration. Maritime trade between China and her traditional trading partners recommenced. However, between 1284 and 1323 the Yuan administration periodically attempted to monopolize Chinese mercantile activities outside the country by forbidding Chinese private traders from going abroad to conduct trade, while providing funds for officially appointed traders and sponsored ships to travel and trade abroad.[35] Private Chinese shipping, which had flourished between the late eleventh and the thirteenth century under the Song court, suffered a serious, if temporary, setback due to the Yuan restrictions. Since the foreigners favored in China during the early decades of Yuan rule were Middle Eastern and Persian, the Malay region's traders also suffered. In addition, at the beginning of the Yuan period, mercantile shipping superintendencies had been reestablished only at Quanzhou, Qingyuan (Ningbo), Shanghai, and Kanfu.[36] Of these, only Quanzhou was suitably located to service the trade arriving from the south.

However, in 1293 superintendencies were reestablished at Shanghai, Wenzhou, Guangdong, and Hangzhou as well.[37] This led to a resumption of regular trade between China and its maritime trading partners in Southeast Asia, the Indian Ocean littoral, and the Middle East. By the third decade of the fourteenth century, maritime trade had stabilized, with private shipping permitted to operate by 1323.

The Chinese import trade in low-value Southeast Asian products continued to develop in the early fourteenth century. The earliest Yuan-period reference to China's trade in Malay products occurs in the *Dade nanhaizhi,* which provides the breakdown of Chinese imports into product categories. Six key categories of products were imported at the beginning of the fourteenth century: luxury items, aromatics, textiles, medicinal products, timber products, and miscellaneous products. Luxury items from the Malay region included hornbill casques, pearls, coral, turtle carapaces, and tortoise shells. Aromatics included chen, su, and huangshou gharuwood incense, damar incense, and lakawood incense. Textiles included both white and decorated foreign cloth. Medicinal products included camphor, cubeb, and cardamoms. Timber products included sappanwood, gharuwood timber, ebony, and a red-purple timber. Miscellaneous products included beeswax, purple rattan, and rattan rods and staffs.[38] Several products were newly introduced, such as hornbill casques, gharuwood timber, and red-purple timber. On the whole, however, the range of types of products imported by China through Guangzhou appears to have decreased by the early fourteenth century, with the same number of types of low-value and high-value products from the Malay region now imported via that port.[39] It is not known whether the value of the trade in low-value products had by this time exceeded that of the high-value products listed. However, given the bulk nature of the trade, the volume of low-value products imported undoubtedly exceeded that of high-value products.

Malay products formed the largest portion of Guangzhou's import trade by the early fourteenth century. Of the sixty-nine products listed in the *Dade nanhaizhi,* twenty-two were probably imported from the Malay region, and others were imported via the Malacca Strait. Thus, the Malay region had become Guangzhou's most important trading partner, within the context in which Southeast Asia as a whole had become the key region with which southern China conducted trade. Forty of the sixty-nine products noted in the *Dade nanhaizhi* were from Southeast Asia.

In the late thirteenth and the early fourteenth century, the only new Southeast Asian products to be introduced to the Chinese market were those from the Malay region, including hornbill casques and jiangzhen. The China–Southeast Asia trade was apparently experiencing a period of stagnation, particularly when compared with the boom in the late eleventh and the twelfth century, during which time large numbers of Southeast Asian products were introduced to the Chinese market. This situation appears to have been the result of the fluctuations in trade regulations and the frequent oscillation of Chinese participation in maritime trade between official monopoly and private trade between 1284 and 1324.

These developments were also accompanied by developments in the larger Asian economic and political context. In the Middle East, the 'Abbasid caliphate, which had been facing a prolonged period of internal political factionalism, eventually capitulated in 1258 under the onslaught of the Mongol forces led by Hulagu Khan. On the Indian subcontinent, the Cholas, in the face of political pressure from the Pandyans of southern India, went into decline as a regional power by the thirteenth century. While the southern Indian kingdom of Pandya carried on the maritime traditions of the Chola Empire during the thirteenth century, political power in southern India gradually shifted inland, toward the southern Deccan Plateau, with the political center based, by the fourteenth century, at Vijayanagar, the capital of the southern Indian empire of Vijayanagara. The general political turmoil in Asia resulted in a general decline in the Asian economy. The only mitigating factor was the close ties between Kublai Khan, the Yuan emperor of China, and the Il-Khans of Persia during the late thirteenth century, which led to regular exchanges between Yuan China and the Middle East via the maritime route.[40] Overall, the maritime-based Asian economy regressed during the late thirteenth and the fourteenth century, in comparison to its efflorescence of the eleventh and twelfth centuries.

This period therefore saw a relative increase in the trade in low-value Southeast Asian products and a decrease in high-value Southeast Asian products trade. The only perceivable exception to this trend, as noted in the historical texts of the Yuan period, was the introduction of hornbill casques as a new luxury trade product. The quick adoption by Chinese traders of a quality-grading system for this product by the mid-fourteenth century suggests that it was eagerly accepted by the Chinese market by the early fourteenth century, The shift toward trade in low-value Southeast Asian products accompanied a decline in China's trade with the Indian Ocean littoral and the Middle East. The list of Middle Eastern and Indian Ocean products noted in the *Dade nanhaizhi* is discernibly shorter than those contained in Song texts.

Despite the relative stagnation in China's sea trade early in the Yuan, there were developments in the trade in low-value Malay products by the beginning of the fourteenth century. A number of new furniture-making materials, grouped under the categories of timber and miscellaneous products, were introduced into the Chinese market during this time. These included gharuwood timber, red-purple timber, and purple rattan, none of which was recorded in Song texts.

The dominance of Southeast Asia's low-value products in China's maritime trade continued into the mid-fourteenth century. Although the level of knowledge of Southeast Asian products among Chinese traders was very high by this time, their marketing strategies remained fairly conservative. China's imports of maritime Southeast Asian products were still largely confined to low-value products on which the Chinese market had already become dependent, such as beeswax, lakawood incense, betel nuts, and gharuwood incense.

Chinese traders plying the Sino-Malay route did not seek to be involved in the general importation of all Malay products. Instead, they continued to specialize in a few products. This practice, evident by the late Song from the cargo of the Quanzhou wreck, continued in the Yuan and was not confined to large-scale traders. Because of his extensive knowledge of specific products and the qualities offered at various ports, the trader Wang Dayuan, for example, appears to have specialized in chen and su gharuwood incense, tortoise shells, and hornbill casques. And he traded in only seven low-value products from the region: beeswax, betel nuts, cotton, lakawood incense, jiangzhen, huangshou gharuwood incense, and tin.

The knowledge possessed by Chinese traders, as seen in the *Daoyi zhilue,* and the grading system used for products in which they specialized, were much more detailed and specific than those recorded in the *Zhufanzhi* in the early thirteenth century. The Chinese market's considerable familiarity with Malay products was not solely the result of Chinese trade activities in the region but was also due to the active promotion by the region's ports of the products that they offered for export. Although trade with the Indian Ocean littoral and Middle East was important to ports in the Malacca Strait in the fourteenth century, the efforts of these ports appear to have been focused largely on the Chinese market. These efforts were reciprocated. The large numbers of Chinese shards found at the sites of ports in the region that were active in the late thirteenth and the fourteenth century attest to this reciprocal commercial relationship between China and the Malay region.

There is currently no known textual record of the volume of Malay products shipped to China during the Yuan. Nonetheless, the context of the China–Southeast Asia trade during this period may allow us to make some tentative conclusions. First, there appears to have been a proliferation of small-scale traders, such as Wang Dayuan. State-sponsored commercial trips do not appear to have continued after the early 1320s, when the power of the Ortaq clique had begun to decline. The participation in Southeast Asian intraregional trade by Chinese traders appears to have increased substantially, possibly because at least some southern Chinese traders relocated abroad during the early decades of Yuan rule. This prolonged commercial engagement in Southeast Asia was also aided by the removal of restrictions on the length of time that Chinese mercantile vessels could remain outside China. The turnaround rate of Chinese mercantile vessels was thus possibly much lower than that experienced during the Song, when the length of time such vessels could remain abroad was limited to approximately nine months, or one monsoon cycle.

While the *Dade nanhaizhi* and the *Daoyi zhilue* portray a sense of continuity in the level of maritime trade that China experienced during the late Song into the Yuan, the scope and value of this trade, in reality, appears to have suffered a relative decline by the fourteenth century. The decline in the sea trade in high-value Middle Eastern and Indian Ocean products during the fourteenth century strongly suggests that the value, if not the volume, of China's maritime trade were reduced by this time. Much of the trade with India and the Middle East appears to have switched to the overland silk route. The rise in importance of the export of low-value Malay products to China appears to have been, in part, a response to the loss of the transshipment trade from the Indian Ocean.

By the late fourteenth century, China's import of Malay products had become centered on a wide range of goods that had become incorporated into the regular consumption patterns of the Chinese market. This was driven by a combination of Southeast Asian export promotion and the mercantile interests of private Chinese maritime traders. This pattern of import trade in Malay products into the Chinese market would come to characterize Sino-Malay economic interaction for the remainder of the second millennium AD.

CONCLUSION

In 1368 a southern Chinese rebellion led by a Buddhist monk named Zhu Yuanzhang brought Yuan rule in China to an end. The period of dynastic rule that followed—the Ming period (1368–1644)—was initially characterized by a shift toward the active projection of Chinese naval power and diplomatic reach in maritime Southeast Asia and the Indian Ocean in the first four decades of the fifteenth century. This was, however, immediately followed first by a turning inward by the Chinese court, away from the outside world, and then by the banning of Chinese maritime shipping, trade, and foreign travel by Chinese citizens from the 1470s on. It was only in 1567, when the maritime ban was eventually lifted, that Chinese maritime trade and overseas travel were once again permitted.

Sino-Malay diplomatic relations initially flourished as a result of the imperial Chinese presence in the Malay region, with regular visits by the Ming imperial fleet during the first four decades of the fifteenth century. Several Malay polities dispatched diplomatic missions, including that of the Malacca sultanate, to the Ming court with the view to benefiting politically and economically from the diplomatic dialogue. However, relations quickly deteriorated from the mid-fifteenth century with the increasingly isolationist stance of the Ming court. By the early sixteenth century, China's lack of interest in projecting its influence beyond its maritime borders had become apparent to the polities of the Malay region, and diplomatic relations were discontinued.

Despite the drastic decline in diplomatic relations between the two regions, the maritime economic interaction that had developed between Chinese traders and Malay ports and traders continued un-abated throughout the Ming. From the late fourteenth century until the advent of colonial rule in Southeast Asia, diplomatic and economic relations between the two regions had developed into separate entities. During the tenth century, on the other hand, diplomatic and economic interactions were intricately intertwined. The period between the tenth and the fourteenth century therefore had a fundamental impact on the nature of Sino-Malay relations in the second millennium.

Far from being static, Sino-Malay relations underwent tremendous changes during the first half of the second millennium AD. The political imperatives that China faced determined the policies that were instituted by the Song and Yuan courts in the administration of maritime trade. However, the effects of changes in the administration of maritime trade continued to unfold so long as those changes remained implemented. Between the tenth and the fourteenth century, China and the Malay region were mutually dependent trading partners. Since the coastal polities of the Malay region depended on China as one of the key economies that determined their economic well-being and political stability, changes in the manner in which China conducted trade had important secondary effects in that region. In turn, China's trade with the Malay region had a significant impact on the society and economy of China at both the state and provincial levels.

Changes in the administrative structures governing trade in China determined the economic and diplomatic approaches that the port-polities of the Malay region adopted in their trade with China. Thus, the Malay region's trade with China changed over time from a trade that was essentially that of a regional power to one that was scattered among individual port-polities. The regional approach had to be initi-ated and maintained by a Malay polity that was sufficiently powerful economically and politically to act as the entrepôt for its sphere of in-fluence. From the thirteenth century on, however, as Chinese traders began to operate actively in the Malay region, and as trade between the two became increasingly diffuse, trade with China was increas-ingly undertaken directly by Malay port-polities in their individual capacities, while diplomatic relations were hardly maintained. The changes in the way China interacted economically and diplomatically with Southeast Asia thus had a fundamental impact in the way the port-polities of the Malay region related to each other as well. The regional political dynamics within the Malay region changed as the Malay polities adapted to changes in China's foreign and economic policies.

The shift in trade from court to port level and the liberalization of private participation in maritime trade by the Song court from the late tenth to late eleventh century shaped Sino-Malay trade into a two-way commercial exchange of products that grew increasingly diverse. The manner in which trade was conducted changed as a result of changes in the administration of China's maritime trade, which evolved from a trade conducted during the tenth century predominantly through trade exchanges at the state, or court, level and within China's borders, to a situation by the thirteenth century in which both Malay state-sponsored trade and Chinese private trade were conducted at the port level, with the commercial activities of the two groups of traders taking place both in China and in the Malay region. The products imported by China and the Malay region also expanded in both range and volume, from a limited number of products mainly of high value or ceremonial significance, to a wide range of nonceremonial products that were mainly of lower value.

In the process, the material circumstances of many Chinese—not just those who were wealthy or were of the scholar-official or gentri-fied classes but those on the lower rungs of the socioeconomic ladder—were dramatically altered by the influx of Southeast Asian products into China. Similarly, the Chinese products imported by the Malay region also changed the nature of material culture in the Malay world. The Malay region benefited from the availability of another source of manufactured products that either required a level of technology or economies of scale that it did not possess. Chinese stoneware, which became perhaps the most important Chinese export commodity to Southeast Asia, satisfied Malay demand for high-fired ceramics that could not be met indigenously because of the absence of the necessary ceramic technology, while Chinese iron products served as a cheap source of iron imports, filling a niche in the Malay region's demand for cheap iron implements in direct competition with the more expensive high quality ironware produced in Southeast Asia and India. The importance of China as an external market to the Malay region, and the pervasiveness of Chinese traders in the region by the thirteenth century, also led to the adoption of Chinese copper cash by a number of port-polities as a form of currency by the late twelfth century.

From the tenth to the fourteenth century, as diplomatic exchanges between China and the Malay region initially intensified and then declined, and as economic interaction between the two regions intensified, the presence of Chinese and Malays had a significant impact on the demography and even administrative policies of the foreign states they each sojourned in. Malay presence at the Chinese ports, particularly Guangzhou and Quanzhou, evolved according to the changing needs of diplomacy and economy. The Malay community in China acted, during the later tenth and the early eleventh century, as a source of political and commercial information for the Srivijayan court and the Malay region, and as facilitators of state-level exchanges. From the later eleventh century on, however, this community gradually served as a commercial interface between the Malay region and Chinese traders operating in the Chinese domestic market. By the thirteenth century the community had split into a number of subcommunities, each acting as an agency for the individual Malay port-polity that had established a direct commercial link with the southern Chinese ports of Guangzhou and Quanzhou. In the process, the political clout that the Malay community had enjoyed in China since the tenth century, under the auspices of Srivijaya, and that reached a peak in the mid-twelfth century, gradually eroded in the thirteenth and fourteenth centuries, giving way to the Middle Easterners, who had by the late thirteenth century become important proxies of the Mongol rulers in China, and the Ortaq cliques operating in the Chinese economy.

In turn, the tenth through the fourteenth century witnessed Chinese traders, in the face of dramatic shifts in the economic and diplomatic contexts, proving them to be highly attuned to their commercial environment and adaptive to the changing circumstances within which they had to operate. Even as circumstances over time became more conducive for private maritime, the commercial practices of these traders continued to evolve, so that trade, and ultimately the procurement of Malay-region products for the Chinese market, became more efficient. In the process, the increasing presence of Chinese traders at Southeast Asian and Malay ports led to the beginnings of a major demographic development among Southeast Asian ports from the fifteenth century on—Chinese settlers whose primary function was to engage in the maritime trade between China and Southeast Asia.

By the late fourteenth century, Sino-Malay trade had evolved far from what it had been in the tenth century. Malay sailors and ships, which had for almost a millennium carried much of the trade between the Malay region and China, no longer did so. Instead, the Malay port-polities sought to engage the Chinese market by attempting to attract Chinese ships and traders that were passing through or arriving at the region's ports. The interaction between the two regions had shifted from China and the southern Chinese ports to the Malay region. This trade had come to consist mainly of low-value Malay products, which were in turn exchanged for low-value Chinese manufactured items. The volume of trade between China and the Malay region had by the fourteenth century increased phenomenally, although its unit value appears to have declined dramatically, since the trade was no longer dominated by high-value products. This became the pattern for economic relations between China and the Malay region for the second half of the second millennium AD.

This book has tried to show that historically, the relationship between maritime Southeast Asia and China was not monolithic but highly complex. China's interaction with the various subregions in maritime Southeast Asia was never homogenous, even though China's policies governing trade and foreign relations were fairly standardized and equitably implemented. The actual impact of these policies, and the varying responses they elicited from the various polities in maritime Southeast Asia, caused China's economic and political relations to vary significantly from subregion to subregion. Southeast Asia is, after all, not a unitary or singular entity geographically, politically, or culturally, but rather a twentieth-century amalgam of subregions. A greater understanding of the complexity of the economic and diplomatic relationship between China and Southeast Asia would thus be attained if it were addressed primarily at the subregional level.

As China rises in economic and political importance in the twenty-first century to assume its historical position as one of the dominant states in Asia, the present study is important in fostering an understanding of the role China has historically played, providing a better idea, from the long cycle of its relationship with Southeast Asia, of the possible trajectory of present-day and future developments. The early Ming period, with particular reference to the Ming voyages initiated in the first four decades of the fifteenth century by the emperor Yongle and led by the admiral Zheng He, has traditionally been viewed as the historical reference point to which the present developments of China–Southeast Asia relations may be compared. However, the parallels between the present and the Song and Yuan periods would be much more apt. The liberalization of the Chinese economy in the Song, particularly that of China's maritime trade, provides a historical reference to the present liberalization of the Chinese economy—including the permitting of private enterprise, coupled with a significant yet diminishing level of involvement on the part of the Chinese government in manufacturing and trade, and a distinction between Chinese economic and diplomatic imperatives at both the state and provincial levels. I have tried to provide historical insight into how states in Southeast Asia would react to, and approach, China's present return to its historical position as a key economy and political entity in Asia.

Although the countries of present-day Southeast Asian have managed to increase their domestic populations significantly as a result of European colonial policies in the region during the nineteenth and twentieth centuries, these countries have remained relatively small; they carry political and economic weight only when they deal with key states as a regional collective under the auspices of the Association of Southeast Asian Nations (ASEAN). As long as China remains the chief location of economic interaction, such a structure remains useful and workable. However, as China gradually engages the Southeast Asian states individually, and as the location of economic interaction begins to shift from China to Southeast Asia, this collective approach may likely give way to a more diffuse approach, and the respective approaches of the Southeast Asian countries toward China would again have to be adapted to fit the changed rules of the economic and diplomatic game. As China's economy, and the administrative structures that govern economic activities, evolve, history may provide valuable lessons in predicting how the maritime Southeast Asian states will react and adapt to the changes in China in order to remain relevant and viable in the twenty-first century.

Appendix A

CHINESE IMPORTS TO THE MALAY REGION, TENTH THROUGH FOURTEENTH CENTURY

Table A.1. Chinese imports to the Malay region, 1225 AD

					bowls, plates
					greenware
Manufactured items					
lacquerware					
stoneware	•	•	•	•	qingbai
	platters				
earthen bowls/alms bowls		•	•		
glass bottles				•	
glass beads				•	
ivory bangles				•	
Foodstuffs					
rice	•	•	•	•	•
wine	•	•	•	•	
sugar		•	•	•	
salt		•	•		
rhizome of Lingusticum wallichii					
galangal		•	•		•
wheat				•	
root of Angelica dahurica					
pond lotuses	•	•	•		•
rhubarb					

Table A.2. Chinese imports to Malay peninsular ports, 1350s

	Item	Tambralingga	Srokam	Malilu	Xialaiwu	Pahang	Kelantan	Trengganu	Jung	Langkasuka
Precious metals	silver								patterned	
Low-value metal items	tin							•	wares	
	copper cauldrons		cauldrons		cauldrons	copper				
	iron		•	cauldrons		wares				
	iron ropes				ropes					
Musical instruments	drums	•								
	drumming boards					•	•			
	zithers						•			
	stringed instruments						•			
Textiles	checkered handkerchiefs						•			(Chinese)
	local (Chinese) printed cloth									•
	colored cloth	red		blue	five-colored	various colored				
	woven silk				red			small and red		(foreign)
Textiles	Javanese cloth	•				•				
	Calicut cloth		•		•		•	•		
	Champa cloth		•		•					
	Hainan Island cloth								•	
	Kunlun cloth									
	Badula cloth									•
Foodstuffs	wine									
Manufactured items	lacquerware					•		•	•	
Ceramics	earthen water jars				coarse					
	bowls						platters			
	greenware	bowls	wares	stoneware platters	wares			stoneware		
	blue-and-white wares						bowls	bowls	bowls	bowls
	patterned ceramics					wares				
	stoneware								bottles and pots	
	Chuzhou stoneware			•						

Source: DYZL, 5a–7b, 8b, and 13a–b.

Table A.3. Chinese imports to Malay and Riau-Lingga archipelago ports, 1350s

	Item	Lambri	Deli	Tamiang	Srivijaya-Jambi	Palembang	Lingga bodhi	Fort Canning (Singapore)	Keppel Straits (Singapore)	Karimata	Semudra
Precious metals	gold	•									
	red gold			•				•	•		
	silver	•		•				•	•		
Low-value metal items	copper cauldrons					•					
	copper and iron woks				•						
	iron rods				•						
	iron: wares	•						•			
	iron cauldrons			•							
Manufactured items	oiled umbrellas						•	•	•		•
Textiles (Chinese)	patterned cloth		•		•				•		
	local (Chinese) printed cloth							•			
	local (Chinese) blue-and-white patterned printed cloth						•				
	colored cloth		five-colored			five-colored					
	colored satin								blue		blue
Textiles (foreign)	West Ocean silk cloth										five-colored
Mineral-based items	sulfur										•
Ceramics	bowls			coarse							
	greenware		coarse							•	
	qingbai wares	bowls	stoneware								
	stoneware					•					
	Chuzhou stoneware							•	•		

Source: DYZL 10a, 13b–15a, 16a–b, 18a–b, 20a–21a.

Appendix B

CERAMICS DATA FROM TEMASIK-PERIOD SITES, SINGAPORE (EMPRESS PLACE AND OLD PARLIAMENT HOUSE)

Table B.1. Ceramics from Old Parliament House, fourteenth century

Percentage by weight	Earthenware	Thai/ Vietnamese/ Burmese wares	Coarse stoneware (Chinese)		Fine stoneware (Chinese)					
						Blue-and-white ware			Whiteware	
			Mercury jar shards	General	Greenware	Yuan	Ming	Dehua	Shufu	Qingbai
Percentage by weight	42 kg	<0.3 kg	89 kg	185 kg	39 kg	0.9 kg	0.9 kg	3 kg	9.5 kg	0.8 kg
In category	—	—	—	—	—	50	50	22.5	71.4	6
In subassemblage	—	—	32.5	67.5	73.3	1.7	1.7	5.6	17.9	1.5
In assemblage	11.4	<0.1	24	49.9	10.5	<0.1	<0.1	0.8	2.6	0.2

Source: Heng, "Economic Interaction," table 4.4.

Table B.2. Ceramics from Empress Place, fourteenth century

Percentage by weight	Earthenware	Coarse stoneware (Chinese)		Greenware (Chinese)		Blue-and-white ware (Chinese)		Whiteware (Chinese)		
		Mercury jar shards	General	Longquan	Others	Yuan	Others	Dehua	Shufu	Others
Percentage by weight	113.6 kg	81 kg	984 kg	58 kg	18.4 kg	0.6 kg	64.8 kg	5.3 kg	6 kg	28.7 kg
In category	—	—	—	—	10.1	0.9	99.1	13.2	15.1	71.7
In subassemblage	—	7.6	92.4	31.9	10.1	0.3	35.6	2.9	3.3	15.8
In assemblage	10	6	72.3	4.3	1.4	<0.1	4.8	0.4	0.4	2.1

Source: Heng, "Economic Interaction," table 4.3.

Appendix C

MALAY IMPORTS TO CHINA, THIRTEENTH AND FOURTEENTH CENTURIES

Table C.1. Indigenous exports by key Malay ports, early thirteenth century

	Item	Barus	Srivijaya	Kompei	Lambri	Langkasuka	Kuala Berang
Luxury items	tortoise shells		•				
	ivory			•	•	•	•
	rhinoceros horns					•	
	pearls			•		•	
Aromatics	camphor	•	•			•	
	jian gharuwood						
	chen gharuwood		low grade				
	su gharuwood		•			•	•
	chan gharuwood		•				
	huangshou gharuwood	•					
	shen gharuwood		•			•	
	lakawood incense		top grade				•
	sandalwood incense	•					•
Medicinals	cloves		•				
	cardamoms		•				
	aniseed						
	pepper						
	safflower						
	cubeb						
	imitation dragon's blood		•				
Misc. goods	red kino gum						
	beeswax		top grade				
Metals	tin			•			
Wood and construction material	ebony						
	sappanwood				•		
	white rattan				•		
Manufactured goods	swords						
	coconut mats		top grade				
Animals	white parrots						

Source: ZFZ 1:5b–10a.

Table C.2. Indigenous exports by Malay peninsular ports, mid-fourteenth century

	Item	Srokam	Pahang	Kelantan	Trengganu	Langkasuka
Metal	tin		patterned	patterned		
	white tin					
Luxury items	tortoise shells	•			•	
	turtle carapaces			•		
	ivory					
	rhinoceros horns					
	crane crests	•		•		•
	kingfisher tails					
	kingfisher feathers					
Medicinal products	cardamoms					
	pepper					
	betel nuts			•		
Aromatics	chen gharuwood	•	•	top grade		superior
	su gharuwood			top grade		
	huangshou gharuwood		•			•
	camphor		•		•	
	grain camphor					
	camphor planks	•				
	lakawood incense			coarse		
	dabai incense		•			
	luozhen incense					
Misc. goods	beeswax			•	•	
	jiangzhen	top grade	coarse		•	•
	sappanwood					
	honey					•

Source: DYZL 6a–7a, 8b, and 13a–b.

Table C.3. Indigenous exports by Malacca Strait ports, mid-fourteenth century

	Item	Tamiang	Lambri	Deli	Jambi	Palembang	Banzu (Singapore)	Longyamen (Singapore)	Semudra
Metal	tin			•				•	•
Luxury items	tortoise shells		•						items
	turtle carapaces		•	•					
	crane crests		•	•		uniquely top grade	top grade		•
Medicinals	betel nuts				•				
Aromatics	chen gharuwood					middle grade			
	su gharuwood					middle grade			
	huangshou gharuwood					•			
	camphor								•
	camphor planks				plum blossom				
	coarse incense								
	lakawood incense	•	superior		middle grade				coarse
Misc. goods	jiangzhen			•		coarse	middle grade	coarse	
	coconuts								
	goats								
	benzoin				•				
	beeswax				•				

Source: DYZL 10a, 13b–14b, 16a–b, 18a–b, and 20a–b.

Abbreviations

Places and dates of publication appear in parentheses.

BEFEO	*Bulletin de l'école française d'extrême-Orient* (Paris)
CFYG	Wang Qinruo 王欽若 and Li Sijing 李嗣京, *Cefu yuangui* 册府元龜 (1013)
DDNHZ	Chen Dazhen 陳大震, *Dade nanhaizhi* 大德南海志 (1306)
DYZL	Wang Dayuan 汪大淵, *Daoyi zhilue* 島夷志略 (ca. 1349)
FMJ	*Federated Museums Journal* (Kuala Lumpur)
HJSYJ	*Haijiaoshi yanjue* 海交史研究 (Quanzhou)
JAOS	*Journal of the American Oriental Society* (New Haven)
JESHO	*Journal of the Economic and Social History of the Orient* (Brussels)
JMBRAS	*Journal of the Malaysian Branch of the Royal Asiatic Society* (Kuala Lumpur)
JSEAH	*Journal of Southeast Asian History* (Singapore)
JSEAS	*Journal of Southeast Asian Studies* (Singapore)
JSSS	*Journal of the South Seas Society* (Singapore)
LSS	Shen Yue 沈約, *Songshu* 宋书 (492–93)
LWDD	Zhou Qufei 周去非, *Lingwai daida* 嶺外代答 (1178)
MIH	*Malaya in History* (Kuala Lumpur)
PZKT	Zhu Yu 朱彧, *Pingzhou ketan* 萍州可談 (1116)
SHY	*Songhuiyao jigao* 宋會要輯稿 (1236)
SMJ	*Sarawak Museum Journal* (Kuching)
SS	Tuo Tuo 托托 et al., *Songshi* 宋史 (1345)
WXTK	Ma Duanlin 馬端臨, *Wenxian tongkao* 文獻通考 (1307)

XTS	Ou Yangxiu 歐陽修 and Song Qi 宋祁, *Xintangshu* 新唐書 (1043–60)
YDZ	*Yuandianzhang* 元典章 (1321–24)
YLMC	Zhao Yanwei 趙彦衛, *Yunlu manchao* 雲麓漫鈔 (1206)
YS	*Yuanshi* 元史 (1370)
ZFZ	Zhao Ruguo 趙汝适, *Zhufanzhi* 諸蕃志 (1225)

Notes

Introduction

1. Wang Gungwu, *The Nanhai Trade: The Early History of Chinese Trade in the South China Sea* (Singapore: Times Academic Press, 1998).

2. Tansen Sen, *Buddhism, Diplomacy, and Trade: The Realignment of Sino-Indian Relations, 600–1400* (Honolulu: University of Hawaii Press, 2003); E. H. Schafer, "Rosewood, Dragon's Blood and Lac," *JAOS* 77, no. 2 (1957): 129–36.

3. Ng Chin Keong, *Trade and Society: The Amoy Network on the China Coast 1683–1735* (Singapore: Singapore University Press, 1983); Wang Gungwu and Ng Chin Keong, eds., *Maritime China in Transition, 1750–1850* (Wiesbaden: Harrassowitz, 2004).

4. For more detailed studies on the history of Srivijaya, see George Coedès, "Le royaume de Crivijaya," *BEFEO* 18, no. 6 (1918): 1–36; Coedès, "Les inscriptions malaises de Crivijaya," *BEFEO* 30, no. 1–2 (1930): 29–80; Coedès, "A propos d'une nouvelle théorie sur le site de Srivijaya," *JMBRAS* 14, no. 3 (1936): 1–9; O. W. Wolters, *Early Indonesian Commerce: A Study of the Origins of Srivijaya* (Ithaca: Cornell University Press, 1967); Wolters, *The Fall of Srivijaya in Malay History* (Kuala Lumpur: Oxford University Press, 1970).

5. For a brief discussion on the key characteristics of Malay port-polities in the premodern era, see Anthony Reid, "The Structure of Cities in Southeast Asia, 15th to 17th Centuries," *JSEAS* 11, no. 2 (1980): 235–50; John N. Miksic, "Urbanisation and Social Change, The Case of Sumatra," *Archipel* 37 (1989): 3–29; Pierre-Yves Manguin, "City-States and City-State Cultures in Pre-15th Century Southeast Asia," in *A Comparative Study of Thirty City-State Cultures: An Investigation Conducted by the Copenhagen Polis Center,* ed. Mogens Herman Hansen (Copenhagen: Historisk-filosofiske Skrifter, Royal Danish Academy of Sciences and Letters, 2000), 409–16.

6. Laurence Junchao Ma, "Commercial Development and Urban Change in Sung China" (PhD diss., Unversity of Michigan, 1971); Wang Shengduo 汪聖鐸, *Liangsong caizhengshi* 兩宋財政史 (Beijing: Zhonghua Shuju, 1995); Yoshinobu Shiba, *Commerce and Society in Sung China,* trans. Mark Elvin (Ann Arbor: Center for Chinese Studies, University of Michigan, 1970); Peng Xinwei 彭信威, *Zhongguo huobishi* 中國貨幣史 (Shanghai: Shanghai Renmin Chubanshe, 1988); Song Lian, *Economic Structure of the Yüan Dynasty,* trans. Herbert Franz Schurmann (Cambridge, MA: Harvard University Press, 1967); Angela Schottenhammer, "Local Politico-economic Particulars of the Quanzhou Region during the Tenth Century," *JSYS* 29 (1999): 1–41; Schottenhammer, "The Maritime Trade of Quanzhou (Zaiton) from the Ninth through the Thirteenth Century," in *Archaeology of Seafaring: The Indian Ocean in the Ancient Period,* Indian Council of Historical Research Monograph Series 1, ed. Himanshu Prabha Ray (Delhi: Pragati, 1999): 271–90.

7. J. Kuwabara, "On P'u Shou-Keng," *Memoirs of the Research Department of the Toyo Bunko,* 1928, no. 2:1–79; Lin Tianwei 林天蔚, *Songdai xiangyao maoyi shigao* 宋代香藥貿易史稿 (Hong Kong: Zhongguo Xueshe, 1959); Yu Changsen 喻常森, *Yuandai haiwai maoyi* 元代海外貿易 (Xian: Xibei daxue Chubanshe, 1994); Guan Luquan 關履權, *Songdai guangzhou de haiwai maoyi* 宋代廣州的海外貿易 (Guangzhou: Guangdong Renmin Chubanshe, 1994); So Kee Long, *Prosperity, Region, and Institutions in Maritime China: The South Fukien Pattern, 946–1368* (Cambridge, MA: Harvard University Asia Center, 2000); Hugh R. Clark, *Community, Trade, and Networks: Southern Fujian Province from the Third to the Thirteenth Century* (Cambridge: Cambridge University Press, 1991).

8. Zhao Ruguo, *Chau Ju-Kua: His Work on the Chinese and Arab Trade in the Twelfth and Thirteenth Centuries, Entitled* Chu-fan-chï, trans. Freidrich Hirth and W. W. Rockhill (New York: Paragon Book Reprint, 1966); Paul Wheatley, *The Golden Khersonese: Studies in the Historical Geography of the Malay Peninsula before AD 1500* (Westport, CT: Greenwood, 1973); Ma Huan, *Ying yai sheng lan, "The Overall Survey of the Ocean's Shores" (1433),* trans. Feng Chengjun (Cambridge: Hakluyt Society, 1970); Roderich Ptak, "The Northern Trade Route to the Spice Islands: South China Sea—Sulu Zone—North Moluccas (14th to Early 16th century)," *Archipel* 43 (1992): 27–56; Fei Xin, *Hsing-ch'a sheng-lan: The Overall Survey of the Star Raft,* trans. J. V. G. Mills, ed. Roderich Ptak (Wiesbaden: Harrassowitz, 1996); Ptak, "From Quanzhou to the Zulu Zone and Beyond: Questions Related to the Early Fourteenth Century," *JSEAS* 29, no. 2 (1998): 269–94.

9. For a brief discussion on the disparity in text-based and archaeology-based scholarship of the Malay region in the premodern era, see Pierre-

Yves Manguin, "Sriwijaya, entre texts historique et terrain archéologique: Un siècle a la recherché d'un état évanescent," *BEFEO* 88 (2001): 331–39.

10. Paul Wheatley, "Geographical Notes on Some Commodities Involved in Sung Maritime Trade," *JMBRAS* 32, no. 2 (1959): 5–140; Roderich Ptak, "Notes on the Word *Shanhu* and Chinese Coral Imports from Maritime Asia c. 1250–1600," *Archipel* 39 (1990): 65–80; Ptak, "China and the Trade in Tortoise-Shell (Sung to Ming Periods)," in *Emporia, Commodities, and Entrepreneurs in Asian Maritime Trade, c. 1400–1750*, ed. Ptak and Dietmar Rothermund (Stuttgart: Franz Steiner, 1991), 195–229; Ptak, "China and the Trade in Cloves, circa 960–1435," *JAOS* 113, no. 1 (1993): 1–13.

11. Bennet Bronson, "Exchange at the Upstream and Downstream Ends: Notes towards a Functional Model of the Coastal State in Southeast Asia," in *Economic Exchange and Social Interaction in Southeast Asia: Perspectives from Prehistory, History and Ethnography*, ed. K. L. Hutterer (Ann Arbor: University of Michigan, 1977), 39–52; Kenneth R. Hall, *Maritime Trade and State Development in Early Southeast Asia* (Honolulu: University of Hawaii Press, 1986).

12. Jan Wisseman-Christie, "Patterns of Trade in Western Indonesia, 9th through 13th Centuries AD," 2 vols. (PhD diss., School of Oriental and African Studies, University of London 1982); Wisseman-Christie, "Trade and Early State Formation in Maritime Southeast Asia: Kedah and Srivijaya," *Jebat* 13 (1985): 43–56; Wisseman-Christie, "Trade and State Formation in the Malay Peninsula and Sumatra, 300 BC–AD 700," in *The Southeast Asian Port and Polity, Rise and Demise*, ed. J. Kathirithamby-Wells and John Villiers (Singapore: Singapore University Press, 1990), 39–61; Wisseman-Christie, "State Formation in Early Maritime Southeast Asia: A Consideration of the Theories and the Data," *Bijdragen tot de taal-, land- en volkenkunde* 151, no. 2 (1995): 235–88; Wisseman-Christie, "The Medieval Tamil-Language Inscriptions in Southeast Asia and China," *JSEAS* 29, no. 2 (1998): 239–268; Wisseman-Christie, "Asian Sea Trade between the Tenth and Thirteenth Centuries and Its Impact on the States of Java and Bali," in *Archaeology of Seafaring: The Indian Ocean in the Ancient Period*, Indian Council of Historical Research Monograph Series 1, ed. Himanshu Prabha Ray (Delhi: Pragati, 1999), 221–70.

13. Wolters, *Early Indonesian Commerce*; Wolters, *Fall of Srivijaya*; Wolters, "A Few and Miscellaneous Pi-Chi Jottings on Early Indonesia," *Indonesia* 34 (1983): 49–65; Wolters, "Restudying Some Chinese Writings on Sriwijaya," *Indonesia* 42 (1986): 1–42.

14. Wolters, *Fall of Srivijaya*; Wolters, "Pi-Chi Jottings"; Wolters: "Restudying Chinese Writings."

15. See Gu Hai 顧海, *Dongnanya gudaishi zhongwen wenxian tiyao* 東南亞古代史中文文獻提要 (Xiamen: Xiamen daxue Chubanshe,

1990). Works in Western languages that contain translated segments of Song texts include W. P. Groeneveldt, *Historical Notes on Indonesia and Malaysia Compiled from Chinese Sources* (Batavia, 1876); Kuwabara, "On P'u Shou-Keng"; Zhao, *Chau Ju-Kua;* Shiba, *Commerce and Society;* Ma, *Commercial Development;* Andrew Watson, ed. and trans., *Transport in Transition: The Evolution of Traditional Shipping in China,* Michigan Abstracts of Chinese and Japanese Works on Chinese History, no. 3 (Ann Arbor: Center for Chinese Studies, University of Michigan, 1972); Wheatley, *Golden Khersonese;* Almut Netolitzky, *Das* Ling-wai tai-ta *von Chou Ch'ü Fei, eine Landeskunde Südchinas aus den 12. Jahrhundert* (Wiesbaden: Franz Steiner, 1977); Wolters, "Pi-Chi Jottings"; So Kee Long, "Dissolving Hegemony or Changing Trade Pattern? Images of Srivijaya in the Chinese Sources of the Twelfth and Thirteenth Centuries," *JSEAS* 29, no. 2 (1998): 295–308; Ptak, "*Word* Shanhu"; Ptak, "China and the Trade in Tortoise-Shell"; Ptak, "Northern Trade Route"; Ptak, "China and the Trade in Cloves"; Ptak, "Ming Maritime Trade to Southeast Asia, 1368–1567: Visions of a 'System,'" in *From the Mediterranean to the China Sea: Miscellaneous Notes,* ed. Claude Guillot, Denys Lombard, and Ptak, South China and Maritime Asia, vol. 7 (Wiesbaden: Harrassowitz, 1998), 157–93; Ptak, "Quanzhou to the Zulu Zone"; Ptak, *China's Seaborne Trade with South and Southeast Asia (1200–1750)* (Aldershot, UK: Ashgate, 1999).

16. The version used in the present study is found in the *Siku quanshu* (*SKQS*) compendium, Zhu Jianmin 朱建民 et al., eds., *Yingjing wenyuange siku quanshu* 印景文淵閣四庫全書 (Taipei: Taiwan Shangwu Yinshuguan Gongsi, 1984), 1038:273–312.

17. The version used here is the one annotated by Tu Youxiang. Tu Youxiang 屠友祥, *Zhou Qufei: Lingwai daida* 周去非: 嶺外代答 (Shanghai: Yuandong Chubanshe, 1996).

18. The version used here is found in the *SKQS.* Zhu et al., Yingjing wenyuange *siku quanshu,* 864:259–409.

19. The version used here is the annotated one published by the Hong Kong University Press. Chen Jiarong 陳佳榮 and Qian Jiang 錢江, *Zhufanzhi zhubu* 諸蕃志注補 (Hong Kong: Hong Kong University Press, 2000).

20. The version used here is Zhonghua Shuju Bianjiaobu 中華書局編輯部, ed., *Songhuiyao jigao* 宋會要輯稿 (Beijing: Zhonghua Shuju, 1957).

21. The version used here is Wang Yunwu 王云五, ed., *Ma Duanlin: Wenxian tongkao* 馬端臨: 文獻通考 (Shanghai: Shangwu Yinshuguan, 1936).

22. The version used here is found in the *SKQS. SKQS* 280:1–288:912.

23. The version used here is found in the *SKQS. SKQS* 292:1–295:739.

24. The version used here is Zhonghua Shuju Bianjiaobu, ed., *Songyuan difangzhi congkan* 宋元地方志叢刊, 8 vols. (Beijing: Zhonghua Shuju, 1990), 8:8413–53.

25. The version used here is found in the *SKQS*. Fudan daxue tushuguan gujibu 復旦大學圖書館古籍部, *Xuxiu siku quanshu* 續修四庫全書 (Shanghai: Shanghai guji Chubanshe, 1995), 787:1–650.

26. The version used here is Su Jiqing 穌繼慶, ed., *Daoyi zhilue jiaoshi* 島夷志略校釋 (Beijing: Zhonghua Shuju, 1981).

27. For a more detailed discussion on this issue, see Derek T. S. Heng, "Economic Exchanges and Linkages between the Malay Region and the Hinterland of China's Coastal Ports during the 10th to 14th Centuries," in *Early Singapore 1300s–1819, Evidence in Maps, Text and Artefacts,* ed. John N. Miksic and Cheryl-Ann Low Mei Gek (Singapore: Singapore History Museum, 2004), 73–85; Heng, "Economic Interaction between China and the Malacca Straits Region, Tenth to Fourteenth Centuries AD" (PhD thesis, Center for Southeast Asian Studies, University of Hull, 2005), 130–62.

28. So Kee Long, "The Trade Ceramics Industry in Southern Fukien During the Sung," *Journal of Sung-Yuan Studies* 24 (1994): 1–19; Ho Chuimei, "The Ceramic Boom in Minnan during Song and Yuan Times," in *The Emporium of the World: Maritime Quanzhou, 1000–1400,* ed. Angela Schottenhammer (Leiden: Brill, 2001), 237–82.

29. Past studies of Chinese ceramics found at Southeast Asian sites that were carried out by Southeast Asianists without access to more recent studies of Chinese kiln sites lack the precision that is now possible. See Eine Moore, "A Suggested Classification of Stonewares of Martabani Type," *SMJ* 18 (1970): 1–78; Barbara Harrisson, *Pusaka: Heirloom Jars of Borneo* (Singapore: Oxford University Press, 1986); Lucas Chin, *Ceramics in the Sarawak Museum* (Kuching: Sarawak Museum, 1988).

30. Michael Flecker and William M. Mathers, eds., *Archaeological Recovery of the Java Sea Wreck* (Annapolis: Pacific Sea Resources, 1997); Flecker, "The Archaeological Recovery of the Tenth-Century Intan Shipwreck" (PhD diss., National University of Singapore, 2001); Abu Ridho and Edmund Edwards McKinnon, *The Pulau Buaya Wreck: Finds from the Song Period,* ed. Sumarah Adhyatman (Jakarta: Ceramic Society of Indonesia, 1998); Roxanna Brown and Sten Sjostrand, Turiang: *A Fourteenth-Century Shipwreck in Southeast Asian Waters* (Pasadena, CA: Pacific Asia Museum, 2000); Douglas Merwin, "Selections from Wen-Wu on the Excavation of a Sung Dynasty Seagoing Vessel in Chuan-Chou," *Chinese Sociology and Anthropology* 9, no. 3 (Spring 1977): 3–106; Nanjing Yaoxueyuan 南京藥學院 et al., "Quanzhouwan chutu songdai muzhao haichuan changnei jiangxiang de xiangwei jianding" 泉州灣出土宋

代木造海船艙內降香的顯微鑒定, *HJSYJ*, 1983, 115–16; Shanghaishi Weishengju Yaoping Yenjiusuo 上海市衛生局藥品檢驗所 et al., "Quanzhouwan chutu songdai muzao haichuan cangnei jiangxiang de huaxue jianding" 泉州灣出土木造海船艙內降香的化學鑒定, *HJSYJ*, 1983, 117–21. Only one of these wrecks is named for a ship, the *Turiang*. The others are named for the location of the site.

31. Edmund Edwards McKinnon, "Kota Cina: Its Context and Meaning in the Trade of Southeast Asia in the Twelfth to Fourteenth Centuries," 2 vols. (PhD thesis, Cornell University, 1984); H. G. Quaritch Wales, "Archaeological Researches on Ancient Indian Culture and Mahayana Buddhism from Sites in Kedah," *JMBRAS* 18, no. 1 (1940): 1–85; D. Wales and Q. Wales, "Further Work on Indian Sites in Malaya," *JMBRAS* 20, no. 1 (1947): 1–11; Alastair Lamb, "Some Notes on the Distribution of Indianised Sites in Kedah," *JSSS* 15, no. 2 (1959): 99–111; Lamb, "Recent Archaeological Work in Kedah, 1958," *JMBRAS* 32, no. 1 (1959): 214–32; Lamb, "Report on the Excavation and Reconstruction of Chandi Bukit Batu Pahat, Central Kedah," *FMJ* 5 (1960): x–108; Lamb, *Chandi Bukit Batu Pahat: A Report on the Excavation of an Ancient Temple in Kedah* (Singapore: Eastern Universities Press, 1961); Lamb, *Chandi Bukit Batu Pahat: Three Additional Notes* (Singapore: Eastern Universities Press, 1966). B. A. V. Peacock, "New Light on the Ancient Settlement of Kedah and Province Wellesley," *MIH* 8, no. 2 (1970): 20–27; Peacock, "Pillar Base Architecture in Ancient Kedah," *JMBRAS* 47, no. 1 (1974): 66–86; Jabatan Muzium dan Antikuiti, Unit Arkeologi, *Ladangan projek penyelidikan arkeologi Candi Sungai Mas (Situs 32) Mukin Kota, daerah Kuala Muda, Kedah Darul Aman,* fasa 8 (Kuala Lumpur: Jabatan Muzium dan Antikuiti, Unit Arkeologi, 1985); S. J. Allen, *Trade, Transportation, and Tributaries: Exchange, Agriculture and Settlement Distribution in Early Historic-Period Kedah, Malaysia* (Michigan: University Microfilms International, 1988); John N. Miksic, *Archaeological Research on the "Forbidden Hill" of Singapore: Excavations at Fort Canning* (Singapore: National Heritage Board, 1985); Miksic, "Beyond the Grave: Excavations North of the Kramat Iskandar Shah, 1988," *Heritage* 10 (1989): 34–56; Marie-France Dupoizat, "La céramique chinoise du site de Lobu Tua à Barus: Premières analyses," *Archipel* 51 (1996): 46–52; Claude Guillot, *Histoire de Barus, Sumatra: Le site de Lobu Tua, sous la direction de Claude Guillot* (Paris: Association Archipel, 1998); Guillot, "La nature du site de Lobu Tua a Barus, Sumatra," in *From the Mediterranean to the China Sea: Miscellaneous Notes,* ed. Claude Guillot, Denys Lombard, and Roderich Ptak (Wiesbaden: Harrassowitz, 1998), 113–30; Edmund Edwards McKinnon and Tengku Luckman Sinar, "A Note on Pulau Kompei in Aru Bay, Northeastern Sumatra," *Indonesia* 32

(1981): 49–73; Hassan Shuhaimi Nik and Othman bin Mohamad Yatim, *Antiquities of the Bujang Valley* (Kuala Lumpur: Museum Association of Malaysia, 1990).

32. Jabatan Muzium–Muzium Brunei, *Sungai Limau Manis: Tapak arkeologi abad ke-10–13 Masihi* (Bandar Seri Begawan, Negara Brunei Darussalam: Jabatan Muzium–Muzium Brunei, Kementerian Kebudayaan, Belia dan Sukan, 2004).

Chapter 1: Sino-Malay Interaction in the First Millennium AD

1. For a detailed discussion on the coastal-hinterland economic symbiosis in the region, see Bennet Bronson, "Exchange at the Upstream and Downstream Ends: Notes towards a Functional Model of the Coastal State in Southeast Asia," in *Economic Exchange and Social Interaction in Southeast Asia: Perspectives from Prehistory, History, and Ethnography,* ed. K. L. Hutterer (Ann Arbor: University of Michigan, 1977), 39–52. For a detailed discussion of the hinterland-coastal economic interaction in Sumatra, see John N. Miksic, "Traditional Sumatran Trade," *BEFEO* 74 (1985): 423–67.

2. Bronson, "Exchange."

3. Kenneth R. Hall, "Economic History of Early Southeast Asia," in *The Cambridge History of Southeast Asia,* vol. 1, *From Early Times to c. 1800,* ed. Nicholas Tarling (Cambridge: Cambridge University Press, 1999), 194.

4. *LSS* 5:15a, 16b.

5. O. W. Wolters, *Early Indonesian Commerce: A Study of the Origins of Srivijaya* (Ithaca: Cornell University Press, 1967), 214.

6. *Tanghuiyao* (Beijing: Zhonghua Shuju, 1956), 100:1782–83.

7. *CFYG* 970:11398b.

8. For an account of the travels of Fa Xian, see Faxian, *Travels of Fah-Hian and Sung-Yun, Buddhist Pilgrims: From China to India (400 AD and 518 AD),* trans. Samuel Beal (Madras: Asian Educational Services, 1993).

9. Wang Gungwu, *The Nanhai Trade: The Early History of Chinese Trade in the South China Sea* (Singapore: Times Academic Press, 1998), 96.

10. J. Kuwabara, "On P'u Shou-Keng," *Memoirs of the Research Department of the Toyo Bunko,* 1928, no. 2:8.

11. Wang, *Nanhai Trade,* 93.

12. Ibid., 96.

13. Wolters, *Early Indonesian Commerce,* 214. For a more detailed discussion of Holing, see W. J. van der Meulen, "In Search of Ho-Ling," *Indonesia* 23 (1977): 86–111.

14. Wolters, *Early Indonesian Commerce,* 214.

15. *Tanghuiyao* 100:1790.

16. Meulen, "Ho-Ling," 90.

17. *XTS* 222:5a; *Tanghuiyao* 100:1799.

18. Wolters, *Early Indonesian Commerce*, 231.

19. Wang, *Nanhai Trade*, 96.

20. See Tansen Sen, *Buddhism, Diplomacy, and Trade: The Realignment of Sino-Indian Relations, 600–1400* (Honolulu: University of Hawaii Press, 2003), 55–107.

21. Wolters, *Early Indonesian Commerce*, 153.

22. Ibid.

23. Ibid., 154.

24. P. Yves Manguin, "The Trading Ships of Insular Southeast Asia: New Evidence from Indonesian Archaeological Sites," in *Pertemuan ilmiah arkeologi V, Yogyakarta*, 4 vols. (Jakarta: Ikatan Ahli Arkeologi Indonesia, 1989), 1:200–220.

25. Wolters, *Early Indonesian Commerce*, 152.

26. For a detailed report on the wreck, see Michael Flecker, "The Archaeological Recovery of the Tenth-Century Intan Shipwreck" (PhD diss., National University of Singapore, 2001). Also see Denis Twitchett and Janice Stargardt, "Chinese Silver Bullion in a Tenth-Century Indonesian Wreck," *Asia Major*, 3rd ser., 15, no. 1 (2002): 23–72.

27. For a detailed account of the Huang Chao rebellion, see Huang Chao, *The Biography of Huang Chao*, trans. Howard Levy (Los Angeles: University of California Press, 1955).

28. For more detailed discussions on the role of Middle Eastern traders in the trade between China Southeast Asia and the Indian Ocean littoral, see Wolters, *Early Indonesian Commerce;* Gabriel Ferrand, *Relations de voyages et texts géographiques arabes, persans et turks relatifs à l'extrême-Orient du VIIIe au XVIIIe siècles*, 2 vols. (Paris: E. Leroux, 1912). For more detailed accounts of Arab navigation in the Malay region and between Maritime Southeast Asia and China, see G. R. Tibbetts, *A Study of the Arabic Texts Containing Material on Southeast Asia* (Leiden: Brill, 1979), 25–65.

29. For a preliminary report on the wreck, see Michael Flecker, "A Ninth-Century AD Arab or Indian Shipwreck in Indonesia: First Evidence for Direct Trade with China," *World Archaeology* 32, no. 3 (2001): 335–54.

30. For an overview of Chinese maritime technology, see Andrew Watson, ed. and trans., *Transport in Transition: The Evolution of Traditional Shipping in China*, Michigan Abstracts of Chinese and Japanese Works on Chinese History, no. 3 (Ann Arbor: Center for Chinese Studies, University of Michigan, 1972); Gang Deng, *Chinese Maritime Activities and Socioeconomic Development, c. 2100 BC–1900 AD* (Westport, CT:

Greenwood, 1997); Gang, *Maritime Sector, Institutions, and Sea Power of Premodern China* (Westport, CT: Greenwood, 1999).

31. See, for example, O. W. Wolters, "Restudying Some Chinese Writings on Sriwijaya," *Indonesia* 42 (1986): 1–42.

32. See, for example, Yao Silian 姚思廉, *Liangshu* 梁書 (Beijing: Zhonghua Shuju, 1973), 33:2b–3a.

33. Kuwabara, "On P'u Shou-Keng," 14.

34. For a list and description of the products imported by China through Southeast Asia during the first millennium AD, see Ji Han, *Nan-fang ts'ao Mu Chuang: A Fourth-Century Flora of Southeast Asia,* trans. Li Hui-Lin (Hong Kong: Chinese University Press, 1979). For a more detailed study of China's trade in maritime Asian products in the late first and early second millennia AD, see Paul Wheatley, "Geographical Notes on Some Commodities Involved in Sung Maritime Trade," *JMBRAS* 32, no. 2 (1959): 5–140. For a more detailed ethnographic study of the uses of these products in the Southeast Asian context, see I. H. Burkill, *A Dictionary of the Economic Products of the Malay Peninsula* (Oxford: Oxford University Press, 1966).

35. For a detailed study on cloves, see Roderich Ptak, "China and the Trade in Cloves, circa 960–1435," *JAOS* 113, no. 1 (1993): 1–13.

36. See Wolters, *Early Indonesian Commerce,* 95–110.

37. See Sumarah Adhyatman, *Antique Ceramics Found in Indonesia* (Jakarta: Ceramic Society of Indonesia, 1990); Abu Ridho, "Penelitian keramik di situs-situs arkeologi provinsi Jambi," in *Laporan: Hasil penelitian arkeologi dan geologi propinsi Jambi, 1994–1995* (Jambi: Pemerintah daerah tingkat I provinsi Jambi, 1995), 198–231; Hassan Shuhaimi Nik and Othman bin Mohamad Yatim, *Antiquities of the Bujang Valley* (Kuala Lumpur: Museum Association of Malaysia, 1990).

38. Flecker, "Arab or Indian Shipwreck," 339–44.

39. For a more detailed discussion of metals as a trade commodity in premodern Southeast Asia, see Bennet Bronson, "Patterns in the Early Southeast Asian Metals Trade," in *Early Metallurgy, Trade and Urban Centers in Thailand and Southeast Asia,* ed. Ian Glover, Pornchai Suchitta, and John Villiers (Bangkok: White Lotus, 1992), 63–114.

40. Flecker, "Arab or Indian Shipwreck," 339.

41. Ibid., 339.

42. See, for example, the finds recovered from the Intan wreck. Flecker, "Intan Shipwreck," 207–11.

43. For a more detailed study of the role of Guangzhou in the first millennium AD, see Guan Luquan 關履權, *Songdai guangzhou de haiwai maoyi* 宋代廣州的海外貿易 (Guangzhou: Guangdong Renmin Chubanshe, 1994), 8–52.

44. For a more detailed discussion of Chinese maritime trade during the interregnum period, see Angela Schottenhammer, "Local Politico-economic Particulars of the Quanzhou Region during the Tenth Century," *JSYS* 29 (1991): 1–41; Schottenhammer, "The Maritime Trade of Quanzhou (Zaiton) from the Ninth through the Thirteenth Century," in *Archaeology of Seafaring: The Indian Ocean in the Ancient Period,* Indian Council of Historical Research Monograph Series 1, ed. Himanshu Prabha Ray (Delhi: Pragati, 1999), 271–90.

45. Hugh R. Clark, *Community, Trade, and Networks: Southern Fujian Province from the Third to the Thirteenth Century* (Cambridge: Cambridge University Press, 1991), 64–70.

46. Guan Luquan 關履權, "Songdai guangzhou de haiwai maoyi yi" 宋代廣州的香料貿易, 48, 49.

47. Clark, *Community, Trade,* 66.

48. *WXTK* 332:2610, 2.

Chapter 2: China's Economic Relations with Maritime Asia

1. The term "Dashi" in the Song texts refers to the 'Abbasid caliphate (750–1258). However, almost all current scholarly publications refer to the Dashi as Arabs, and I follow that convenion here.

2. *SHY zhiguan* (ZG) 44:1a; *WXTK* 20:200, 3; *SS* 186:23a. Detailed discussions of the identification of these place names may be found in Chen Jiarong 陳佳榮, *Gudai nanhai diming huishi* 古代南海地明會史 (Beijing: Zhonghua Shuju, 1986).

3. *SHY* ZG 44:1b.

4. Ibid.

5. Ibid.; *SS* 186:24a.

6. *SS* 186:23b.

7. *SHY* ZG 44:2a,b.

8. These eight products were tortoise shells, ivory, rhinoceros horns, steel, turtle carapaces, coral, agate, and frankincense. *SHY* ZG 44:2a,b.

9. *WXTK* 20:200, 3.

10. Ibid., 20:201, 1.

11. Ibid., 339:2664, 1.

12. *SHY* ZG 44:2b.

13. Ibid., ZG 44:3a–b.

14. O. W. Wolters, "Restudying Some Chinese Writings on Sriwijaya," *Indonesia* 42 (1986): 36.

15. *WXTK* 20:201, 1.

16. *SS* 186:24a.

17. Ibid.

18. Hugh R. Clark, "The Politics of Trade and the Establishment of the Quanzhou Trade Superintendency," in *China and the Maritime Silk Route,* ed. Quanzhou International Seminar on China and the Maritime Routes of the Silk Roads Organization Committee (Fujian: Fujian People's Publishing House, 1991), 387; Paul Wheatley, "Geographical Notes on Some Commodities Involved in Sung Maritime Trade," *JMBRAS* 32, no. 2 (1959): 24.

19. For a detailed study on the impact of the Wang Anshi reforms on the Song salt monopoly, see Cecilia Lee-Fang Chien, *Salt and State: An Annotated Translation of the Songshi Salt Monopoly Treatise* (Ann Arbor: Center for Chinese Studies, University of Michigan, 2004), 3–90.

20. H. R. Williamson, *Wang An Shih: A Chinese Statesman and Educationalist of the Sung Dynasty,* 2 vols. (London: Arthur Probsthain, 1935).

21. Arjan van Aelst, "Majapahit Picis: The Currency of a 'Moneyless' Society," *Bijdragen tot de taal-, land- en volkenkunde* 151, no. 3 (1995): 361–62; Jan Wisseman-Christie, "Money and Its Uses in the Javanese States of the Ninth to Fifteenth Centuries AD," *JESHO* 39, no. 3 (1996): 268–71.

22. *WXTK* 20:201, 1; *SS* 186:24a.

23. *SS* 186:24a.

24. *WXTK* 20:201, 1.

25. Ibid.

26. Yoshinobu Shiba, "Sung Foreign Trade: Its Scope and Organization," in *China among Equals: The Middle Kingdom and Its Neighbours, 10th–14th Centuries,* ed. Morris Rossabi (Berkeley: University of California Press, 1983), 92.

27. Van Aelst, "Majapahit Picis," 374; Brigitte Borell, "Money in Fourteenth-Century Singapore," paper presented at the Seventh International Conference of the European Association of Southeast Asian Archaeologists, Berlin, September 1996, table 2.

28. Van Aelst, "Majapahit Picis"; Borell, "Money," 7; Edmund Edwards McKinnon, "Kota Cina: Its Context and Meaning in the Trade of Southeast Asia in the Twelfth to Fourteenth Centuries," 2 vols. (PhD diss., Cornell University, 1984), 106–12; Derek T. S. Heng, "Export Commodity and Regional Currency: The Role of Chinese Copper Coins in the Malacca Straits Region, Tenth to Fourteenth Centuries," *JSEAS* 37, no. 2 (2006): 179–203.

29. Robert Hartwell, "The Evolution of the Early Northern Sung Monetary System, AD 960–1025," *JAOS* 87, no. 3 (1967): 284; Jerome Chen, "Sung Bronzes: An Economic Analysis," *Bulletin of Oriental and African Studies* 28, no. 3 (1968): 619.

30. Grace Wong, *A Commentary on the Tributary Trade between China and Southeast Asia, and the Place of Porcelain in This Trade during the Period*

of the Song Dynasty in China, Southeast Asian Ceramics Society (Singapore) Transaction 7 (Singapore: Southeast Asian Ceramics Society, 1979), 10, 16, 18.

31. *SS* 489:14090; *WXTK* 332:2610, 2.

32. *SHY ZG* 44:27.

33. Ibid., 44:11a–b, 44:27a–28a.

34. *WXTK* 20:200, 3.

35. *SHY ZG* 44:8a–b.

36. Ibid., 44:8a; *SS* 186:26a; *WXTK* 62:563, 1. For a discussion of the establishment of the Quanzhou mercantile shipping superintendency and its impact on Chinese maritime trade, see Clark, *Community, Trade, and Networks: Southern Fujian Province from the Third to the Thirteenth Century* (Cambridge: Cambridge University Press, 1991), 127–35; Clark, "Politics of Trade."

37. *WXTK* 20:200, 3.

38. *PZKT* 2:2a–4a. Watson, *Transport in Transition.*

39. For a more detailed discussion of the development of China's import trade in Southeast Asian and Malay products, see chapter 6.

40. *PZKT* 2:1b; *SHY ZG* 44:27.

41. *SHY ZG* 44:27a–28a.

42. C. P. Fitzgerald, *China: A Short Cultural History* (London: Barrie and Jenkins, 1978), 392.

43. Ibid., 392–94.

44. Wisseman, "Money and Its Uses," 269.

45. *SHY ZG* 44:11b–12a; *WXTK* 20:201, 3.

46. *SHY ZG* 44:12a–b; *WXTK* 62:563, 1.

47. *SHY ZG* 44:17a.

48. *SS* 185:32a; *SHY ZG* 44:19b.

49. *WXTK* 20:201, 3; *SS* 185:32a.

50. *SHY ZG* 44:12a–b.

51. Ibid., 44:19b–20b; *SS* 185:32a.

52. *SHY ZG* 44:19b–20b; *SS* 185:32a.

53. *SHY ZG* 44:24a–b.

54. Ibid., 44:17b–19b.

55. Ibid., 44:19b–20b.

56. Ibid., 44:21a–23a.

57. Ibid.

58. Ibid., 44:25b–26b.

59. Ibid., 44:19b–20b, 44:20b–21a, 44:26b–27a.

60. Ibid., 44:20b.

61. *WXTK* 20:201; *SHY ZG* 44:26a.

62. For a more detailed study of the economic activities of the hinterlands of the Chinese coastal port-cities, and in particular that of the southern Fujian and Quanzhou, see Clark, *Community, Trade,* 141–67.

63. *SHY* ZG 44:24b–25a; *WXTK* 62:563:2.

64. *SHY* ZG 44:27a–28a.

65. Ibid.; *WXTK* 20:201:3.

66. *SHY* ZG 44: 27a–28a; *WXTK* 20:201:3.

67. *SHY* ZG 44:2a.

68. Ibid., 44:27a–28a; *WXTK* 20:201:3.

69. *SS* 186:32a.

70. *SHY* ZG 44:27a–28a.

71. Tu Youxiang 屠友祥, *Zhou Qufei: Lingwai daida* 周去非: 嶺外代答 (Shanghai: Yuandong Chubanshe, 1996), 141–210.

72. So Kee Long, "Dissolving Hegemony or Changing Trade Pattern? Images of Srivijaya in the Chinese Sources of the Twelfth and Thirteenth Centuries," *JSEAS* 29, no. 2 (1998): 303.

73. *SHY* ZG 44:27a–28a.

74. So, "Dissolving Hegemony," 303; Chen Jiarong 陳佳榮 and Qian Jiang 錢江, *Zhufanzhi zhubu* 諸蕃志注補 (Hong Kong: Hong Kong University Press, 2000), 46, 47, 319.

75. Su Jiqing 穌繼慶, ed., *Daoyi zhilue jiaoshi* 島夷志略校釋 (Beijing: Zhonghua Shuju, 1981), 141, 187.

76. *DDNHZ* 7:18a.

77. *YS* 94:25a.

78. Ibid., 94:26a.

79. Ibid., 94:26b.

80. Ibid.

81. Ibid.

82. Ibid.

83. Ibid., 94:25a.

84. Ibid., 94:25a–26b.

85. Song Lian, *Economic Structure of the Yüan Dynasty,* trans. Herbert Franz Schurmann (Cambridge, MA: Harvard University Press, 1967), 224.

86. Ibid.

87. Billy So Kee Long, *Prosperity, Region, and Institutions in Maritime China: The South Fukien Pattern, 946–1368* (Cambridge, MA: Harvard University Asia Center, 2000), 107–17.

88. For a more detailed discussion of the role of locally born Middle Eastern merchant families in the Chinese ports during the Yuan, see So, *Prosperity, Region,* 206–8; John Chaffee, "Diasporic Identities in the

Historical Development of the Maritime Muslim Communities of Song-Yuan China," *JESHO* 49, no. 4 (2006): 412–16.

89. *YS* 94:24a.

90. *YDZ* 22:71a–79b.

91. *YS* 94:24b.

92. Schurmann, *Economic Structure,* 225.

93. *YDZ* 22:71a–79b.

94. Yu Changsen 喻常森, *Yuandai haiwai maoyi* 元代海外貿易 (Xian: Xibei daxue Chubanshe, 1994), 91.

95. *YS* 94:26b.

96. Ibid.

97. Ibid.

Chapter 3: The Malay Region's Diplomatic and Economic Interactions with China

1. *SHY* ZG 44:2b; *SS* 186:23b.

2. See Wang Gungwu, *The Nanhai Trade: The Early History of Chinese Trade in the South China Sea* (Singapore: Times Academic Press, 1998); Paul Wheatley, *The Golden Khersonese: Studies in the Historical Geography of the Malay Peninsula before AD 1500* (Westport, CT: Greenwood, 1973), chs. 1–5.

3. *WXTK* 339:2663, 3.

4. For a more detailed discussion of this apparent focus by the Malay region on a specific port of call in China during the tenth to the twelfth centuries, see chapter 4.

5. Champa's mission was the second to arrive in China, three months after Srivijaya's, while the Arab's inaugural mission arrived in 968. Grace Wong, *A Commentary on the Tributary Trade between China and Southeast Asia, and the Place of Porcelain in This Trade during the Period of the Song Dynasty in China,* Southeast Asian Ceramics Society (Singapore) Transaction 7 (Singapore: Southeast Asian Ceramics Society, 1979), 6, 13, 17.

6. The Chinese historical texts are currently the only known sources to contain references to the names of the Srivijayan kings of the tenth to the twelfth centuries. The only exception pertains to a temple inscription found in Nagapattinam, which mentions the names of two Srivijayan kings who reigned at the beginning of the eleventh century. George Coedès, "Le royaume de Crivijaya," *BEFEO* 18, no. 6 (1918): 7.

7. *SS* 489:14088; *SHY* FY 7:1a. The location of the reception of tribute, the tribute items, and the reciprocal gifts were not recorded.

8. *SS* 489:14088; *SHY* FY 7:2a; *WXTK* 332:2610, 2. The location of the reception of tribute, the tribute items, and the reciprocal gifts were not recorded for either occasion.

9. *WXTK* 332:2610, 2; *SS* 489:14088. The location of the reception of tribute and the tribute items were not recorded. However, it was noted that the envoys were awarded two sets of harnesses, as well as white-yak tails, white stoneware, lacquerware, and silks.

10. *WXTK* 332:2610, 2; *SS* 489:14088. Glass crystals and a petroleum product were presented as tribute. The location of the reception of tribute and the reciprocal gifts were not noted.

11. *WXTK* 332:2610, 2; *SS* 489:14089. No details of the tribute mission have been recorded.

12. *WXTK* 332:2610, 2, *SS* 489:14089. Tribute of elephant tusks, frankincense, rosewater, dates, white granulated sugar, crystals, glass bottles, and branches of coral were presented. The location of the reception of tribute and the reciprocal gifts were not noted.

13. *SS* 489:14089; *WXTK* 332:2610, 2. Tribute of produce of the land was presented. The location of the reception of tribute was not noted. The mission envoy was rewarded with a splendid headdress, gold- and silverware, and copper cash.

14. *SS* 489:14089; *WXTK* 332:2610, 2. The mission presented aromatic products, rhinoceros horns, and elephant tusks. The place of reception and the reciprocal gifts were not noted.

15. *SS* 489:14089. The tribute included Arabian brocade, Yuelue cloth, rhinoceros horns, glass bottles, elephant tusks, aromatics, and a crystal Buddha. The place of reception and the reciprocal gifts were not noted.

16. *WXTK* 332:2610, 2; *SS* 489:14089. The envoy, a ship captain named Jin Huayi, arrived with tribute consisting of produce of the land. The place of reception and the reciprocal gifts were not recorded.

17. *SS* 489:14089. No details concerning the mission were recorded.

18. *SHY* FY 7:12b; *SS* 489:14089; *WXTK* 332:2610, 2. The tribute consisted of a Buddhist sutra in a green wooden box; amber, red, green, and white crystals, 1 red and 1 black wooden rosary in an inlaid box; 5 deerskin baskets; 1 swing of red silk with bronze and iron studs; incise-decorated cups and various drinking vessels; boxes inlaid with gold; boxes covered with deer fur; an inlaid scroll table; gold and copper water vessels; iron swords; 20 bat wings; a pair of inlaid comb boxes, one of which contained 270 wooden combs and the other a dragon-bone comb; several pieces of white cloth with coins (attached?); a pair of camphor screens; an inlaid saddle, and 700 *jin* (catty) of sulfur (the jin was a unit of weight equal to 16 *liang* [tael], or 500 grams). The mission was headed by four persons. Each bore a document, one of which listed the items and quantities of the tribute; another was a memorial from the Srivijayan king. The place of reception and the reciprocal gifts were not recorded.

19. *WXTK* 332:2610, 2. No information on the mission has been recorded.

20. Wong, *Tributary Trade*, 13.

21. *WXTK* 332:2606, 2–3; *SHY* FY 4:97a–98a.

22. *SHY* ZG 44:2a–b.

23. *WXTK* 332:2610, 2; *SS* 489:15a.

24. For a more detailed discussion of the Srivijayan community sojourning at China's port-cities of Guangzhou and Quanzhou, see chapter 4.

25. *WXTK* 332:2610, 2.

26. *SHY* ZG 44:1a–b.

27. Wong, *Tributary Trade*, 17; *WXTK* 339:2663, 3.

28. *SS* 489:14089.

29. Some scholars feel that the missions dispatched by Srivijaya were often led by envoys who were non-Malays. In particular, Middle Eastern individuals appear to have served often as Srivijayan envoys to China during the tenth to twelfth centuries. As such, it may appear at first glance that the use of the phrase "home-based political elite" may be erroneous. However, the place of non-Malay individuals as the political elite of such Malay coastal polities as Srivijaya needs to be understood within the context of premodern coastal Malay societies. The coastal port-polities had, until the establishment of the modern nation-state in the twentieth century, been political entities that were open to the influx of people from outside the indigenous fold. They included individuals from such places as India, the Middle East, Southeast Asia, and China, who, as *orang kaya,* or land-based elites, became based in a Malay coastal port-polity and became engaged in a patron-client relationship with the polity's ruler. In other words, they became, and were regarded as, an integral part of the port-polity's society. It would therefore not be surprising that non-Malay individuals, as the land-based elite of a Malay coastal port-polity, would be tasked by the ruler of a Malay polity, such as Srivijaya, to lead a state-level mission to China. For a more in-depth discussion of premodern Malay sociopolitical structures, see O. W. Wolters, *History, Culture and Region in Southeast Asian Perspectives* (Singapore: Institute of Southeast Asian Studies, 1999), 43; A. C. Milner, *The Malay Raja: A Study of Malay Political Culture in East Sumatra and the Malay Peninsula in the Early Nineteenth Century* (Ann Arbor: University Microfilms International, 1977), 74, 75, 77; J. M. Gullick, *Indigenous Political Systems of Western Malaya* (London: Athlone, 1958), 44–61, 65–94. For a discussion of the possible role of Middle Eastern persons in the Srivijayan state-level missions to China, see Tansen Sen, *Buddhism, Diplomacy and Trade: The Realignment of Sino-Indian Relations, 600—1400* (Honolulu: University of Hawaii Press, 2003), 167.

30. *PZKT* 2:2a–b.

31. *WXTK* 332:2610, 2; *SS* 489:14089.

32. George Coedès, *The Indianised States of Southeast Asia,* trans. Susan Brown Cowing, ed. Walter F. Vella (Kuala Lumpur: University of Malaya Press, 1968), 88–94.

33. Ibid., 132.

34. Wong, *Tributary Trade,* 16–17.

35. *SHY* FY 4:97a–98a; *WXTK* 332:2606, 2–3.

36. *SS* 489:14089; *WXTK* 332:2610, 2.

37. *SS* 489:14089; *WXTK* 332:2610, 2.

38. *SS* 489:14089; *WXTK* 332:2610, 2.

39. O. W. Wolters, "Tambralingga," *Bulletin of the School of Oriental and African Studies* 21, no. 3 (1958): 605.

40. Coedès, "Crivijaya," 5.

41. B. C. Chandra, Department of Archaeology, *Annual Report on Indian Epigraphy for 1956–57* (New Delhi: Manager of Publications, 1957), 15.

42. *SHY* ZG 44:2a-b.

43. Ibid., 44:2b–3b.

44. *WXTK* 339:2664, 1.

45. For discussions on the Chola raids on the Malacca Strait and their ramifications for Srivijaya, see Hermann Kulke, "Rivalry and Competition in the Bay of Bengal in the Eleventh Century and Its Bearing on Indian Ocean Studies," in *Commerce and Culture in the Bay of Bengal, 1500–1800,* ed. Om Prakash and Denys Lombard (New Delhi: Manohar, 1999), 17–35; George Spencer, *The Politics of Expansion: The Chola Conquest of Sri Lanka and Sri Vijaya* (Madras: New Era, 1983). Also see Tan Yeok Seong, "The Sri Vijayan Inscription of Canton (AD 1079)," *JSEAH* 5, no. 2 (1964): 20.

46. Tan, "Sri Vijayan Inscription," 17–25.

47. Ibid., 23.

48. Ibid., 17–25.

49. Tu Youxiang 屠友祥, *Zhou Qufei: Lingwai daida* 周去非: 嶺外代答 (Shanghai: Yuandong Chubanshe, 1996), 42.

50. *SHY* ZG 44:6b; *SS* 489:14090.

51. Coedès, "Crivijaya," 1–36.

52. Charles O. Hucker, *A Dictionary of Official Titles in Imperial China* (Stanford: Stanford University Press, 1985), 301.

53. *SHY* FY 4: 91b–92a.

54. *SS* 489:14090.

55. *SHY* ZG 44:6b; *SS* 489:14090.

56. *SHY* ZG 44:9a.

57. *PZKT* 2:4b–5a.
58. Ibid., 2:6b–7a.
59. Ibid., 2:5a–b.
60. Ibid., 2:5a–b.
61. Wong, *Tributary Trade,* 3, 10, 15, 19.
62. *SHY* ZG 44:11a–b.
63. Ibid., 44:4b–5a; *ZG* 44:11a–b.
64. *SHY* ZG 44:9b–10a.
65. Ibid., 44:9a.
66. Ibid., 44:11a–b.
67. Ibid., 44:12a–b.
68. *WXTK* 62:563, 1.
69. The tribute presented comprised pearls, elephant tusks, ambergris, coral, and aromatics. The reciprocal gifts consisted of a saddled horse, ceremonial clothes, a belt, and a silver vase. The Srivijayan king was also granted an honorary title. The place of the tribute has not been recorded. *SS* 119:25a.

70. *SS* 489:14090; *SHY* FY 7:28a. The tribute presented comprised 1 piece of ambergris weighing 36 jin, 113 liang of pearls, 1 coral tree weighing 240 liang, 8 rhinoceros horns, 3 plum-blossom camphor pieces, 200 liang of plum-blossom camphor planks, 39 pieces of glassware, 39 diamond, cat's-eye, and green-agate rings, 13 large pearls, civet, 28 bolts of foreign textiles, sugar in 4 Arabian glass bottles, 168 jin of rose water, 9 long jeweled steel swords, 6 short steel swords, 81,680 jin of frankincense, 87 elephant tusks weighing 4,065 jin, liquid storax, 278 jin of pachak (roots used as incense), 117 jin of cloves, 30 jin of dragon's blood, 58 jin of asafoetida, 127 jin of nutmeg, 2,674 jin of pepper, 10,750 jin of sandalwood incense, and 19,935 jin of jian gharuwood incense. The mission was received by the Song court. The title of "commandant who instructs loyalty" was conferred upon the chief envoy, while the two assistant envoys were also granted the title of commandant. The mission envoys were also paid cash equal to the value of the tribute.

71. *SHY* FY 7:55b–56a; *WXTK* 332:2610, 3. The tribute presented comprised 81.7 liang of pearls, 4 plum-blossom camphor planks weighing 14 jin, 23 liang of ambergris, 1 box containing 40 liang of coral, 189 pieces of glassware, 10 Guangyin bottles, 4 green glass bottles, 6 green-lipped glass bottles, 5 glass bottles with narrow and wide lips, 2 round glass bottles, 2 glass bottles with small rim-lips, 4 clear glass bottles, 42 glass bottles, 8 shallow trays, 3 square trays, 38 round trays, 1 long tray, 2 dishes, 2 clear glass bottles with gold inlay, 1 set of lidded wine cups with gold inlay, 1 water bottle with gold inlay, 3 wine vessels, 2 small wine vessels, 1 incense burner, 22 small and large jars, 33 small and large pots, 4 small and large

dishes, 2 small and large sunflower dishes, foreign sugar, foreign dates in 3 glass bottles weighing 8 jin, gardenia flowers, 4 glass bottles weighing 180 liang, 60 elephant tusks weighing 2,109 jin, 1,550 jin of pepper, 85 jin of a mixture of jian and su gharuwood incense, 3,009 jin of rosewater, 80 jin of nutmeg, 230 jin of asafoetida, 280 jin of myrrh, 210 jin of benzoin, 150 jin of tortoise shells, 85 jin of pachak, 1,570 jin of sandalwood incense, 11 cat's eyes, and 15 foreign swords. The mission was received at Quanzhou. The reciprocal gift was not recorded.

72. *SHY* FY 7:48b.

73. *PZKT* 2:5a–b.

74. *WXTK* 20:201, 3.

75. *SHY* ZG 44:24b–25a.

76. Ibid., 44:21a–23a.

77. Tu, *Zhou Qufei*, 42, 69.

78. Ibid., 69.

79. *WXTK* 332:2610, 3: *SS* 119:25a–b.

80. *WXTK* 332:2610, 3.

81. *SS* 489:18a. According to the text, "The emperor said, 'Distant people regard [our] culture with admiration, only this is to be praised, [and] not the benefit of attracting produce of the land.'"

82. *WXTK* 332:2610, 3.

83. *SHY* FY 7:55b–56a; *WXTK* 332:2610, 3.

84. Wolters, "Tambralingga," 605.

85. Herbert Franke, "Sung Embassies: Some General Observations," in *China Among Equals: The Middle Kingdom and Its Neighbours, 10th–14th centuries,* ed. Morris Rossabi (Berkeley: University of California Press, 1983), 119–20.

86. *WXTK* 332:2606, 3; *SHY* FY 4:97a–98a.

87. Chen Jiarong 陳佳榮 and Qian Jiang 錢江, *Zhufanzhi zhubu* 諸蕃志注補 (Hong Kong: Hong Kong University Press, 2000), 26.

88. Guo Zhengzhong, *Liangsong shixiang shangpin huo-bi jingji kaolue* 兩宋城鄉商品貿幣經濟考略 (Beijing: Jingji guanli Chubanshe, 1997), 389–405.

89. *YLMC* 5:88.

90. Ibid.

91. So Kee Long, "Dissolving Hegemony or Changing Trade Pattern? Images of Srivijaya in the Chinese Sources of the Twelfth and Thirteenth Centuries," *JSEAS* 29, no. 2 (1998): 303; Chen and Qian, *Zhufanzhi zhubu,* 46, 47, 319.

92. Su Jiqing 穌繼慶, ed., *Daoyi zhilue jiaoshi* 島夷志略校釋 (Beijing: Zhonghua Shuju, 1981), 141, 187.

93. *DDNHZ* 7:18a.

94. For the location of these port-polities, see map 3.1. For more detailed discussions of these port-polities, including the archaeological research conducted at their respective sites, see Edmund Edwards McKinnon, "Early Polities in Southern Sumatra: Some Preliminary Observations Based on Archaeological Evidence," *Indonesia* 40 (1985): 1–36; Edwards McKinnon and Sinar, "A Note on Pulau Kompei in Aru Bay, Northeastern Sumatra," *Indonesia* 32 (1981): 49–73.

95. *YS* 13:10a.

96. Ibid., 210:4670.

97. Ibid., 131:20b.

98. Ibid., 13:10a, 13:18a.

99. Ibid., 12:8a–9b.

100. W. W. Rockhill, "Notes on the Relations and Trade of China with the Eastern Archipelago and the Coasts of the Indian Ocean during the Fourteenth Century," *T'oung pao* 15 (1914): 428–47; *YS* 12:8a–9b, 14:13b.

101. *YS* 12:8a–9b.

102. O. W. Wolters, *The Fall of Srivijaya in Malay History* (Kuala Lumpur: Oxford University Press, 1970), 45.

Chapter 4: Malay and Chinese Foreign Representation and Commercial Practices Abroad

1. *SHY* ZG 44:1a–b.

2. Ibid.

3. Ibid., 44:4a–b.

4. Ibid.

5. Ibid., 44:5b–6a.

6. Hugh R. Clark, "The Politics of Trade and the Establishment of the Quanzhou Trade Superintendency," in *China and the Maritime Silk Route,* ed. Quanzhou International Seminar on China and the Maritime Routes of the Silk Roads Organization Committee (Fujian: Fujian People's Publishing House, 1991), 378–81.

7. *SHY* ZG 44:5b–6a.

8. Chen Dasheng 陳達生, "Zhongguo dongnan yanhai diqu yisilan beiming yanjiu gangyao" 中國東南沿海地區伊斯蘭碑銘研網要, in *China and the Maritime Silk Route,* ed. Quanzhou International Seminar on China and the Maritime Routes of the Silk Roads Organization Committee (Fujian: Fujian People's Publishing House, 1991), 158–82.

9. *PZKT* 2:6b.

10. *SHY* ZG 44:8b–9a; *SS* 186:26a.

11. *PZKT* 2:10a.

12. Ibid.

13. For a more detailed discussion of marriages between Song imperial clanswomen and foreigners resident in China, see John W. Chaffee, *Branches of Heaven: A History of the Imperial Clan of Sung China* (Cambridge, MA: Harvard University Press, 1999), 92–93.

14. *SHY* ZG 44:9b and 10a.

15. Ibid., 44:8b.

16. B. C. Chandra, Department of Archaeology, *Annual Report on Indian Epigraphy for 1956–57* (New Delhi: Manager of Publications, 1957), 15.

17. Tan Yeok Seong, "The Sri Vijayan Inscription of Canton (AD 1079)," *JSEAH* 5, no. 2 (1964): 17–26.

18. *PZKT* 2:6b–7a.

19. So, "Dissolving Hegemony," 305.

20. Ibid.

21. Ibid.

22. *YLMC* 5:88.

23. Fu Zongwen 傅宗文, "Houtu guchuan: Song ji nanwai zongsi haiwai jingshang di wuzheng" 后渚古船宋及南外宗司海外經商的物征, *HJSYJ,* 1989, no. 2:79, 80.

24. *YS* 94:25a.

25. *SHY* ZG 44:27a–28a.

26. *PZKT* 2:1b.

27. Michael Flecker and William M. Mathers, eds., *Archaeological Recovery of the Java Sea Wreck* (Annapolis: Pacific Sea Resources, 1997), 77–94; Abu Ridho and Edmund Edwards McKinnon, *The Pulau Buaya Wreck: Finds from the Song Period,* ed. Sumarah Adhyatman (Jakarta: Ceramic Society of Indonesia, 1998), 64.

28. Douglas Merwin, "Selections from Wen-Wu on the Excavation of a Sung Dynasty Seagoing Vessel in Chuan-Chou," *Chinese Sociology and Anthropology* 9, no. 3 (Spring 1977): 18, table 1.

29. So Kee Long, *Prosperity, Region, and Institutions in Maritime China: The South Fukien Pattern, 946–1368* (Cambridge, MA: Harvard University Asia Center, 2000), 210–20.

30. *PZKT* 2:3a.

31. Ibid., 2:4a.

32. Ibid.

33. *SHY* ZG 44:25b–26b.

34. Fu, "Houtu guchuan," 77–83.

35. Quanzhouwan Songdai Haichuan Fajue Baogao Bianxiezhu 泉州灣宋代海船發掘報告編寫組, "Quanzhouwan songdai haichuan fajue jianbao" 泉州灣宋代海船發掘簡報, *Wenwu,* 1975, no. 10:11.

36. So, *Prosperity, Region,* 217.

37. Su Jiqing 穌繼慶, ed., *Daoyi zhilue jiaoshi* 島夷志略校釋 (Beijing: Zhonghua Shuju, 1981), 93, 99, 102, 123; Heng, "Economic Interaction between China and the Malacca Straits Region, Tenth to Fourteenth Centuries AD" (PhD thesis, Center for Southeast Asian Studies, University of Hull, 2005), 328–33.

38. Roxanna Brown and Sten Sjostrand, Turiang: *A Fourteenth-Century Shipwreck in Southeast Asian Waters* (Pasadena, CA: Pacific Asia Museum, 2000), 32–34.

39. Ibid., 18.

40. Ibid., 17.

41. *SHY* FY 4:97a.

42. *PZKT* 2:10a. On the Song imperial clan and their impact on the ports of China, see John W. Chaffee, "The Impact of the Song Imperial Clan on the Overseas Trade of Quanzhou," in *The Emporium of the World: Maritime Quanzhou, 1000–1400,* ed. Angela Schottenhammer (Leiden: Brill, 2001), 13–46.

43. *PZKT* 2:10a.

44. Ibid.

45. Wolters, "Tambralingga," 605.

46. Ibid.

47. *SHY* ZG 44:8b–9a; *SS* 186:26a.

48. Su, *Daoyi zhilue jiaoshi,* 55.

49. Ibid.

50. Ibid., 213.

51. For a detailed discussion on this economic area during the fourteenth century AD, see Derek T. S. Heng, "Temasik as an International and Regional Trading Port in the Thirteenth and Fourteenth Centuries: A Reconstruction Based on Recent Archaeological Data," *JMBRAS* 72, no. 1 (1999): 113–24.

52. Roderich Ptak, "From Quanzhou to the Zulu Zone and Beyond: Questions Related to the Early Fourteenth Century," *JSEAS* 29, no. 2 (1998): 269–94.

53. Merwin, *Selections from Wen-Wu,* 18, table 1.

54. Janice Stargardt, "Behind the Shadows: Archaeological Data on Two-Way Sea Trade between Quanzhou and Satingpra, South Thailand, 10th–14th Century," in *The Emporium of the World: Maritime Quanzhou, 1000–1400,* ed. Angela Schottenhammer (Leiden: Brill, 2001), 372–73.

55. Ibid., 373.

56. Merwin, *Selections from Wen-Wu,* 18.

57. *SHY* ZG 44:17b–19b.

58. Ibid.

59. Ibid., 44:21a–23a.

60. *DDNHZ* 7:19a–20b.

61. Ibid.

62. Ibid., 7:20a–b.

63. Marie-France Dupoizat, "The Ceramic Cargo of a Song Dynasty Junk Found in the Philippines and Its Significance in the China–Southeast Asia Trade," in *South East Asia and China: Art, Interaction and Commerce,* Colloquies in Art and Archaeology in Asia, no. 17, School of Oriental and African Studies, ed. Rosemary Scott and John Guy (London: School of Oriental and African Studies, University of London, 1995), 205–24; Roxanna M. Brown, *Guangdong Ceramics from Butuan and Other Philippine Sites* (Manila: Oriental Ceramic Society of the Philippines, 1989); Kerry Nguyen Long, "History Behind the Jar," in *A Thousand Years of Stoneware Jars in the Philippines,* eds. Cynthia Valdes, Long, and Artemio C. Barbosa (Manila: Jar Collectors, 1992), 25–69.

64. Wolters, "Tambralingga," 587–607.

65. *DDNHZ* 7:17b–18b.

66. Derek T. S. Heng, "The Trade in Lakawood Products between South China and the Malay World from the Twelfth to Fifteenth Centuries AD," *JSEAS* 32, no. 2 (2001): 136–42.

67. *SHY* ZG 44:17b–19b, 21a–23a.

68. Heng, "Lakawood Products," 136–42.

69. Su, *Daoyi zhilue,* 58, 70, 89, 118.

Chapter 5: China as a Source of Manufactured Products for the Malay Region

1. *SHY* ZG 44:1a–b; *SS* 186:23a.

2. Ibid., 44:1a.

3. Ibid., 44:1a–b; *SS* 186:23a.

4. *SHY* ZG 44:2b.

5. *SS* 489:14089; *WXTK* 332:2610:2.

6. Denis Twitchett and Janice Stargardt. "Chinese Silver Bullion in a Tenth-Century Indonesian Wreck," *Asia Major,* 3rd ser., 15, no. 1 (2002): 35–56.

7. Angela Schottenhammer, "The Role of Metals and the Impact of the Introduction of Huizi Paper Notes in Quanzhou on the Development of Maritime Trade in the Song Period," in *The Emporium of the World: Maritime Quanzhou, 1000–1400,* ed. Schottenhammer (Leiden: Brill, 2001), 105; Robert S. Wicks, *Money, Markets, and Trade in Early Southeast Asia: The Development of Indigenous Monetary Systems to AD 1400* (Ithaca: Southeast Asian Program, Cornell University, 1982), 303.

8. Paul Wheatley, *The Golden Khersonese: Studies in the Historical Geography of the Malay Peninsula before AD 1500* (Westport, CT: Greenwood, 1973), xxi.

9. B. C. Chandra, Department of Archaeology, *Annual Report on Indian Epigraphy for 1956–57* (New Delhi: Manager of Publications, 1957), 15.

10. *SHY* ZG 44:4a–b.

11. *SS* 489:14090; *WXTK* 332:2610, 2.

12. Grace Wong, *A Commentary on the Tributary Trade between China and Southeast Asia, and the Place of Porcelain in This Trade during the Period of the Song Dynasty in China.* Southeast Asian Ceramics Society (Singapore) Transaction 7 (Singapore: Southeast Asian Ceramics Society, 1979), 14.

13. Ibid., 3, 14.

14. *SHY* ZG 44:12a–b; Wong, *Tributary Trade,* 19.

15. *SS* 186:33a.

16. Ibid.

17. Ibid., 185:32b.

18. *YS* 94:25a.

19. See app. A, table A.3.

20. See app. A, table A.2.

21. Bennet Bronson, "The Iron Industry and Trade," in *Archaeological Recovery of the Java Sea Wreck,* ed. Michael Flecker and William M. Mathers (Annapolis: Pacific Sea Resources, 1997), 101–2. Also see Jerome Chen, "Sung Bronzes: An Economic Analysis," *Bulletin of Oriental and African Studies* 28, no. 3 (1968): 613–26.

22. Michael Flecker, "The Archaeological Recovery of the Tenth-Century Intan Shipwreck" (PhD diss., National University of Singapore, 2001), 208.

23. *SS* 186:33a.

24. Chen Jiarong 陳佳榮 and Qian Jiang 錢江, *Zhufanzhi zhubu* 諸蕃志注補 (Hong Kong: Hong Kong University Press, 2000), 73, 46–47, 89, 273.

25. See app. A, table A.1.

26. *YS* 94:25a.

27. Ibid., 94:26a.

28. The *Daoyi zhilue* indicates that Chinese iron products were being exported to most ports in the region. See app. A, tables A.2, A.3.

29. Schottenhammer, "Role of Metals," 144; Peng Xinwei 彭信威, *Zhongguo huobishi* 中國貨幣史 (Shanghai: Shanghai Renmin Chubanshe, 1988), 382; H. R. Williamson, *Wang An Shih, a Chinese Statesman and Educationalist of the Sung Dynasty,* 2 vols. (London: Arthur Probsthain, 1935), 243.

30. Bronson, "Iron Industry," 95–102.

31. Claudine Salmon, "A Tentative Interpretation of the Chinese Inscription (1231) Engraved on a Bronze Gong Recovered in Muara Jambi (Central Sumatra)," *Archipel* 66 (2003): 91–112; Salmon, "La diffusion du gong en Insulinde vue essentiellement a travers diverses épaves orientales (période Song-Ming)," in *Mirabilia Asiatica: Produtos raros no comércio marítimo,* ed. Jorge M. dos Santos Alves, Claude Guillot, and Roderich Ptak, 2 vols. (Wiesbaden: Harrassowitz, 2005), 88–116.

32. Flecker, "Intan Shipwreck," 135–41.

33. Abu Ridho and Edmund Edwards McKinnon, *The Pulau Buaya Wreck: Finds from the Song Period,* ed. Sumarah Adhyatman (Jakarta: Ceramic Society of Indonesia, 1998), 78; Salmon, "Diffusion du gong," 89–98.

34. *WXTK* 332:2, 566; ibid., 332:2610, 3; Claudine Salmon, "Srivijaya, la Chine et les marchands chinois (Xe–XIIe s.): Quelques reflexions sur la société de l'empire sumatranais," *Archipel* 63 (2002): 70.

35. Williamson, *Wang An Shih,* 246–47. For a detailed discussion on the exchange rate of Chinese copper coins to other metal currencies in circulation in the Song Chinese economy, and the role of these coins in China's maritime trade during the Song, see Peng Xinwei 彭信威, *Zhongguo huobishi* 中國貨幣史 (Shanghai: Shanghai Renmin Chubanshe, 1988), 382; Schottenhammer, "Role of Metals," 95–176; Chen, "Sung Bronzes," 613–26.

36. *SHY ZG:* 4:2b–3a.

37. *WXTK* 20:201, 1; *SS* 186:24a. Yoshinobu Shiba, "Sung Foreign Trade: Its Scope and Organization," in *China among Equals: The Middle Kingdom and Its Neighbours, 10th–14th Centuries,* ed. Morris Rossabi (Berkeley: University of California Press, 1983), 92.

38. Arjan van Aelst, "Majapahit Picis: The Currency of a 'Moneyless' Society," *Bijdragen tot de taal-, land- en volkenkunde* 151, no. 3 (1995): table 2.

39. Abu Ridho, "Penelitian Keramik di Situs–Situs Arkeologi Provinsi Jambi," in *Laporan: Hasil penelitian arkeologi dan geologi propinsi Jambi, 1994–1995,* 198–231. (Jambi: Pemerintah daerah tingkat I provinsi Jambi, 1995), 198–231.

40. Flecker, "Intan Shipwreck," 148–51.

41. *SS* 133:2, 4; van Aelst, "Majapahit Picis," 361–62; Jan Wisseman-Christie, "Money and Its Uses in the Javanese States of the Ninth to Fifteenth Centuries AD," *JESHO* 39, no. 3 (1996): 268–71; Paul Wheatley, "Geographical Notes on Some Commodities Involved in Sung Maritime Trade," *JMBRAS* 32, no. 2 (1959): 37.

42. Robert Hartwell, "The Evolution of the Early Northern Sung Monetary System, AD 960–1025," *JAOS* 87, no. 3 (1967): 284; Chen, "Sung Bronzes," 619.

43. Wong, *Tributary Trade,* 10, 16, 18.

44. *SS* 489:14090; *WXTK* 332:2610, 2.

45. *SS* 11186:26a; *SHY* ZG 44:8a.

46. Hong Zun, 洪遵, *Quanzhi,* 泉志 (Taibei: Xin wen feng chuban gongsi, 1984), 12:1b.

47. Michael Mitchiner, *The History and Coinage of South East Asia until the Fifteenth Century* (London: Hawkins, 1998), 219–20; Wicks, *Money, Markets,* 235–38, 241.

48. Wisseman-Christie, "Money and Its Uses," 267–68.

49. For a detailed study of these early silver coins, see Jan Wisseman-Christie, *A Preliminary Survey of Early Javanese Coinage Held in Javanese Collections* (Jakarta: Kundika, 1994).

50. Jan Wisseman-Christie, pers. comm., 2004.

51. *SHY* ZG 44:12a, 17a.

52. *SS* 489:14090.

53. The 1134 Arab mission, for instance, converted the copper coins that were paid by the Song court for the tribute it had presented into six hundred lumps of silver, wares of gold and silver, and bolts of silk. Wong, *Tributary Trade,* 19.

54. *SS* 186:33a.

55. Chen and Qian, *Zhufanzhi zhubu,* 88, 101.

56. Wisseman-Christie, "Money and Its Uses," 270; van Aelst, "Majapahit Picis," 376–89.

57. Ridho, "Penelitian Keramik," 198–231.

58. Hassan Shuhaimi Nik and Othman bin Mohamad Yatim, *Antiquities of the Bujang Valley* (Kuala Lumpur: Museum Association of Malaysia, 1990).

59. S. J. Allen, *Trade, Transportation and Tributaries: Exchange, Agriculture, and Settlement Distribution in Early Historic-Period Kedah, Malaysia* (Ann Arbor: University Microfilms International, 1988).

60. Edmund Edwards McKinnon and Tengku Luckman Sinar, "A Note on Pulau Kompei in Aru Bay, Northeastern Sumatra," *Indonesia* 32 (1981): 49–73.

61. Edmund Edwards McKinnon, "Kota Cina: Its Context and Meaning in the Trade of Southeast Asia in the Twelfth to Fourteenth Centuries," 2 vols. (PhD diss., Cornell University, 1984), 106–12.

62. Brigitte Borell, "Money in Fourteenth-Century Singapore," paper presented at the Seventh International Conference of the European Association of Southeast Asian Archaeologists, Berlin, September 1996, 7.

63. Edwards McKinnon, "Kota Cina," 362–63.

64. See Derek T. S. Heng, "Export Commodity and Regional Currency: The Role of Chinese Copper Coins in the Malacca Straits Region, Tenth to Fourteenth Centuries," *JSEAS* 37, no. 2 (2006): 197–202.

65. Quanzhouwan Songdai Haichuan Fajue Baogao Bianxiezhu 泉州灣宋代海船發掘報告編寫組, "Quanzhouwan songdai haichuan fajue jianbao" 泉州灣宋代海船發掘簡報, *Wenwu*, 1975, no. 10:14, table 4.

66. Kim Wondong, *Chinese Ceramics from the Wreck of a Yuan Ship in Sinan, Korea—with Particular Reference to Celadon Wares*, 2 vols. (Ann Arbor: University Microfilms International, 1989), 1:179–185.

67. Wong, *Tributary Trade*, 6.

68. *SHY* ZG 44:2b.

69. For a detailed study of the types of Chinese and Southeast Asian textiles traded from the Song to the Ming, see Lee Chor Lin, "Textile Trade between China and Southeast Asia during the Song, Yuan and Ming Dynasties" (master's thesis, University of Singapore, 1994). On textiles in medieval Java, see Jan Wisseman-Christie, "Texts and Textiles in 'Medieval' Java," *BEFEO* 80 (1993): 181–211.

70. *SHY* ZG 44:1a–b; *SS* 186:23a.

71. *SS* 489:14089; *WXTK* 332:2610, 2.

72. *WXTK* 332:2610, 3; *SS* 489:14090.

73. *WXTK* 332:2610, 3; *SS* 489:14090.

74. *SS* 185:32b.

75. See app. A, table A.1.

76. See app. A, tables A.2, A.3. The *DYZL* does not specify the type of material that the handkerchiefs and printed cloth were made from, so it is possible that the fabric was not silk but cotton, which was, by the mid-Song period, grown and woven in Hainan and parts of southern China. Lee, *Textile Trade*, 30.

77. See app. A, tables A.2, A.3.

78. Michael Flecker, "A Ninth-Century AD Arab or Indian Shipwreck in Indonesia: First Evidence for Direct Trade with China," *World Archaeology* 32, no. 3 (2001): 335–54.

79. *SS* 489:14088; *SHY* FY 7:2a; *WXTK* 332:2610:2.

80. *SHY* ZG 44:1a–b; *SS* 186:23a.

81. Chen and Qian, *Zhufanzhi zhubu*, 88.

82. Ibid., 46.

83. See app. A, tables A.2, A.3.

84. *PZKT* 2:3a.

85. Kerry Nguyen Long, "History behind the Jar," in *A Thousand Years of Stoneware Jars in the Philippines*, ed. Cynthia Valdes, Long, and Artemio C. Barbosa (Manila: Jar Collectors, 1992), 30.

86. *SS* 185:32b.

87. See Ho Chuimei, "The Ceramic Boom in Minnan during Song and Yuan Times," in *The Emporium of the World: Maritime Quanzhou,*

1000–1400, ed. Angela Schottenhammer (Leiden: Brill, 2001), 237–82; So Kee Long, "The Trade Ceramics Industry in Southern Fukien during the Sung," *JSYS* 24 (1994): 1–19.

88. See Flecker, "Intan Shipwreck," 248–84.

89. Liu Liangyu, *Sung Wares,* vol. 2 of *A Survey of Chinese Ceramics* (Taipei: Aries Gemini, 1991), 168.

90. See Ridho and Edwards McKinnon, *Pulau Buaya Wreck,* 6–64.

91. Flecker and Mathers, *Java Sea Wreck,* 116–71.

92. Leong Sau Heng, "A Study of Ceramic Deposits from Pengkalan Bujang, Kedah" (master's thesis, University of Malaya, 1973), 130–219.

93. See Edwards McKinnon, "Kota Cina," 106–18.

94. See app. B, tables B.1, B.2.

95. Edwards McKinnon, "Kota Cina," 196–280.

96. See app. B, table B.2.

97. For a detailed discussion of collection centers in the region, see Leong Sau Heng, "Collecting Centers, Feeder Points and Entrepots in the Malay Peninsula, c. 1000 BC–AD 1400," in *The Southeast Asian Port and Polity, Rise and Demise,* ed. J. Kathirithamby-Wells and John Villiers (Singapore: Singapore University Press, 1990), 17–38.

98. John N. Miksic, "Recently Discovered Chinese Green Glazed Wares of the Thirteenth and Fourteenth Centuries in Singapore and the Riau Islands," in *New Light on Chinese Yue and Longquan Wares,* ed. Ho Chuimei (Hong Kong: Centre of Asian Studies, University of Hong Kong, 1994), 231; Derek T. S. Heng, "Temasik as an International and Regional Trading Port in the Thirteenth and Fourteenth centuries: A Reconstruction Based on Recent Archaeological Data," *JMBRAS* 72, no. 1 (1999): 119–120.

99. John N. Miksic, "Beyond the Grave: Excavations North of the Kramat Iskandar Shah, 1988," *Heritage* 10 (1989): 39; see also app. B, tables B.1, B.2.

100. Southeast Asian Ceramics Society, *A Ceramic Legacy of Asia's Maritime Trade* (Selangor: Southeast Asian Ceramics Society, W. Malaysia Chapter, 1985), 147.

101. *YLMC* 5:88.

102. Su, *Daoyi zhilue,* 96, 99, 102.

103. Edwards McKinnon, "Kota Cina," 189.

104. See app. B, tables B.1, B.2.

105. Edwards McKinnon, "Kota Cina," 185.

106. Ibid., 189.

107. Leong, "Ceramic Deposits," 109.

108. See app. B, tables B.1, B.2.

109. Miksic, "Beyond the Grave," 39.

110. Edwards McKinnon, "Kota Cina," 116–18, 129–286; Edwards McKinnon, "Mediaeval Tamil Involvement in Northern Sumatra, C11–C14 (The Gold and Resin Trade)," *JMBRAS* 69, no. 1 (1996): 85–99; Claude Guillot, *Histoire de Barus, Sumatra: Le site de Lobu Tua, sous la Direction de Claude Guillot* (Paris: Association Archipel, 1998), 113–30; K. P. Rao, "Kottapatnam—A South Indian Port Trading with Eastern Lands," in *In search of Chinese Ceramic-Sherds in South India and Sri Lanka,* ed. Noboru Karashima (Tokyo: Taisho University Press, 2004), 9–15, plate 5.2; Viswas D. Gogteand, "The Chandraketugarh-Tamluk Region of Bengal: Sources of the Early Historic Rouletted Ware from India and South East Asia," *Man and Environment* 22, no. 1 (1997): 69–85.

111. Leong, *Ceramic Deposits,* 132–85.

112. Southeast Asian Ceramics Society, *Ceramic Legacy,* 76, 119.

113. Flecker, "Intan Shipwreck," 281–84.

114. Roxanna Brown and Sten Sjostrand, Turiang: *A Fourteenth-Century Shipwreck in Southeast Asian Waters* (Pasadena, CA: Pacific Asia Museum, 2000), 18.

115. Eine Moore, "A Suggested Classification of Stonewares of Martabani Type," *SMJ* 18 (1970): 8. The suggestion that these jars may have been used to store mercury was first made by F. E. Treloar, who noted that these jars had heavily potted bases and lower walls, which would have allowed them to be used to contain liquids of high density. The trace residues in the samples Treloar examined, which were from Sarawak Museum, suggest that one of the uses of these jars may have been, at least in north Borneo, the storage of mercury. Subsequent finds from Southeast Asia do not suggest that these jars were used in the storage and transportation of mercury in other Southeast Asian areas, but "mercury jar" has remained a term for classifying this type of jar within the Southeast Asian archaeological context. F. E. Treloar, "Stoneware Bottles in the Sarawak Museum: Vessels for Mercury Trade?" *SMJ* 20 (1972): 377–84.

116. Xu Qingquan 許清泉, "Songchuan chutu de xiaokou taoping niandai he yongtu de tantao" 宋船出土的小口陶瓶年代和用途的探討, *HJSYJ,* 1983, no. 1:112–14.

117. See Roxanna M. Brown, "The Ming Gap and Shipwreck Ceramics in Southeast Asia (PhD diss., UCLA, 2004).

Chapter 6: China's Evolving Trade in Malay Products

1. *SHY ZG* 44:1a–b.

2. Ibid.

3. For a more detailed study on China's trade in tortoise shells, see Roderich Ptak, "China and the Trade in Tortoise-Shell (Sung to Ming

Periods)," in *Emporia, Commodities, and Entrepreneurs in Asian Maritime Trade, c. 1400–1750,* ed. Roderich Ptak and Dietmar Rothermund (Stuttgart: Franz Steiner, 1991), 195–229.

4. *SHY* ZG 44:2a–b.

5. Grace Wong, *A Commentary on the Tributary Trade between China and Southeast Asia, and the Place of Porcelain in This Trade during the Period of the Song Dynasty in China,* Southeast Asian Ceramics Society (Singapore) Transaction 7 (Singapore: Southeast Asian Ceramics Society, 1979), 6–8.

6. Ibid.,16.

7. Ibid., 17–19.

8. For a more detailed study of the trade of lakawood incense, see Derek T. S. Heng, "The Trade in Lakawood Products between South China and the Malay World from the Twelfth to Fifteenth Centuries AD," *JSEAS* 32, no. 2 (2001): 133–50.

9. Paul Wheatley, "Geographical Notes on Some Commodities Involved in Sung Maritime Trade," *JMBRAS* 32, no. 2 (1959): 67.

10. Chen Jiarong 陳佳榮 and Qian Jiang 錢江, *Zhufanzhi zhubu* 諸蕃志注補 (Hong Kong: Hong Kong University Press, 2000), 354.

11. Tu Youxiang 屠友祥, *Zhou Qufei: Lingwai daida* 周去非: 嶺外代答 (Shanghai: Yuandong Chubanshe, 1996), 141.

12. Chen and Qian, *Zhufanzhi zhubu,* 368.

13. *SHY* ZG 44:1a–b.

14. For a more detailed study of China's trade in cloves, see Roderich Ptak, "China and the Trade in Cloves, circa 960–1435," *JAOS* 113, no. 1 (1993): 1–13.

15. *SS* 489:14090; *WXTK* 332:2610, 2.

16. *WXTK* 332:2610, 3; *SS* 489:14090.

17. *WXTK* 332:2610, 3; *SS* 489:14090.

18. *WXTK* 332:2610, 1.

19. *SHY* ZG 44:21a–23a.

20. Ibid.

21. Ibid.

22. Ibid., 44:24b–25a.

23. Ibid.

24. Wong, *Tributary Trade,* 8–10, 14.

25. *SHY* ZG 44:27a–28a.

26. Ibid., 44:21a–23a.

27. Ibid., 44:27a–28a.

28. *SS* 489:14090; *SHY* FY 7:28a.

29. *SHY* FY 7:55b–56a; *WXTK* 332:2610, 3.

30. Chen and Qian, *Zhufanzhi zhubu*, 80.

31. Ibid., 78. This was certainly a reexport of tin from sources on the western coast of the Malay Peninsula.

32. Chen and Qian, *Zhufanzhi zhubu*, 46–47.

33. Douglas Merwin, "Selections from Wen-Wu on the Excavation of a Sung Dynasty Seagoing Vessel in Chuan-Chou," *Chinese Sociology and Anthropology* 9, no. 3 (Spring 1977): 18, table 1.

34. Fu Zongwen 傅宗文, "Houtu guchuan: Song ji nanwai zongsi haiwai jingshang di wuzheng" 后渚古船: 宋及南外宗司海外經商的物征, *HJSYJ*, 1989, no. 2:77–83.

35. Song Lian, *Economic Structure of the Yüan Dynasty*, trans. Herbert Franz Schurmann (Cambridge, MA: Harvard University Press, 1967), 225.

36. Ibid., 223.

37. Ibid., 224.

38. *DDNHZ* 7:17a–18b.

39. Ibid.

40. For a more detailed discussion of the economic and diplomatic relations between Yuan China and the Il-Khans of Persia, and the special importance that this relationship accorded to the maritime route in China's eyes, see Thomas T. Allsen, *Culture and Conquest in Mongol Eurasia* (Cambridge: Cambridge University Press, 2001), chs. 4, 5.

Bibliography

Works in Chinese

Chen Dasheng 陳達生. "Zhongguo dongnan yanhai diqu yisilan beiming yanjiu gangyao" 中國東南沿海地區伊斯蘭碑銘研網要. In *China and the Maritime Silk Route: UNESCO Quanzhou International Seminar on China and the Maritime Routes of the Silk Roads,* edited by Quanzhou International Seminar on China and the Maritime Routes of the Silk Roads Organization Committee, 15–182. Fujian: Fujian People's Publishing House, 1991.

Chen Gaohua 陳高華. "Yuandai de hanghai shijia ganpu yangshi" 元代的航海世家澉浦楊氏. *HJSYJ*, 1995, no. 1:4–18.

Chen Guangyao 陳光耀. *Zhongguo gudai duiwai maoyishi* 中國古代對外貿易史. Guangdong: Guangdong Renmin Chubanshe, 1985.

Chen Jiarong 陳佳榮. *Gudai nanhai diming huishi* 古代南海地明會史. Beijing: Zhonghua Shuju, 1986.

Chen Jiarong 陳佳榮 and Qian Jiang 錢江. *Zhufanzhi zhubu* 諸蕃志注補. Hong Kong: Hong Kong University Press, 2000.

Chen Lianqing 陳連慶. "Dade nanhaizhi suojian siyi nanhai zhuguo kaoshi" 大德南海志所見四夷南海諸國考實. *Wenshi*, 1986, no. 27:145–64.

Chen Limin 曾麗民. "Quanzhou yi liuqiu de minsu ganxi" 泉州與琉球的民俗關係. *HJSYJ*, 1994, no. 2:105–11.

Chen Xiyu 陳希育. *Zhongguofanchuan yi haiwai maoyi* 中國帆船與海外貿易. Fujian: Xiamen Daxue Chubanshe, 1991.

Chen Yuanjing 陳元勁. *Shilin guangji* 事林廣記. Beijing: Zhonghua Shuju, 1990.

Chen Yujing 陳裕菁. *Pushougeng kao* 浦壽庚考. Beijing: Zhonghua Shuju, 1954.

Deng Duanben 鄧端本. "Lun 'guanghuo' zai haishang sichouzhilu de jueqi" 論'廣貨'在海上絲綢之路的崛起. In *China and the Maritime*

Silk Route: UNESCO Quanzhou International Seminar on China and the Maritime Routes of the Silk Roads, edited by the Quanzhou International Seminar on China and the Maritime Routes of the Silk Roads Organization Committee, 64–71. Fujian: Fujian People's Publishing House, 1991.

Fang Zuyou 方祖猷 and Yu Xinfang 俞信芳. "Wudai song mingzhou shibo jigou chujian shijian ji yanbian kao" 五代宋明州市舶機构初建時間及演變考. *HJSYJ,* 1996, no. 2:76–82.

Foshan City Museum. "Guangdong shiwan guyaozhi diaocha" 廣動石灣古窯址調查. *Kaogu,* 1978, no. 3:195–99.

Fu Zongwen 傅宗文. "Houtu guchuan: Song ji nanwai zongsi haiwai jingshang di wuzheng" 后渚古船: 宋及南外宗司海外經商的物征. *HJSYJ,* 1989, no. 2:77–83.

———. "Zhongguo gudai haiwai maoyi de guanli chuantong yu zaoqi haiguan" 中國古代海外貿以易的管理傳統與早期海關. *HJSYJ,* 1987, no. 1:1–9.

Fudan Daxue Tushuguan Gujibu 復旦大學圖書館古籍部. *Xuxiu siku quanshu* 續修四庫全書. Shanghai: Shanghai Guji Chubanshe, 1995.

Gu Hai 顧海. *Dongnanya gudaishi zhongwen wenxian tiyao* 東南亞古代史中文文獻提要. Xiamen: Xiamen Daxue Chubanshe, 1990.

Guan Luquan 關履權. *Songdai guangzhou de haiwai maoyi* 宋代廣州的海外貿易. Guangzhou: Guangdong Renmin Chubanshe, 1994.

———. "Songdai Guangzhou de xiangliao maoyi" 宋代廣州的香料貿易. *Wenshi,* 1963, no. 3:205–19.

Guangdong Provincial Museum. *Chaozhou Bijiashan songdai yaozhi fajue baogao* 潮州筆架山宋代發掘報告. Beijing: Wenwu Chubanshe, 1981.

———. "Foshan shiwan, Yangjiang shiwan guyao guanxi chutan" 佛山石灣揚江石灣古窯關系初探. In *Shiwan taozhan* 石灣陶展, edited by Fengpingshan bowuguan 馮平山博物館, 119–68. Hong Kong: Guangdong Provincial Museum, 1979.

Guo Zhengzhong 郭正忠. *Liangsong shixiang shangpinhuobi jingji kaolue* 兩宋城鄉商品貿幣經濟考略. Beijing: Jingji Guanli Chubanshe, 1997.

Han Zhenhua 韓振華. "Quanzhou tumenjie qingzhensi yi tonghuaijie qingjingsi" 泉州涂門街清真寺與通淮街清净寺. *HJSYJ,* 1996, no. 1:62–76.

———. "Songdai quanzhou yisilan de qingjingsi" 宋代泉州伊斯蘭的清净寺. *HJSYJ,* 1997, no. 1:68–74.

———. "Songyuan shidai zhuanru quanzhou de waiguo zongjiao guji" 宋元時代傳入泉州的外國宗教古跡. *HJSYJ,* 1995, no. 1:96–110.

Hong Zun 洪遵. *Quanzhi* 泉志. Taibei: Xin wen feng chuban gongsi, 1984.

Huang Wanli 黃萬里. *Zhongguo huobishi* 中國貨幣史. Hong Kong: Yingshua Huadong Yinshuguan, 1953.

Jingdezhen Taoci Lishi Bowuguan 景德鎮陶瓷歷史博物館. "Jingdezhen hutianyao kaocha jiyao" 景德鎮湖田窯考查記要. *Wenwu,* 1980, no. 11:39–49.

Jinjiangxian Wenguanhui Bowuguan 晉江縣文管會博物館. *Cizao yaozhi* 磁灶窯址. Fujian: Yanjiangxian Wenguanhui Bowuyuan, 1987.

Li Wanquan 李萬權 and Zhu Jianqiu 朱鋻秋. "Zhenghe hanghaitu de zonghe yanjiu" 鄭和航海圖的綜合研究. In *China and the Maritime Silk Route: UNESCO Quanzhou International Seminar on China and the Maritime Routes of the Silk Roads,* edited by the Quanzhou International Seminar on China and the Maritime Routes of the Silk Roads Organization Committee, 260–65. Fujian: Fujian People's Publishing House, 1991.

Lin Tianwei 林天蔚. *Songdai xiangyao maoyi shigao* 宋代香藥貿易史稿. Hong Kong: Zhongguo Xueshe, 1959.

Liu Jingcheng 劉精誠. *Zhongguo huobishi* 中國貨幣史. Taipei: Wenjin Chubanshe, 1994.

Liu Mingshu 劉銘恕. "Zaidu zhenghe hanghaitu" 再讀鄭和航海圖. *HJSYJ,* 1999, no. 1:102–3.

Luo Xianglin 羅香林. *Pu Shou Geng zhuan* 浦壽庚傳. Taipei: Zhonghua Wenhua Chubanshe Ye Weiyuanhui, 1955.

———. *Pushougeng yanjiu* 浦薩壽庚研究. Hong Kong: Zhongguo Xueshe, 1958.

Nanjing Yaoxueyuan 南京藥學院 et al. "Quanzhouwan chutu songdai muzhao haichuan changnei jiangxiang de xiangwei jianding" 泉州灣出土宋代木造海船艙內降香的顯微鑒定. *HJSYJ* (1983): 115–16.

Peng Xinwei 彭信威. *Zhongguo huobishi* 中國貨幣史. Shanghai: Shanghai Renmin Chubanshe, 1988.

Peng Yuxin 彭雨新 and Yang Mingyuan 湯明橡. *Zhongguo fengjianshehui jingjishi* 中國封建社會經濟史. Wuchang: Wuhan Daxue Chubanshe, 1994.

Quanzhouwan Songdai Haichuan Fajue Baogao Bianxiezhu 泉州灣宋代海船發掘報告編寫組, "Quanzhouwan songdai haichuan fajue jianbao" 泉州灣宋代海船發掘簡報. *Wenwu,* 1975, no. 10:1–28.

Shanghaishi Weishengju Yaoping Yenjiusuo 上海市衛生局藥品檢驗所 et al. "Quanzhouwan chutu songdai muzao haichuan cangnei jiangxiang de huaxue jianding" 泉州灣出土木造海船艙內降香的化學鑒定. *HJSYJ,* 1983, no. 1:117–21.

Su Jiqing 穌繼慶, ed. *Daoyi zhilue jiaoshi* 島夷志略校釋. Beijing: Zhonghua Shuju, 1981.

Tu Youxiang 屠友祥. *Zhou Qufei: Lingwai daida* 周去非: 嶺外代答. Shanghai: Yuandong Chubanshe, 1996.

Wang Shengduo 汪聖鐸. *Liangsong caizhengshi* 兩宋財政史. Beijing: Zhonghua Shuju, 1995.

Wang Yunhai 王雲海. *Songhuiyao jigao kaojiao* 宋會要輯稿考校. Shanghai: Shanghai Guji Chubanshe, 1986.

Wang Yunwu 王云五. *Ma Duanlin: Wenxian tongkao* 馬端臨: 文獻通考. Shanghai: Shangwu Yinshuguan, 1936.

Wuxishi Bowuguan 無錫市博物館. "Wuxishi huanchenghe gujing qingli" 無錫市環城河古井清理. *Wenwu*, 1983, no. 5:45–53.

Xu Qingquan 許清泉. "Songchuan chutu de xiaokou taoping niandai he yongtu de tantao" 宋船出土的小口陶瓶年代和用途的探討. *HJSYJ*, 1983, no. 1:112–14.

Yang Guozhen 楊國楨. "Mingdai minnan tong liuqiu hanglu shishi gou chen" 明代閩南通琉球航路史事鉤沉. *HJSYJ*, 1991, no. 2:16–30.

———. "Yuandai quanzhou yu nanyindu guanxi xinzheng" 元代泉州與南印度關奚新証. In *China and the Maritime Silk Route: UNESCO Quanzhou International Seminar on China and the Maritime Routes of the Silk Roads,* edited by the Quanzhou International Seminar on China and the Maritime Routes of the Silk Roads Organization Committee, 194–207. Fujian: Fujian People's Publishing House, 1991.

Yao Silian 姚思廉. *Liangshu* 梁書. Beijing: Zhonghua Shuju, 1973.

Yu Changsen 喻常森. *Yuandai haiwai maoyi* 元代海外貿易. Xian: Xibei Daxue Chubanshe, 1994.

Zeng Guangyi 曾廣意. "Guangdong chao'an bijia tangdai yaozhi" 廣東潮安筆架唐代窯址. *Kaogu,* 1964, no. 4:194–95.

———. "Guangdong huiyang baimashan gucitao diaochaji" 廣東惠陽白馬山古瓷陶調查記. *Kaogu,* 1962, no. 8:414–15.

———. "Guangdong huiyang xin'ancun gucitao fajue jianbao" 廣東惠陽新庵村古瓷陶發掘簡報. *Kaogu,* 1964, no. 4:196–99.

———. "A Study of the Characteristics of Tang and Song Ceramics of Guangdong." In *Ceramic Finds from Tang and Song Kilns in Guangdong,* edited by Fung Ping Shan Museum, 63–80. Hong Kong: University of Hong Kong, 1985.

Zhonghua Shuju Bianjiaobu 中華書局編輯部. *Songhuiyao jigao* 宋會要輯稿. Beijing: Zhonghua Shuju, 1957.

———. *Songyuan difangzhi congkan* 宋元地方志叢刊. Beijing: Zhonghua Shuju, 1990.

Zhu Jianmin 朱建民 et al., eds. *Yingjing wenyuange siku quanshu* 印景文淵閣四庫全書. Taipei: Taiwan Shangwu Yinshuguan Gongsi, 1984.

Zhu Jianqiu 朱鑒秋. *Xinbian zhenghe hanghaituji* 新編政合航海圖集. Beijing: Renmin Jiaotong Chubanshe, 1988.

Other Works

Abdul Aziz, Abdul Rashid. *Laporan penyelidikan dan ekskavasi arkeologi tapak 32,* Kampung Sungai Mas, Kuala Muda, Kedah Darul Aman, Fasa 8, 1995. Kuala Lumpur: Jabatan Muzium dan Antikuiti, 1995.

Abu-Lughod, Janet L. *Before European Hegemony: The World System AD 1250–1350.* Oxford: Oxford University Press, 1989.

Addis, J. M. Chinese Ceramics from Datable Tombs and Some Other Dated Material. London: Sotheby Parke Bernet, 1978.

Adhyatman, Sumarah. *Antique Ceramics Found in Indonesia: Various Uses and Origins.* Jakarta: Ceramic Society of Indonesia, 1990.

Adhyatman, Sumarah, and Abu Ridho. *Martavans in Indonesia.* Jakarta: Ceramic Society of Indonesia, 1984.

Allen, S. J. Trade, Transportation, and Tributaries: Exchange, Agriculture, and Settlement Distribution in Early Historic-Period Kedah, Malaysia. Ann Arbor: University Microfilms International, 1988.

Allsen, Thomas T. *Culture and Conquest in Mongol Eurasia.* Cambridge: Cambridge University Press, 2001.

Ayers, John. Chinese Ceramics in the Topkapi Saray Museum, Istanbul: A Complete Catalogue. London: Sotheby's, 1986.

Bastin, John. *Travellers' Singapore: An Anthology.* Kuala Lumpur: Oxford University Press, 1994.

Beal, Samuel. Travels of Fah-Hian and Sung-Yun, Buddhist Pilgrims: From China to India (400 AD and 518 AD). Madras: Asian Educational Services, 1993.

Beamish, Jane. "The Significance of Yuan Blue and White Exported to Southeast Asia." In *South East Asia and China: Art, Interaction and Commerce,* Colloquies on Art and Archaeology in Asia, no. 17, edited by Rosemary Scott and John Guy, 225–51. London: University of London, School of Oriental and African Studies, 1995.

Borell, Brigitte. "Money in Fourteenth-Century Singapore." Paper presented at the Seventh International Conference of the European Association of Southeast Asian Archaeologists, Berlin, September 1996.

Bronson, Bennet. "Exchange at the Upstream and Downstream Ends: Notes towards a Functional Model of the Coastal State in Southeast Asia." In *Economic Exchange and Social Interaction in Southeast Asia: Perspectives from Prehistory, History, and Ethnography,* edited by K. L. Hutterer, 39–52. Ann Arbor: University of Michigan, 1977.

———. "The Iron Industry and Trade." In *Archaeological Recovery of the Java Sea Wreck,* edited by Michael Flecker and William M. Mathers, 95–102. Annapolis: Pacific Sea Resources, 1997.

————. "Patterns in the Early Southeast Asian Metals Trade." In *Early Metallurgy, Trade and Urban Centers in Thailand and Southeast Asia,* edited by Ian Glover, Pornchai Suchitta, and John Villiers, 63–114. Bangkok: White Lotus, 1992.

Bronson, Bennet, and Wisseman, Jan. "Palembang as Srivijaya: The Lateness of Early Cities in Southern Southeast Asia." *Asian Perspectives* 19, no. 2 (1978): 220–39.

Brown, C. C. *Sejarah Melayu; or, Malay Annals.* London: Oxford University Press, 1970.

Brown, Roxanna M. *Guangdong Ceramics from Butuan and Other Philippine Sites.* Manila: Oriental Ceramic Society of the Philippines, 1989.

————. "The Ming Gap and Shipwreck Ceramics in Southeast Asia." PhD diss., UCLA, 2004.

Brown, Roxanna, and Sten Sjostrand. Turiang: *A Fourteenth-Century Shipwreck in Southeast Asian Waters.* Pasadena, CA: Pacific Asia Museum, 2000.

Burkill, I. H. A Dictionary of the Economic Products of the Malay Peninsula. Oxford: Oxford University Press, 1966.

Chaffee, John W. *Branches of Heaven: A History of the Imperial Clan of Sung China.* Cambridge, MA: Harvard University Press, 1999.

————. "Diasporic Identities in the Historical Development of the Maritime Muslim Communities of Song-Yuan China." *JESHO* 49, no. 4 (2006): 395–420.

————. "The Impact of the Song Imperial Clan on the Overseas Trade of Quanzhou." In *The Emporium of the World: Maritime Quanzhou, 1000–1400,* edited by Angela Schottenhammer, 13–46. Leiden: Brill, 2001.

Chandra, B. C. Department of Archaeology. *Annual Report on Indian Epigraphy for 1956–57.* New Delhi: Manager of Publications, 1957.

Chen, Jerome. "Sung Bronzes: An Economic Analysis." *Bulletin of Oriental and African Studies* 28, no. 3 (1968): 613–26.

Cheng Te-K'un. *Archaeology in Sarawak.* Toronto: University of Toronto Press, 1969.

Chien, Cecilia Lee-Fang. *Salt and State: An Annotated Translation of the Songshi Salt Monopoly Treatise.* Ann Arbor: Center for Chinese Studies, University of Michigan, 2004.

Chin, Lucas. *Ceramics in the Sarawak Museum.* Kuching: Sarawak Museum, 1988.

Ching, Francis D. K. *A Visual Dictionary of Architecture.* New York: Van Nostrand Reinhold, 1995.

Chou Ta Kuan. *Notes on the Customs of Cambodia.* Translated from French version of Paul Pelliot by J. Gilman D'Arcy Paul. Bangkok: Social Science Association, 1967.

Clark, Hugh R. Community, Trade, and Networks: Southern Fujian Province from the Third to the Thirteenth Century. Cambridge: Cambridge University Press, 1991.

———. "The Politics of Trade and the Establishment of the Quanzhou Trade Superintendency." In *China and the Maritime Silk Route,* edited by Quanzhou International Seminar on China and the Maritime Routes of the Silk Roads Organization Committee, 375–94. Fujian: Fujian People's Publishing House, 1991.

Coedès, George. "A propos d'une nouvelle théorie sur le site de Srivijaya." *JMBRAS* 14, no. 3 (1936): 1–9.

———. *The Indianized States of Southeast Asia.* Translated from the French by Susan Brown Cowing. Edited by Walter F. Vella. Kuala Lumpur: University of Malaya Press, 1968.

———. "Les inscriptions malaises de Crivijaya." *BEFEO* 30, nos. 1–2 (1930): 29–80.

———. "Le royaume de Crivijaya." *BEFEO* 18, no. 6 (1918): 1–36.

Cowan, C. D., and O. W. Wolters, eds. *Southeast Asian History and Historiography: Essays Presented to D. G. E. Hall.* Ithaca: Cornell University Press, 1976.

Crawfurd, John. Journal of an Embassy from the Governor-General of India to the Courts of Siam and Cochin-China. London: Colburn, 1828.

Das, S. C. Indian Pandits in the Land of Snow. Calcutta: n.p., 1893.

Dupoizat, Marie-France. "The Ceramic Cargo of a Song Dynasty Junk Found in the Philippines and Its Significance in the China–Southeast Asia Trade." In *South East Asia and China: Art, Interaction and Commerce,* Colloquies on Art and Archaeology in Asia, no. 17, edited by Rosemary Scott and John Guy, 205–24. London: School of Oriental and African Studies, University of London, 1995.

———. "La céramique chinoise du site de Lobu Tua à Barus: Premières analyses." *Archipel* 51 (1996): 46–52.

Ecke, Gustav. *Chinese Domestic Furniture.* Hong Kong: Hong Kong University Press, 1962.

Edwards McKinnon, Edmund. "A Brief Note on Maura Kumpeh Hilir: An Early Port Site on the Batang Hari." *SPAFA Digest* 3, no. 2 (1982): 37–40.

———. "Early Polities in Southern Sumatra: Some Preliminary Observations Based on Archaeological Evidence." *Indonesia* 40 (1985): 1–36.

———. "Kota Cina: Its Context and Meaning in the Trade of Southeast Asia in the Twelfth to Fourteenth Centuries." 2 vols. PhD diss., Cornell University, 1984.

――――. "Mediaeval Tamil Involvement in Northern Sumatra, c11–c14 (The Gold and Resin Trade)." *JMBRAS* 69, no. 1 (1996): 85–99.

――――. "Research at Kota Cina, a Sung-Yuan Period Trading Site in East Sumatra." *Archipel* 14 (1977): 19–32.

Edwards McKinnon, Edmund, and Tengku Luckman Sinar. "A Note on Pulau Kompei in Aru Bay, Northeastern Sumatra." *Indonesia* 32 (1981): 49–73.

Ellsworth, Robert Hatfield. Chinese Furniture: Hardwood Examples of the Ming and Ching Dynasties. New York: Random House, 1973.

Faxian. *Travels of Fah-Hian and Sung-Yun, Buddhist Pilgrims: From China to India (400 AD and 518 AD)*. Translated by Samuel Beal. Madras: Asian Educational Services, 1993.

Fei Xin. *Hsing-ch'a sheng-lan: The Overall Survey of the Star Raft*. Translated by J. V. G. Mills. Edited by Roderich Ptak. Wiesbaden: Harrassowitz, 1996.

Ferrand, Gabriel. Relations de voyages et texts géographiques arabes, persans et turks relatifs à l'extrême-Orient du VIIIe au XVIIIe siècles. 2 vols. Paris: E. Leroux, 1912.

Fitzgerald, C. P. *China: A Short Cultural History*. London: Barrie and Jenkins, 1978.

Flecker, Michael. "The Archaeological Recovery of the Tenth-Century Intan Shipwreck." PhD diss., National University of Singapore, 2001.

――――. "The Bakau Wreck: An Early Example of Chinese Shipping in Southeast Asia." *International Journal of Nautical Archaeology* 30, no. 2 (2001): 221–30.

――――. "A Ninth-Century AD Arab or Indian Shipwreck in Indonesia: First Evidence for Direct Trade with China." *World Archaeology* 32, no. 3 (2001): 335–54.

Flecker, Michael, and William M. Mathers, eds. *Archaeological Recovery of the Java Sea Wreck*. Annapolis: Pacific Sea Resources, 1997.

Franke, Herbert. "Sung Embassies: Some General Observations." In *China among Equals: The Middle Kingdom and Its Neighbours, 10th–14th Centuries*, edited by Morris Rossabi, 116–48. Berkeley: University of California Press, 1983.

Franke, Wolfgang. "China's Overseas Communications with Southeast Asia as Reflected in Chinese Epigraphic Materials, 1264–1800." In *China and the Maritime Silk Route*, UNESCO Quanzhou International Seminar on China and the Maritime Routes of the Silk Roads, edited by Quanzhou International Seminar Organization Committee, 309–22. Fujian: Fujian People's Publishing House, 1991.

Fung Ping Shan Museum. *Dehua Wares*. Hong Kong: Fung Ping Shan Museum, 1990.

————. Exhibition of Ceramic Finds from Ancient Kilns in China. Hong Kong: Fung Ping Shan Museum, 1981.

Gang Deng. Chinese Maritime Activities and Socioeconomic Development, c. 2100 BC–1900 AD. Westport, CT: Greenwood, 1997.

————. Maritime Sector, Institutions, and Sea Power of Premodern China. Westport, CT: Greenwood, 1999.

Glover, Ian C. "Beads and Bronzes: Archaeological Indicators of Trade between Thailand and the Early Buddhist Civilization of Northern India." In *Asian Trade Routes, Continental and Maritime,* edited by Karl Reinhold Haellquist, 117–41. London: Curzon, 1991.

————. "Recent Archaeological Evidence for Early Maritime Contacts between India and Southeast Asia." In *Tradition and Archaeology Early Maritime Contacts in the Indian Ocean,* Proceedings of the International Seminar, Techno-archaeological Perspectives of Seafaring in the Indian Ocean, 4th Century BC–15th Century AD, edited by Himanshu Prabha Ray and Jean-François Salles, 129–58. New Delhi: Manohar, 1996.

Gogteand, Viswas D. "The Chandraketugarh-Tamluk Region of Bengal: Sources of the Early Historic Rouletted Ware from India and South East Asia." *Man and Environment* 22, no. 1 (1997): 69–85.

Goodrich, Carrington. "Recent Discoveries at Zayton." *JAOS* 77, no. 3 (1957): 161–65.

Groeneveldt, W. P. Historical Notes on Indonesia and Malaysia Compiled from Chinese Sources. Batavia, 1876.

Gu Yunquan. "A Study of the Development of Ceramics Production in Guangdong during the Tang-Song Period." In *Ceramic Finds from Tang and Song Kilns in Guangdong,* edited by Fung Ping Shan Museum, 11–21. Hong Kong: University of Hong Kong. 1985.

Guillot, Claude. Histoire de Barus, Sumatra: Le site de Lobu Tua, sous la Direction de Claude Guillot. Paris: Association Archipel, 1998.

————. "La nature du site de Lobu Tua a Barus, Sumatra." In *From the Mediterranean to the China Sea: Miscellaneous Notes,* edited by Claude Guillot, Denys Lombard, and Roderich Ptak, 113–30. Wiesbaden: Harrassowitz, 1988.

Gullick, J. M. Indigenous Political Systems of Western Malaya. London: Athlone, 1958.

Hall, Kenneth R. "Economic History of Early Southeast Asia." In *The Cambridge History of Southeast Asia.* Vol. 1, *From Early Times to c. 1800,* edited by Nicholas Tarling, 183–275. Cambridge: Cambridge University Press, 1999.

————. Maritime Trade and State Development in Early Southeast Asia. Honolulu: University of Hawaii Press, 1986.

Harrisson, Barbara. *Pusaka: Heirloom Jars of Borneo.* Singapore: Oxford University Press, 1986.

Hartwell, Robert. "The Evolution of the Early Northern Sung Monetary System, AD 960–1025." *JAOS* 87, no. 3 (1967): 280–89.

He Li. Chinese Ceramics: The New Standard Guide. London: Thames and Hudson, 1996.

Heng, Derek T. S. "Economic Exchanges and Linkages between the Malay Region and the Hinterland of China's Coastal Ports during the 10th to 14th Centuries." In *Early Singapore, 1300s—1819: Evidence in Maps, Text and Artefacts,* edited by John N. Miksic and Cheryl-Ann Low Mei Gek, 73–85. Singapore: Singapore History Museum, 2004.

———. "Economic Interaction between China and the Malacca Straits Region, Tenth to Fourteenth Centuries AD." PhD thesis, Center for Southeast Asian Studies, University of Hull, 2005.

———. "Export Commodity and Regional Currency: The Role of Chinese Copper Coins in the Malacca Straits Region, Tenth to Fourteenth Centuries." *JSEAS* 37, no. 2 (2006): 179–203.

———. "Temasik as an International and Regional Trading Port in the Thirteenth and Fourteenth Centuries: A Reconstruction Based on Recent Archaeological Data." *JMBRAS* 72, no. 1 (1999): 113–24.

———. "The Trade in Lakawood Products between South China and the Malay World from the Twelfth to Fifteenth Centuries AD." *JSEAS* 32, no. 2 (2001): 133–50.

Hinckley, F. Lewis. *Directory of the Historic Cabinet Woods.* New York, Crown, 1960.

Ho Chuimei. "The Ceramic Boom in Minnan during Song and Yuan Times." In *The Emporium of the World: Maritime Quanzhou, 1000–1400,* edited by Angela Schottenhammer, 237–82. Leiden: Brill, 2001.

Hucker, Charles O. *A Dictionary of Official Titles in Imperial China.* Stanford: Stanford University Press, 1985.

Jabatan Muzium dan Antikuiti. Unit Arkeologi. *Ladangan projek penyelidikan arkeologi Candi Sungai Mas (Situs 32) Mukin Kota, daerah Kuala Muda, Kedah Darul Aman, fasa 8.* Kuala Lumpur: Unit Arkeologi, Jabatan Muzium dan Antikuiti, 1995.

Jabatan Muzium–Muzium Brunei. *Sungai Limau Manis: Tapak arkeologi abad ke-10–13 Masihi.* Bandar Seri Begawan, Negara Brunei Darussalam: Jabatan Muzium–Muzium Brunei, Kementerian Kebudayaan, Belia dan Sukan, 2004.

Jacq-Hergoualc'h, Michel. La civilization de ports-entrepôts du Sud Kedah (Malaysia), Vème—XIVème siècle. Paris: Editions L'Harmattan, 1992.

Ji Han. *Nan-fang ts'ao mu chuang: A Fourth-Century Flora of Southeast Asia.* Translated by Li Hui-Lin. Hong Kong: Chinese University Press, 1979.

Jones, Antoinette M. Barrett. *Early Tenth Century Java from the Inscriptions.* Dordrecht: Foris, 1984.

Jung-Pang Lo. "The Emergence of China as a Sea Power during the Late Sung and Early Yuan Periods." *Far Eastern Quarterly* 14, no. 4 (1955): 489–503.

———. "Maritime Commerce and Its Relation to the Sung Navy." *JESHO* 12, no. 1 (1969): 57–101.

Kim Wondong. Chinese Ceramics from the Wreck of a Yuan Ship in Sinan, Korea—with Particular Reference to Celadon Wares. 2 vols. Ann Arbor: University Microfilms International, 1989.

Kulke, Hermann. "Rivalry and Competition in the Bay of Bengal in the Eleventh Century and Its Bearing on Indian Ocean Studies." In *Commerce and Culture in the Bay of Bengal, 1500–1800,* edited by Om Prakash and Denys Lombard, 17–35. New Delhi: Manohar, 1999.

Kuwabara, J. "On P'u Shou-Keng." *Memoirs of the Research Department of the Toyo Bunko,* 1928, no. 2:1–79.

Kwan, K. K., and Jean Martin. "Canton, Pulau Tioman and Southeast Asian Maritime Trade." In A Ceramic Legacy of Asia's Maritime Trade: Song Dynasty Guangdong Wares and Other 11th to 19th Century Trade Ceramics Found on Tioman Island, Malaysia, edited by Southeast Asian Ceramics Society, 49–63. Selangor: Southeast Asian Ceramics Society, 1985.

———. "Introduction to the Finds from Pulau Tioman." In A Ceramic Legacy of Asia's Maritime Trade: Song Dynasty Guangdong Wares and Other 11th to 19th Century Trade Ceramics Found on Tioman Island, Malaysia, edited by Southeast Asian Ceramics Society, 69–82. Selangor: Southeast Asian Ceramics Society, 1985.

Kwee Hui Kian. "*Dao Yi Zhi Lue* as a Maritime Traders' Guidebook: A Contribution to the Study of Private Enterprise in Maritime Trade during the Yuan Period, 1279—1360." Honors thesis, National University of Singapore, 1997.

Lam, Peter Y. K. "Decorative Techniques and Styles in Guangdong Trade Wares of the Song Period." In *Guangdong Ceramics from Butuan and Other Philippine Sites,* edited by Roxanna M. Brown, 47–60. Manila: Oriental Ceramic Society of the Philippines, 1989.

———. "Northern Song Guangdong Wares." In A Ceramic Legacy of Asia's Maritime Trade: Song Dynasty Guangdong Wares and Other 11th to 19th Century Trade Ceramics Found on Tioman Island,

Malaysia, edited by Southeast Asian Ceramics Society, 1–30. Selangor: Southeast Asian Ceramics Society, 1985.

Lamb, Alastair. Chandi Bukit Batu Pahat: A Report on the Excavation of an Ancient Temple in Kedah. Singapore: Eastern Universities Press, 1961.

———. *Chandi Bukit Batu Pahat: Three Additional Notes.* Singapore: Eastern Universities Press, 1966.

———. "Recent Archaeological Work in Kedah, 1958." *JMBRAS* 32, no. 1 (1959): 214–32.

———. "Report on the Excavation and Reconstruction of Chandi Bukit Batu Pahat, Central Kedah." *FMJ* 5 (1960): x–108.

———. "Some Notes on the Distribution of Indianised Sites in Kedah." *JSSS* 15, no. 2 (1959): 99–111.

Lee Chor Lin. "Textile Trade between China and Southeast Asia during the Song, Yuan and Ming Dynasties." Master's thesis, University of Singapore, 1994.

Lee, Arthur Joo-Jock. "Geographical Setting." In *A History of Singapore,* edited by Ernest C. T. Chew and Edwin Lee, 3–14. Singapore: Oxford University Press, 1991.

Le May, Reginald. *The Culture of South-East Asia: The Heritage of India.* London: George Allen and Unwin, 1954.

Leong Sau Heng. "Collecting Centers, Feeder Points and Entrepots in the Malay Peninsula, c. 1000 BC–AD 1400." In *The Southeast Asian Port and Polity, Rise and Demise,* edited by J. Kathirithamby-Wells and John Villiers, 17–38. Singapore: Singapore University Press, 1990.

———. "A Study of Ceramic Deposits from Pengkalan Bujang, Kedah." Master's thesis, University of Malaya, 1973.

Liu Liangyu. Liao, His-Hsia, Chin and Yuan Wares. Vol. 3 of A Survey of Chinese Ceramics. Taipei: Aries Gemini, 1991.

———. *Sung Wares.* Vol. 2 of *A Survey of Chinese Ceramics.* Taipei: Aries Gemini, 1992.

Lo, K. S. The Stonewares of Yixing: From the Ming Period to the Present Day. New York: Sotheby's, 1986.

Long, Kerry Nguyen. "History behind the Jar." In *A Thousand Years of Stoneware Jars in the Philippines,* edited by Cynthia Valdes, Kerry Nguyen Long, and Artemio C. Barbosa, 25–69. Manila: Jar Collectors, 1992.

Ma Huan. *Ying-yai sheng-lan: "The Overall Survey of the Ocean's Shores" (1433).* Translated by Feng Chengjun. Cambridge: Hakluyt Society, 1970.

Ma, Laurence Junchao. "Commercial Development and Urban Change in Sung China." PhD diss., University of Michigan, 1971.

Manguin, Pierre-Yves. "City-States and City-State Cultures in Pre-15th Century Southeast Asia." In *A Comparative Study of Thirty City-State Cultures: An Investigation Conducted by the Copenhagen Polis Center,* edited by Mogens Herman Hansen, 409–16. Copenhagen: Historisk-filosofiske Skrifter, Royal Danish Academy of Sciences and Letters, 2000.

————. "Sriwijaya, entre texts historique et terrain archéologique: Un siècle a la recherché d'un état évanescent." *BEFEO* 88 (2001): 331–39.

————. "The Trading Ships of Insular Southeast Asia: New Evidence from Indonesian Archaeological Sites." In *Pertemuan ilmiah arkeologi V, Yogyakarta.* Vol. 1, 200–220. Jakarta: Ikatan Ahli Arkeologi Indonesia, 1989.

Merwin, Douglas. "Selections from Wen-Wu on the Excavation of a Sung Dynasty Excavation of a Sung Dynasty Seagoing Vessel in Chuan-Chou." *Chinese Sociology and Anthropology* 9, no. 3 (Spring 1977): 3–106.

Meulen, W. J. van der. "In Search of Ho-Ling." *Indonesia* 23 (1977): 86–111.

Miksic, John N. Archaeological Research on the "Forbidden Hill" of Singapore: Excavations at Fort Canning. Singapore: National Heritage Board, 1985.

————. "Archaeology and Palaeogeography in the Straits of Malacca." In *Economic Exchange and Social Interaction in Southeast Asia: Perspectives from Prehistory, History and Ethnography,* edited by Karl L. Hutterer, 155–76. Ann Arbor: Center for South and Southeast Asian Studies, University of Michigan, 1977.

————. "Beyond the Grave: Excavations North of the Kramat Iskandar Shah, 1988." *Heritage* 10 (1989): 34–56.

————. "Fourteenth Century Chinese Glass Found in Singapore and the Riau Archipelago." In *South East Asia and China: Art, Interaction and Commerce,* Colloquies in Art and Archaeology in Asia, no. 17, edited by Rosemary Scott and John Guy, 252–73. London: School of Oriental and African Studies, 1995.

————. "Fourteenth-Century Singapore: A Port of Trade." In *Early Singapore 1300s—1819, Evidence in Maps, Texts and Artefacts,* edited by John N. Miksic and Cheryl-Ann Low Mei Gek, 41–54. Singapore: Singapore History Museum, 2004.

————. "Recently Discovered Chinese Green Glazed Wares of the Thirteenth and Fourteenth Centuries in Singapore and the Riau Islands." In *New Light on Chinese Yue and Longquan Wares,* edited by Ho Chuimei, 229–50. Hong Kong: University of Hong Kong, 1994.

————. "Traditional Sumatran Trade." *BEFEO* 74 (1985): 423–67.

————. "Urbanisation and Social Change, The Case of Sumatra." *Archipel* 37 (1989): 3–29.

Mills, J. V. C. "Chinese Navigators in Insulinde about AD 1500." *Archipel* 18 (1979): 69–94.

Milner, A. C. The Malay Raja: A Study of Malay Political Culture in East Sumatra and the Malay Peninsula in the Early Nineteenth Century. Ann Arbor: University Microfilms International, 1977.

Mitchiner, Michael. The History and Coinage of South East Asia until the Fifteenth Century. London: Hawkins, 1998.

Mokhtar bin abu Bakar, Mohamad. "The Finds from Kampung Juara." In A Ceramic Legacy of Asia's Maritime Trade: Song Dynasty Guangdong Wares and other 11th to 19th Century Trade Ceramics Found on Tioman Island, Malaysia, edited by Southeast Asian Ceramics Society, 66–68. Selangor: Southeast Asian Ceramics Society, 1985.

Moore, Eine. "A Suggested Classification of Stonewares of Martabani Type." *SMJ* 18 (1970): 1–78.

Netolitzky, Almut. Das Ling-wai tai-ta von Chou Ch'u-Fei: Eine Landeskunde Südchinas aus dem 12. Jahrhundert. Wiesbaden: Franz Steiner, 1977.

Ng Chin-Keong. Trade and Society: The Amoy Network on the China Coast, 1683—1735. Singapore: Singapore University Press, 1983.

Nik, Hassan Shuhaimi. "Art, Archaeology and the Early Kingdoms of the Malay Peninsula and Sumatra, c. 400–1400 AD." PhD thesis, School of Oriental and African Studies, University of London, 1984.

Nik, Hassan Shuhaimi, and Othman bin Mohamad Yatim. *Antiquities of the Bujang Valley.* Kuala Lumpur: Museum Association of Malaysia, 1990.

Nik, Hassan Shuhaimi, and Kamaruddin bin Zakaria. "Recent Archaeological Discoveries in Sungai Mas, Kuala Muda, Kedah." *JMBRAS* 66, no. 2 (1993): 73–80.

Peacock, B. A. V. "New Light on the Ancient Settlement of Kedah and Province Wellesley." *MIH* 8, no. 2 (1970): 20–27.

————. "Pillar Base Architecture in Ancient Kedah." *JMBRAS* 47, no. 1 (1974): 66–86.

————. "Recent Archaeological Discoveries in Malaya (1957)." *JMBRAS* 31, no. 1 (1958): 180–87.

Pires, Tomé, and Francisco Rodrigues. *The Suma Oriental of Tomé Pires and The Book of Francisco Rodrigues.* Translated and edited by Armando Cortesão. 2 vols. London: Hakluyt Society, 1944.

Polo, Marco. *The Travels of Marco Polo.* Ware, Hertfordshire: Wordsworth Classics, 1997.

————. *Voyages and Travels of Marco Polo.* London: Cassell, 1886.

Pope, John Alexander. *Chinese Porcelains from the Ardebil Shrine.* Washington, DC: Smithsonian Institution, 1956.

Ptak, Roderich. "China and the Trade in Cloves, circa 960–1435." *JAOS* 113, no. 1 (1993): 1–13.

————. "China and the Trade in Tortoise-Shell (Sung to Ming Periods)." In *Emporia, Commodities, and Entrepreneurs in Asian Maritime Trade, c. 1400–1750,* edited by Roderich Ptak and Dietmar Rothermund, 195–229. Stuttgart: Franz Steiner, 1991.

————. *China's Seaborne Trade with South and Southeast Asia (1200–1750).* Aldershot, UK: Ashgate, 1999.

————. "From Quanzhou to the Zulu Zone and Beyond: Questions Related to the Early Fourteenth Century." *JSEAS* 29, no. 2 (1998): 269–94.

————. "Images of Maritime Asia in Two Yuan Texts: *Daoyi zhilue* and *Yiyu zhi.*" *JSYS* 25 (1995): 47–75.

————. "Ming Maritime Trade to Southeast Asia, 1368–1567: Visions of a 'System.'" In *From the Mediterranean to the China Sea: Miscellaneous Notes,* edited by Claude Guillot, Denys Lombard, and Roderich Ptak, 157–93. Wiesbaden: Harrassowitz, 1998.

————. "The Northern Trade Route to the Spice Islands: South China Sea—Sulu Zone—North Moluccas (14th to Early 16th Century)." *Archipel* 43 (1992): 27–56.

————. "Notes on the Word *Shanhu* and Chinese Coral Imports from Maritime Asia c. 1250—1600." *Archipel* 39 (1990): 65–80.

Rabinowitz, L. Jewish Merchant Adventurers: A Study of the Radanites. London: Edward Goldston, 1948.

Rao, K. P. "Kottapatnam—A South Indian Port Trading with Eastern Lands." In *In Search of Chinese Ceramic-Sherds in South India and Sri Lanka,* edited by Noboru Karashima, 9–15. Tokyo: Taisho University Press, 2004.

Reid, Anthony. "The Structure of Cities in Southeast Asia, 15th to 17th Centuries." *JSEAS* 11, no. 2 (1980): 235–50.

————. "Trade Goods and Trade Routes in Southeast Asia: C. 1300–1700." In Final Report, Consultative Workshop on Research on Maritime Shipping and Trade Networks in Southeast Asia (I-W7), Cisarua, West Java, 1984, edited by SEAMEO Project in Archaeology and Fine Arts, 249–72. Bangkok: SPAFA Coordinating Unit [1984].

Ridho, Abu. "Penelitian Keramik di Situs-Situs Arkeologi Provinsi Jambi." In *Laporan: Hasil Penelitian Arkeologi dan Geologi Propinsi Jambi 1994–1995,* 198–231. Jambi: Pemerintah Daerah Tingkat I Provinsi Jambi, 1995.

Ridho, Abu, and Edmund Edwards McKinnon. *The Pulau Buaya Wreck: Finds from the Song Period.* Edited by Sumarah Adhyatman. Jakarta: Ceramic Society of Indonesia, 1998.

Ridley, Henry N. *The Flora of the Malay Peninsula.* London: L. Reeve, 1922.

Rockhill, W. W. "Notes on the Relations and Trade of China with the Eastern Archipelago and the Coasts of the Indian Ocean during the Fourteenth Century." *T'oung pao* 15 (1914): 419–47.

———. "Notes on the Relations and Trade of China with the Eastern Archipelago and the Coasts of the Indian Ocean during the Fourteenth Century: Part II." *T'oung pao* 16 (1915): 61–159, 236–71, 374–92, 435–67, 604–26.

Salmon, Claudine. "La diffusion du gong en Insulinde vue essentiellement a travers diverses épaves orientales (période Song-Ming)." In *Mirabilia Asiatica: Produtos raros no comércio marítimo,* 2 vols., edited by Jorge M. dos Santos Alves, Claude Guillot, and Roderich Ptak, 2:8–116. Wiesbaden: Harrassowitz, 2005.

———. "Srivijaya, la Chine et les marchands chinois (Xe–XIIe s.): Quelques reflexions sur la société de l'empire sumatranais." *Archipel* 63 (2002): 57–78.

———. "A Tentative Interpretation of the Chinese Inscription (1231) Engraved on a Bronze Gong Recovered in Muara Jambi (Central Sumatra)." *Archipel* 66 (2003): 91–112.

Salmon, Claudine, and Denys Lombard. "Un vaisseau du XIIIème siècle retrouvé avec sa cargaison dans la rade de 'Zaiton,'" *Archipel* 18 (1979): 57–68.

Sandhu, Kernial Singh. Early Malaysia: Some Observations on the Nature of Indian Contacts with Pre-British Malaya. Singapore: University Education Press, 1973.

Sarkar, H. B. Trade and Commercial Activities of Southern India in the Malayo-Indonesian World, up to AD 1511. Calcutta: Firma KLM, 1986.

Sastri, K. A. *Nilakanta: History of Srivijaya.* Madras: University of Madras, 1949.

Schafer, E. H. *The Golden Peaches of Samarkand.* Berkeley: University of California Press, 1963.

———. "Rosewood, Dragon's Blood and Lac." *JAOS* 77, no. 2 (1957): 129–36.

Schottenhammer, Angela. "Local Politico-economic Particulars of the Quanzhou Region during the Tenth Century." *JSYS* 29 (1999): 1–41.

———. "The Maritime Trade of Quanzhou (Zaiton) from the Ninth through the Thirteenth Century." In *Archaeology of Seafaring: The*

Indian Ocean in the Ancient Period, Indian Council of Historical Research Monograph Series 1, edited by Himanshu Prabha Ray, 271–90. Delhi: Pragati, 1999.

————. "The Role of Metals and the Impact of the Introduction of Huizi Paper Notes in Quanzhou on the Development of Maritime Trade in the Song Period." In *The Emporium of the World: Maritime Quanzhou, 1000–1400,* edited by Angela Schottenhammer, 95–176. Leiden: Brill, 2001.

Sen, Tansen. *Buddhism, Diplomacy, and Trade: The Realignment of Sino-Indian Relations, 600—1400.* Honolulu: University of Hawaii Press, 2003.

Sengupta. "Archaeology of Coastal Bengal." In *Tradition and Archaeology: Early Maritime Contacts in the Indian Ocean,* Proceedings of the International Seminar, Techno-archaeological Perspectives of Seafaring in the Indian Ocean 4th Century BC–15th Century AD, edited by Himanshu Prabha Ray and Jean-François Salles, 115–28. New Delhi: Manohar, 1996.

Shiba, Yoshinobu. *Commerce and Society in Sung China.* Translated by Mark Elvin. Ann Arbor: Center for Chinese Studies, University of Michigan, 1970.

————. "Sung Foreign Trade: Its Scope and Organization." In *China among Equals: The Middle Kingdom and Its Neighbours, 10th–14th Centuries,* edited by Morris Rossabi, 89–115. Berkeley: University of California Press, 1983.

Sieveking, G. De G. "Recent Archaeological Discoveries in Malaya (1955)." *JMBRAS* 29, no. 1 (1956): 200–211.

So, Billy Kee Long. "Dissolving Hegemony or Changing Trade Pattern? Images of Srivijaya in the Chinese Sources of the Twelfth and Thirteenth Centuries." *JSEAS* 29, no. 2 (1998): 295–308.

————. "Financial Crisis and Local Economy: Chuan-Chou in the Thirteenth Century." *T'oung pao* 77 (1991): 119–37.

————. Prosperity, Region, and Institutions in Maritime China: The South Fukien Pattern, 946–1368. Cambridge, MA: Harvard University Asia Center, 2000.

————. "The Trade Ceramics Industry in Southern Fukien during the Sung." *JSYS* 24 (1994): 1–19.

Soerianegara, Ishemat, and R. H. M. J. Lemmens. *Timber Trees: Major Commercial Timbers.* Plant Resources of South-East Asia, no. 5 (1). Wageningen: Pudoc Scientific, 1993.

Song Lian. *Economic Structure of the Yüan Dynasty.* Translated by Herbert Franz Schurmann. Cambridge, MA: Harvard University Press, 1967.

Southeast Asian Ceramics Society. *A Ceramic Legacy of Asia's Maritime Trade*. Selangor: Southeast Asian Ceramics Society, W. Malaysia Chapter, 1985.

Spencer, George. The Politics of Expansion: The Chola Conquest of Sri Lanka and Sri Vijaya. Madras: New Era, 1983.

Stargardt, Janice. "Behind the Shadows: Archaeological Data on Two-Way Sea Trade between Quanzhou and Satingpra, South Thailand, 10th–14th Century." In *The Emporium of the World: Maritime Quanzhou, 1000–1400,* edited by Angela Schottenhammer, 309–94. Leiden: Brill, 2001.

Subbarayalu, Y. "Chinese Ceramics of Tamilnadu and Kerala Coasts." In *Tradition and Archaeology Early Maritime Contacts in the Indian Ocean,* Proceedings of the International Seminar, Techno-archaeological Perspectives of Seafaring in the Indian Ocean 4th Century BC–15th Century AD, edited by Himanshu Prabha Ray and Jean-François Salles, 109–14. New Delhi: Manohar, 1996.

Tan Yeok Seong. "The Sri Vijayan Inscription of Canton (AD 1079)." *JSEAH* 5, no. 2 (1964): 17–26.

Tibbetts, G. R. A Study of the Arabic Texts Containing Material on Southeast Asia. Leiden: Brill, 1979.

Treloar, F. E. "Stoneware Bottles in the Sarawak Museum: Vessels for Mercury Trade?" *SMJ* 20 (1972): 377–84.

Twitchett, Denis, and Janice Stargardt. "Chinese Silver Bullion in a Tenth-Century Indonesian Wreck." *Asia Major,* 3rd ser., 15, no. 1 (2002): 23–72.

Vainker, S. J. *Chinese Pottery and Porcelain*. New York: George Braziller, 1991.

Valdes, Cynthia O., Kerry Nguyen Long, and Artemio C. Barbosa, eds. *A Thousand Years of Stoneware Jars in the Philippines*. Manila: Jar Collectors, 1992.

van Aelst, Arjan. "Majapahit Picis: The Currency of a 'Moneyless' Society." *Bijdragen tot de taal-, land- en volkenkunde* 151, no. 3 (1995): 357–93.

Wales, H. G. Quaritch. "Archaeological Researches on Ancient Indian Culture and Mahayana Buddhism from Sites in Kedah." *JMBRAS* 18, no. 1 (1940): 1–85.

Wales, D., and Q. Wales. "Further Work on Indian Sites in Malaya." *JMBRAS* 20, no. 1 (1947): 1–11.

Wang Gungwu. The Nanhai Trade: The Early History of Chinese Trade in the South China Sea. Singapore: Times Academic Press, 1998.

Wang Gungwu and Ng Chin Keong, eds. *Maritime China in Transition, 1750–1850*. Wiesbaden: Harrassowitz, 2004.

Wang Shixiang. Connoisseurship of Chinese Furniture: Ming and Early Ching Dynasties, vol. 1. Chicago: Art Media Resources, 1990.

Watson, Andrew, ed. and trans. *Transport in Transition: The Evolution of Traditional Shipping in China.* Michigan Abstracts of Chinese and Japanese Works on Chinese History, no. 3. Ann Arbor: Center for Chinese Studies, University of Michigan, 1972.

Watt, James C. Y. "Hsi-Ts'un, Ch'ao-an and Other Ceramic Wares of Kwangtung in the Northern Song Period." In *Guangdong Ceramics from Butuan and other Philippine Sites,* edited by Roxanna M. Brown, 35–46. Manila: Oriental Ceramic Society of the Philippines, 1989.

Wheatley, Paul. "Geographical Notes on Some Commodities Involved in Sung Maritime Trade." *JMBRAS* 32, no. 2 (1959): 5–140.

———. The Golden Khersonese: Studies in the Historical Geography of the Malay Peninsula before AD 1500. Westport, CT: Greenwood, 1973.

Wicks, Robert S. Money, Markets, and Trade in Early Southeast Asia: The Development of Indigenous Monetary Systems to AD 1400. Ithaca: Southeast Asian Program, Cornell University, 1992.

Williamson, H. R. Wang An Shih, a Chinese Statesman and Educationalist of the Sung Dynasty. 2 vols. London: Arthur Probsthain, 1935.

Winstedt, R. O. "Gold Ornaments Dug Up at Fort Canning, Singapore." *JMBRAS* 6, no. 4 (1926): 1–4.

Wisseman-Christie, Jan. "Asian Sea Trade between the Tenth and Thirteenth Centuries and Its Impact on the States of Java and Bali." In *Archaeology of Seafaring: The Indian Ocean in the Ancient Period.* Indian Council of Historical Research Monograph Series 1, edited by Himanshu Prabha Ray, 221–70. Delhi: Pragati, 1999.

———. "The Medieval Tamil-Language Inscriptions in Southeast Asia and China." *JSEAS* 29, no. 2 (1998): 239–68.

———. "Money and Its Uses in the Javanese States of the Ninth to Fifteenth Centuries AD." *JESHO* 39, no. 3 (1996): 243–86.

———. "Patterns of Trade in Western Indonesia: Ninth through Thirteenth Centuries AD." 2 vols. PhD diss., School of Oriental and African Studies, University of London, 1982.

———. A Preliminary Survey of Early Javanese Coinage Held in Javanese Collections. Jakarta: Kundika, 1994.

———. "State Formation in Early Maritime Southeast Asia: A Consideration of the Theories and the Data." *Bijdragen tot de taal-, land- en volkenkunde* 151, no. 2 (1995): 235–88.

———. "Texts and Textiles in 'Medieval' Java." *BEFEO* 80, no. 1 (1993): 181–211.

———. "Trade and Early State Formation in Maritime Southeast Asia: Kedah and Srivijaya." *Jebat* 13 (1985): 43–56.

―――. "Trade and State Formation in the Malay Peninsula and Sumatra, 300 BC–AD 700." In *The Southeast Asian Port and Polity, Rise and Demise*, edited by J. Kathirithamby-Wells and John Villiers, 39–61. Singapore: Singapore University Press, 1990.

Wolters, O. W. Early Indonesian Commerce: A Study of the Origins of Srivijaya. Ithaca: Cornell University Press, 1967.

―――. *The Fall of Srivijaya in Malay History.* Kuala Lumpur: Oxford University Press, 1970.

―――. "A Few and Miscellaneous Pi-Chi Jottings on Early Indonesia." *Indonesia* 34 (1983): 49–65.

―――. "Restudying Some Chinese Writings on Sriwijaya." *Indonesia* 42 (1986): 1–42.

―――. *History, Culture and Region in Southeast Asian Perspectives.* Singapore: Institute of Southeast Asian Studies, 1999.

―――. "Tambralingga." Bulletin of the School of Oriental and African Studies 21, no. 3 (1958): 587–607.

Wong, Grace. A Commentary on the Tributary Trade between China and Southeast Asia, and the Place of Porcelain in This Trade during the Period of the Song Dynasty in China. Southeast Asian Ceramics Society (Singapore) Transaction 7. Singapore: Southeast Asian Ceramics Society, 1979.

Xiu Ouyang and Qi Song. *Biography of Huang Chao.* Translated by Howard Levy. Los Angeles: University of California Press, 1955.

Yamamoto, Tatsuro. "Re-examination of Historical Texts Concerning Srivijaya." Paper presented at the conference of the International Association of Historians of Asia, Kuala Lumpur, 1980.

Yang Shaoxiang. "A Brief Account of Ceramics Exports from Guangdong during the Tang and Song Dynasties." In *Ceramic Finds from Tang and Song Kilns in Guangdong*, edited by Fung Ping Shan Museum, 22–31. Hong Kong: University of Hong Kong, 1985.

Yijing. A Record of the Buddhist Religion: As Practised in India and the Malay Archipelago (AD 671–695). Translated by Junjiro Takakusu. New Delhi: Munshiram Manoharlal, 1982.

Zeng Fan. "An Archaeological Study of Ceramics from the Dehua Kilns in Fujian." In *Dehua Wares*, edited by Fung Ping Shan Museum, 26–36. Hong Kong: Fung Ping Shan Museum, 1990.

Zhao Ruguo. *Chau Ju-Kua: His Work on the Chinese and Arab Trade in the Twelfth and Thirteenth Centuries, Entitled Chu-fan-chï.* Translated by Friedrich Hirth and W. W. Rockhill. New York: Paragon Book Reprint, 1966.

Index

ceramics (*cont.*)
    recovered from Southeast Asian settle-
      ment sites, 9, 16, 33, 159, 179–90
    sancai, 33
    Thai, 129, 189
    white, 33, 171–72, 174–79, 182
    Xicun, 181, 183, 186
    Yaozhou, 176, 181, 183
    Yixing, 183, 186, 188
    Yue-type, 33, 174–76
    Zhangpu, 176
Champa, 39, 81, 99, 102, 107, 125, 133
    missions to China, 42, 77, 87, 92, 94–95,
      101, 167–68, 192
    textile production, 128, 170
    transshipment trade to China, 59, 193,
      194, 198
Chang Qing Chen, 28
Chen Dazhen, 11
    Dade nanhaizhi, 11, 128, 138–39,
      205–7, 209
Cholas, 42, 85, 87–88
    conflict with Malacca Strait region, 85,
      87–88, 90, 92
    missions to China, 47, 91, 163
    Rajaraja I, 85
    Rajendra I, 85
Christie, Jan Wisseman, 7
circuits, administrative
    Guangnan, 54, 57, 63
    Liangzhe, 42, 54, 57, 95, 180
cloves, 32, 58, 82, 194, 198
coconut fiber mats, 137, 197, 200
combs, 78, 243
compulsory purchases, 40–41, 45–47, 51,
    55–57, 59, 60–61, 67, 103, 162,
    197–98, 200
copper, 33, 54, 152, 155, 156, 158, 158–61
    export embargo on, 45, 46, 160
copper cash, 14, 16, 46, 47, 79, 154, 161–67,
    173, 195, 214
coral, 59, 78, 192, 197, 205
Coromandel Coast (Tianzhu), 193
crane's crest, 140–41
cubeb, 206
customs duties, Chinese, 40–41, 46–47, 49,
    56–61, 64, 67, 69, 197–98
    classification system (high- and low-
      value products), 57
    coarse products, 51, 67, 172, 197
    fine products, 67, 97, 172, 177, 179–80,
      182, 184–86, 197–98
    luxury items, 54–55, 58–62, 103, 152,
      195, 198–200, 205, 207, 224–25

Dade nanhaizhi (Chen Dazhen), 11, 128,
    138–39, 205–7, 209
Damar incense, 196–97, 206
Daoyi zhilue (Wang Dayuan), 11, 65, 128,
    133, 139–40, 169–72, 208–9
dates, 32, 82
Deli, 107, 170
Dihua Jialuo, 88
Dinghai, 113
dragon's blood, 32
    imitation dragon's blood, 202

ebony, 51, 192, 206
elephant tusks. *See* ivory

foodstuffs, 16, 32, 33, 58, 186–89
    grain, 63, 197
    salt, 44, 63, 153
    Southeast Asian, 129
    tea, 63
    wine, 188–89
foreign headman, 91–93, 96, 115, 118–19
foreign official, 35, 78, 96–97, 117, 119
foreign residents
    in China, 60, 66, 68, 70, 78–79, 114–20, 122
    Chinese abroad, 126–30, 209
    commandants, 91–92
    foreign quarters (China), 114–23
    at Guangzhou, 78–79, 81, 83, 89–93, 96,
      112–19, 195
    at Quanzhou, 107, 116, 120
frankincense, 32–33, 47, 55–56, 58–59,
    64–65, 78, 82, 93, 96–98, 106, 152,
    155, 163
Fujian, 30, 188
    ceramics, 13, 172–79, 183, 186
    economy, 13, 32, 107, 113, 163, 172–77,
      187–89
    kilns, 13, 175, 179
    in Song period, 36, 37, 54, 57, 96
    in Yuan period, 63, 66, 107, 205
Funan, 21, 22
    Oc Eo, 22
furniture, 78, 199, 208
Fuzhou, 34, 113, 154

gems, 32
gharuwood, 32, 193, 202–3, 208
    chen (sinking), 58, 140, 192–93, 197–98,
      201–2, 205, 208
    huangshou, 192–93, 197, 206, 208
    jian (steamed), 192, 194, 197–98
    mature, 202
    su, 140, 192, 194, 197–98, 202, 206, 208
    timber, 206, 208